"Any publication by Rabbi Reuven Hammer is cause for celebration. His wisdom, warmth, and depth are treasures. *A Year with the Sages* is exceptional—the contemporary sage, Rabbi Hammer, guides us in walking the path of the ancient sages."

—**Rabbi Bradley Shavit Artson**, dean of the Ziegler School of Rabbinic Studies, American Jewish University

"Reuven Hammer examines a portion of each week's Torah and holiday readings in a unique tri-partite fashion—Explanation, Exposition of Sages, and Personal Reflections—offering us his in-depth knowledge of Torah, erudite mastery of Rabbinic sources, and enlightening reflections, respectively. The end result—*A Year with the Sages*—is a truly valuable contribution to us all."

—**Shalom M. Paul**, professor emeritus of Bible studies, Hebrew University in Jerusalem

"*A Year with the Sages* offers a learned, relevant and eloquent reaction to each among the entire year of weekly Torah portions. These essays are insightful in preparing for Bible Study classes, for sermonic presentations, and for an on-going rhythm of engagement with sacred texts. Rabbi Hammer's breadth of knowledge combines scholarship with current-day life wisdom. This is a worthy addition to both personal and communal Jewish libraries."

—**Rabbi Alan Silverstein**, president of Mercaz Olami, past president of the International Rabbinical Assembly and of Masorti Olami

"Hammer sheds insightful light on the meaning of Torah for both the rabbinic period and our time."

—**Rabbi Steven Reuben**, senior rabbi emeritus of Kehillat Israel Reconstructionist Congregation in Pacific Palisades, California

"Hammer has chosen his rabbinic texts wisely; his comments are both scholarly and contemporary, and offer us meaningful life lessons."

—**Rabbi Vernon Kurtz**, North Suburban Synagogue Beth El in Highland Park, Illinois, and author of *Encountering Torah: Reflections on the Weekly Portion*

A Year with the Sages

JPS Daily Inspiration Series

University of Nebraska Press
Lincoln

A Year with the Sages

Wisdom on the Weekly Torah Portion

RABBI REUVEN HAMMER

The Jewish Publication Society
Philadelphia

Library of Congress Cataloging-in-Publication Data
Names: Hammer, Reuven, author.
Title: A year with the Sages: wisdom on the weekly
Torah portion / Rabbi Reuven Hammer.
Description: Lincoln: University of Nebraska Press;
Philadelphia: The Jewish Publication Society, [2019] |
Series: JPS daily inspiration series | "Published by the
University of Nebraska Press as a Jewish Publication
Society book." | Includes bibliographical references.
Identifiers: LCCN 2018047889
ISBN 9780827613119 (cloth: alk. paper)
ISBN 9780827617896 (epub)
ISBN 9780827617902 (mobi)
ISBN 9780827617919 (pdf)
Subjects: LCSH: Bible. Pentateuch—Commentaries. |
Fasts and feasts—Judaism. | Aggada.
Classification: LCC BS1225.53 .H3574 2019+
| DDC 222/.107—dc23 LC record available at
https://lccn.loc.gov/2018047889.

Set in Merope Basic by Mikala R. Kolander.

To the memory of my mother-in-law,
Shirley Robbins Kotin,
a woman of independence and a loving
mother, grandmother, and great-grandmother,
on the fifteenth anniversary of her death.

She girds herself with strength
and performs her tasks with vigor.

—Proverbs 31:17

Contents

III. LEVITICUS (VA-YIKRA')

IV. NUMBERS (BE-MIDBAR)

V. DEUTERONOMY (DEVARIM)

VI. HOLIDAYS

Acknowledgments

Since my student days at the Jewish Theological Seminary (JTS) and throughout my career as a rabbi and an academic, the writings of the Sages have been the primary focus of my studies.

My interest in midrash arose through study of the Sages' writings with such superb teachers as Prof. Judah Goldin and Prof. Max Kadushin. Under the wise tutelage of Prof. Louis Finkelstein I wrote my doctoral thesis on the theology of the Sages. The opportunity to teach Rabbinic literature at the Jerusalem branch of the JTS, as well as at other institutions, deepened my understanding of the Sages' works. Prof. Gershon Cohen, then JTS chancellor, also furthered my knowledge by encouraging my first major work on the Sages: *Sifre: A Tannaitic Commentary on the Book of Deuteronomy*, a translation and commentary on Sifre Deuteronomy. From my students I learned more than I had already known.

I want to express my appreciation to Rabbi Barry Schwartz and Joy Weinberg of the Jewish Publication Society for their help and guidance throughout the writing of this volume and for the many suggestions they made that were incorporated into the final product. And, as with all my writings, here too my appreciation goes to my first reader and finest critic, my wife, Raḥel, who went over every page and always found the places that needed improvement and elucidation. I am most appreciative of the opportunity to have this work published under the distinguished auspices of the University of Nebraska Press.

To all those who helped and inspired this work, my deepest appreciation.

Introduction

In 2015 the Jewish Publication Society (JPS) published my study of the life and teachings of one of the greatest Sages, Rabbi Akiva (*Akiva: Life, Legend, Legacy*). Therefore, a new invitation from JPS to write *A Year with the Sages* was most welcome. It gave me yet another opportunity to delve into the writings of the Sages, to probe the ways in which they chose to interpret the Torah, and to demonstrate how their thinking is still relevant to our contemporary lives as Jews. It is not an exaggeration to say that our Judaism would not exist without their work.

If I had a choice, I would spend much more than a year with the Sages, this group of hundreds of men—unfortunately, there are no women among them—whose lives spanned a period of some thousand years. They were the creators of Rabbinic Judaism, the very foundation of the Judaism we know today. What a fascinating group of individuals they were, coming from vastly different backgrounds and having varying approaches to Judaism, but united in the attempt to interpret and understand the Torah, adapt it to the needs of their times, and inspire people to lead a meaningful life guided by the love of God, Israel, and all humankind.

Known in Hebrew as ḤAZAL—the first letters of *Hakhamenu Zikhrom L'vrakha*—our Sages (wise men) of blessed memory viewed themselves as the direct heirs of Moses, Joshua, the elders, and the prophets. According to the historiography of the Sages as recorded in the opening lines of the tractate *Avot*, they considered themselves to have inherited the oral teachings God had transmitted to Moses, which were passed on to the "men of the Great Assembly," a legendary group of scribes and scholars who gathered around Ezra (fifth century BCE).

They in turn transmitted these teachings—Torah—and the right to interpret them to each subsequent generation.

The true history of the growth of the tradition from the time of Moses (thirteenth century BCE) until the time of Ezra (fifth century BCE) is undoubtedly much more complicated. According to current scholarship, the Torah as we know it, that is, the Five Books of Moses, was not actually put into its present form until the time of Ezra. He was the Scribe, that is, the master of the texts, meaning the collection of teachings from different schools that the people of Judea carried into exile in Babylonia. Bible scholars believe that Ezra then edited the texts into one unified collection and proclaimed them to be the authoritative teaching of the Lord. Ezra read this "scroll of the Teachings of Moses with which the Lord had charged Israel" aloud to the people at a great convocation in Jerusalem held on the first of the seventh month (Tishrei) ca. 444 BCE, and there the people accepted the teachings as sacred Scripture (Nehemiah 8). The men of the Great Assembly whom Ezra had assembled became the keepers of the tradition, the authoritative interpreters of the Torah. The generations of teachers that followed, known as the Pharisees, were the forefathers of the Sages. Many centuries later, in the first century CE, these teachers became known as Rabbis.

Although we know the names of a few of the early Sages (second century BCE), such as Antigonos of Soko, Simeon the Righteous, Simeon ben Shetah, Shemaiah, and Avtalion, the rest remain anonymous. Aside from their sayings and teachings we know very little of their lives.

More is recorded about the Sages who lived in the first century BCE, such as Hillel and Shammai, and those who came thereafter. Until the destruction of the Temple and Jerusalem in 70 CE these Sages were identified with the Pharisaic movement, the most popular of the Jewish sects during Second Temple times. Unlike the other major sect, the Sadducees, the Pharisees considered the oral traditions, and not only the written Torah, to be sacred. This belief transformed the Torah into a living, ever-advancing document pertinent to new times and new conditions.

The Pharisees as an organized group disappeared with the destruction of the Temple. The abolition of Jewish independence and the collapse of organized Jewish society seem to have included the breakdown in organized religious groupings as well. The nobility and priesthood that comprised the Sadducean group lost its power. The Essenes were no longer in existence, and the Pharisees, who had always represented the majority of Jews, simply became the only religious authorities of any importance, but they were no longer a separate political body.

The Pharisees' last leader, Rabban Yohanan ben Zakkai, almost single-handedly saved Judaism after the destruction. He gathered other Sages together in Yavneh (near the coastal area of the land of Israel), where he formed a school of study that also functioned as a quasi Sanhedrin, finding ways to adapt Judaism to the people's realities — living without any control of their homeland and without the center of Jewish life and worship embodied by the Temple. He forged the path of the future for a people now devoid of the instruments of sovereignty.

The Sages who continued the basic principles of Pharisaic teaching after the destruction, such as Rabbi Eliezer, Rabbi Akiva, Rabbi Ishmael, Rabbi Meir, and Rabbi Judah the Prince, are known as *tannaim*, from the Aramaic "to teach" or "to study." They lived and taught in the Land of Israel. Their teachings are found principally in the Mishnah, the collection of Jewish law assembled into order by Rabbi Akiva and edited in its final form by Rabbi Judah the Prince around 200 CE. Other traditions and teachings of the *tannaim* that had not been incorporated into the Mishnah were later collected in a compilation of Jewish law called the Tosefta and in the classical midrashim, Rabbinic commentaries on the Torah created by the schools of Rabbi Akiva and Rabbi Ishmael (ca. 300 CE).

The later Sages who continued their work through their discussions of the Mishnah as recorded in the Talmud (the text of the Mishnah followed by accounts of the discussions on it, called the Gemora) are known as *amoraim*, from the word meaning "to speak" or "to interpret." Those who lived in the Land of Israel created the Jerusalem Talmud in the mid-fourth century CE, while those in Babylonia, where great academies of learning had been established, created the Babylonian Talmud in the sixth century CE.

The unusual thing about these Sages of Israel is that they were so diverse. While some came from wealthy patrician families, many others were from poor plebeian backgrounds. Akiva, for example, is said to have come from unlettered, unobservant, country stock. His rival, Ishmael, was said to be the descendant of the High Priest. Their ways of thinking were equally diverse. Akiva, a mystic, viewed the Torah as a book of supernatural origins, whereas Ishmael gloried in reason and said the Torah was written in purely human language. One other example: Hillel was a man of patience representing the poorer class, whereas Shammai was always impatient and defended the interests of the wealthy landowners.

Indeed, if there is one thing that truly characterizes the literature of the Sages, it is their passion for questioning and disagreement. This is true in matters of both interpreting and understanding texts (*aggadah*), as well as in matters of practice (*halakhah*). The Mishnah is not simply a list of laws to be observed; it is replete with multiple opinions. It begins with a question and then gives a multiplicity of possible answers. The midrashim that comment on the books of Scripture often offer multiple interpretations of the same verse. The Talmud is basically the record of passionate discussions and arguments based upon the Mishnah.

Yet, for all the great diversity found in the Sages' teachings, some underlying concepts do constitute the consensus opinion of the Sages. The Rabbinic scholar Max Kadushin, who coined the phrase "value-concepts," believed that the Sages' method of thinking, which he termed "organic thinking," was different from Greek philosophical methodology. Whereas the Greek philosophers relied on logic in their argumentation, Kadushin taught that the Sages employed "organic thinking," which was rooted in invoking and applying certain underlying concepts to various situations. Kadushin singled out four primary concepts: God's justice, God's love, Torah, and Israel. He also enumerated other subconcepts, such as humility, honesty, loving-kindness, reverence, prayer, and repentance (the list is too long to reproduce).

Many of these value-concepts are embedded in the passages cited in this volume. For example, in the essay concerning Sukkot, the Sages' comments concerning the symbolic meaning of the four species apply the value-concept of Israel. Similarly, the importance of the loving-kindness subconcept is stressed in the teaching of this midrash, cited in the Simḥat Torah selection: "Rabbi Simlai explained: The Torah begins and ends with acts of loving kindness. It begins with acts of loving kindness, as it is said, 'And the Lord God made garments of skins for Adam and his wife, and clothed them' (Genesis 3:21). It ends with acts of loving kindness, as it is said, 'He [God] buried him in the valley of the land of Moab, near Beth-peor . . .' (Deuteronomy 34:6)" (Sotah 14a).

The sayings in this book are drawn from the vast literature of the Sages—all of the periods mentioned above, as well as some later compilations based on the works of the earlier Sages. I have attempted to choose sayings and legends that both illuminate the Sages' thinking and are particularly relevant to our lives today. For each Shabbat and holiday reading I offer a commentary, a teaching of the Sages, an exposition of that teaching, and a personal reflection, all intended to generate thought and discussion and eventually move one to action.

The importance of the Sages' teachings cannot be overestimated. One cannot even begin to understand Judaism without a knowledge of their work. Just as the Torah and the entire Hebrew Bible are the foundations of Judaism, the Sages' teachings are the structures of Jewish belief and practice that have been erected upon that foundation. The one is incomplete without the other.

A Year with the Sages gives you, the reader, the opportunity to be exposed to a vast range of the Sages' words, including both law and lore and ranging over many centuries. The selections often emphasize the innovative ways in which the Sages reinterpreted the words of the Torah in order to make them relevant to their times—and even to emphasize different concepts that they felt were important to bring to the fore. I hope this opportunity will inspire you to continue to interact with the Sages—to fully experience the depth and the breadth of their thinking in their own profound writings. For this I would suggest both reading about their ideas in books such as those recommended in this volume's selected bibliography and reading their actual words in collections of their sayings and translations of these works. You might also consider joining adult education classes that emphasize midrash and Talmud. These classes are widely available today through many synagogues and institutions of Jewish studies.

The writings of the Sages have always inspired me. It is my hope that through this volume they will inspire you as well and encourage you to keep delving into the heritage of Rabbinic thought, which is at the very core of Jewish life and belief.

A Year with the Sages

I

Genesis (Bere'shit)

Bere'shit

A Fence Too Tall

GENESIS 1:1–6:8

And the Lord God commanded the man, saying, "Of every tree of the garden you are free to eat; but as for the tree of knowledge of good and bad, you must not eat of it; for as soon as you eat of it, you shall die."... [The serpent] said to the woman, "Did God really say: 'You shall not eat of any tree of the garden'?" The woman replied to the serpent, "We may eat of the fruit of the other trees of the garden. It is only about fruit of the tree in the middle of the garden that God said: 'You shall not eat of it or touch it, lest you die.'" And the serpent said to the woman, "You are not going to die."

—Genesis 2:16–17, 3:1–4

P'shat: Explanation

The creation of the world in Genesis 1 is described as filled with goodness and promise. Then, in Genesis 2, man—*adam*—is created and placed in the ideal world.

Now, for the first time, a limitation has been placed upon what he is permitted to do. And with this prohibition comes the possibility it will be disobeyed. Indeed, this is what happens.

The question is, What brought about the transgression? Who was responsible for it? The Torah's account does not elaborate. It says that the serpent told Eve, who, unlike Adam, had not heard God's prohibition, that if she and Adam ate the fruit of the tree of knowledge of good and bad, they would not die but become like divine beings. Eve was somehow persuaded, ate fruit from the tree, and gave the fruit to Adam to eat. For this they were all punished.

This story of Adam and Eve's expulsion from Eden, commonly known in the Western world as "the fall of man" because of its emphasis on the sinful nature of human beings, became a central pillar of belief in Christianity and Western culture. In later Judaism, however, it plays almost no role. On the contrary, the Jewish view is that humans are not inherently sinful. Jews traditionally recite this prayer daily: "The soul that You have implanted in us is pure." At Jewish weddings one of the seven recited blessings even includes a positive reference to Adam and Eve: "Let these loving companions [the bride and groom] rejoice even as You made Your creatures in the Garden of Eden [Adam and Eve] rejoice."

D'rash: Exposition of the Sages

The members of the Great Assembly said . . .
Create a fence around the Torah.
—*Avot* 1:1

It is said, "And the Lord God commanded the man, saying, 'Of
every tree of the garden you are free to eat; but as for the tree
of knowledge of good and bad, you must not eat of it; for as
soon as you eat of it, you shall die'" (Genesis 2:16–17). Primal
Adam, however, . . . told her, ". . . from the fruit of the tree in
the middle of the Garden God said: 'You shall not eat of it or
touch it, lest you die'" (Genesis 3:3). At that very moment,
the wicked serpent began to plot, thinking "Since I cannot
foil the man, I will foil Eve!" . . . He stood and touched the
tree with his hands and feet, shaking it until its fruit fell to
the ground. . . . Then he said to [Eve], "If you say, 'The Holy
One has commanded us not to eat from it,' watch how I eat
from it and do not die! So too can you eat from it and not die!"
What did Eve think to herself? "Whatever my Master (Adam)

commanded me from the very beginning is nothing but lies . . ."
and she immediately took from it, ate it and gave it to Adam
who ate it. . . . So what caused her to touch it? The barrier that
Primal Adam created around his words. From this we learn:
One should not add to the words one has heard. Rabbi Yosi
said: A barrier of ten handbreadths that remains standing
is preferable to one a hundred cubits high that collapses.
—Avot de-Rabbi Natan A 1

The saying concerning a fence around the Torah is attributed to the
"men of the Great Assembly," a legendary body about which we know
very little. It seems to have been a group of Sages gathered together
by Ezra in the fifth century BCE to help create and codify the text of
the Torah, which was then accepted as Judaism's official law in a great
ceremony held in Jerusalem in 444 BCE. They then continued the work
of interpreting and teaching the Torah to the populace.

"Create a barrier around the Torah" is usually understood to mean
that in order to make certain that the Torah's commands will be
observed and not violated, even unintentionally, a barrier or fence—
that is, additional prohibitions—are to be added to whatever the
Torah commands. For example, if the Torah commanded there be
no commerce on the Sabbath, the Sages added that it was prohibited
to even handle money. If the Sabbath is to begin at sunset, then we
should begin it even earlier just to be sure it will not be violated. If
the evening *Sh'ma* could be recited until the beginning of the dawn,
the Sages decreed that it should be completed before midnight so
that we would not postpone it until it was too late.

Avot de-Rabbi Natan (*The Fathers According to Rabbi Nathan*), a third-
century commentary on *Avot*, details many such barriers illustrating
the general rule to "keep far from what is hideous or even seems hideous." One barrier mentioned there, however, is different because it
had a negative effect: the barrier Adam created.

The Sages noted the difference between what God said to Adam
and what Eve relays to the serpent. Eve adds the prohibition against

touching the tree, which was not part of God's command. Wondering where she got that idea, they decided she was only repeating what Adam had told her. Because he did not trust her, he added a "fence" to God's command, assuming that if she did not touch the tree, then she surely would not eat fruit from it. But that very "fence" proved to be Adam and Eve's undoing, because the "wicked serpent" took advantage of it to trip her up.

This Rabbinic midrash (interpretation) also addresses the question, Who was ultimately responsible for the first transgression of humankind and the expulsion from Eden? In Western culture it is indubitably Eve, the ultimate temptress responsible for Adam's actions and a perpetual symbol of the femme fatale. One has only to read Milton's *Paradise Lost* or look in any gallery of medieval art to see Eve holding the apple out to Adam.

Yet our Sages took a different view of the matter. In their Rabbinic retelling, the man, Adam, not the woman, Eve, is to blame. By adding an unneeded prohibition, Adam brought about the couple's expulsion from Eden.

Rabbi Yosi summed up the Sages' conclusion: we must be careful about adding too many prohibitions, because if there are too many, in the end none will be observed. Piling up restrictions may lead to contempt for what is truly important.

D'rash: Personal Reflection

A FENCE RESTRICTING JEWISH RIGHTS

For many years I was the head of the Rabbinical Court of the Rabbinical Assembly of Israel, affiliated with the Masorti (Conservative) movement. We handled matters of personal status and conversion. On a number of occasions, we received appeals from immigrants born in the former Soviet Union who had been denied a Jewish marriage by the Chief Rabbinate of Israel because they could not prove their

Jewishness to the Chief Rabbinate's satisfaction. They were being asked for documentation that simply did not exist in Soviet Russia.

Yet Jewish law does not require such documentation. The law stipulates that one is to take the word of a person whom the Jewish community has regarded as a Jew unless there is a very good reason to doubt it. Thus, by adding strictures that were not only unrequired but impossible to uphold, the Chief Rabbinate of Israel was denying these people their rights as Jews.

Our rabbinical court would therefore investigate the matter by asking questions about the couple's family and speaking to friends who had known them for years. In most cases, we had no reason to doubt their testimony and proceeded to officiate at their marriages.

A very learned expert in Jewish law once told me that when asked if something is permissible or forbidden in Judaism, the easiest response is to say, "It is forbidden." The greater challenge is to prove that it is permitted.

Similar situations occurred regarding conversions. The most serious case concerned a group of non-Orthodox parents, many of whom were observant of Jewish tradition and who had adopted non-Jewish infants from various European countries. When they tried to have these babies converted to Judaism, the Chief Rabbinate told them that unless they themselves adopted an ultra-Orthodox lifestyle, their children would not be converted. In desperation they came to us.

Again we discovered that nothing in Jewish law required this of them. As long as they wished their children to be Jews and promised to arrange for them to become bar or bat mitzvah, we told them, we would convert the babies, and indeed we did. The mass conversion ceremony we conducted became headline news, but, more importantly, we were able to create Jewish families in accord with Jewish law. It was one of the finest days of celebration I have ever had.

Noaḥ

Human Nature

GENESIS 6:9–11:32

The Lord smelled the pleasing odor, and the Lord said to Himself: "Never again will I doom the earth because of man, since the devisings of man's mind are evil from his youth; nor will I ever again destroy every living being as I have done."
—Genesis 8:21

P'shat: Explanation

At the beginning of the portion God is said to have decided to "put an end to all flesh, for the earth is filled with lawlessness because of them" (Genesis 6:12). Now, after the Flood, God vows never again to destroy all living beings. It seems as if God has had a change of mind. Why this new position? After all, nothing has really changed. Human beings are the same after the Flood as they were before, and there is no reason to think they will not "fill the earth with lawlessness" once again. Indeed, we have seen that very occurrence in modern times.

If there is a change, it is not in human nature but in God's understanding of it and in God's willingness to deal with it. In this verse God clearly acknowledges that evil is an integral part of human beings from their youth, and therefore the struggle against human evil will never cease. If man were nothing but good, man would not be man. To be human is to learn to overcome the potential evil that exists in oneself. It is almost as if God is saying, "Well, what did I expect? I created humans with the inclination toward evil."

D'rash: Exposition of the Sages

Rabbi Hiyya Rabba says: How unfortunate is the dough
when he who created it testifies that it is truly bad—
the devisings of man's mind are evil from his youth."
Antoninus asked Rabbi Judah the Prince, "When is the
evil impulse planted within a person, before or after the
child emerges from the mother's womb?" He answered him,
"Before he emerges from the mother's womb." He said to
him, "No, for if it were implanted before birth, the infant
would tear up the mother's insides in order to emerge
immediately." Rabbi Judah accepted that opinion since it
agreed with what the verse says, "... from his youth."
—Genesis Rabbah 34:10

The evil impulse begins to develop in the mother's
womb and is born with the person. . . . Thirteen years
later the good impulse is born. . . . If he goes to commit
a terrible transgression it reprimands him.
—Avot de-Rabbi Natan A 16

The figure of Antoninus, a Roman emperor of the Antonines dynasty, appears often in Rabbinic literature in friendly discussion with Rabbi Judah the Prince, the head of the Jewish community at the end of the second and beginning of the third century CE. Rabbi Judah was in close touch with the Roman authorities, but we are not certain of who Antoninus was, including whether he was a real person or a literary creation representing Roman officials who were in touch with Rabbi Judah. The midrash's positive attitude toward him can be seen by Rabbi Judah's willingness to accept Antoninus's opinions over his own.

Rabbi Hiyya Rabba, a student of Rabbi Judah, is often found in Rabbi Judah's company. Here he comments on the fact that God, the creator of human impulses, pronounces God's very own work to be "evil." Rabbi Hiyya compares the evil impulse to the leaven in the dough, which causes it to ferment. On Passover, when we remove all leaven—hametz—from our homes, many Haggadot contain this reflection, "Just as I have removed the leaven from my home, so may I be worthy to remove the evil inclination from my heart and so may You remove all evil from the world."

Rabbi Hiyya then references a discussion of the evil impulse by Rabbi Judah and a Roman official. He cites Genesis 8:21, where, for the first time, the two words comprising the expression yetzer ha-ra (the evil inclination) appear in the Torah. The Hebrew for the English word "devisings" is yetzer. This verse is the source of this concept the Sages developed, which depicts the impulses in human nature that can lead to evil if not properly controlled. The discussion concluded that the evil impulse comes into being at the moment of birth. It is an integral part of human beings from the moment they emerge into this world. In contrast, the good impulse is said to develop much later—only when one reaches maturity, defined as age thirteen, the traditional time of bar mitzvah.

According to this point of view, children are neither good nor evil; they are simply unformed and undisciplined. The evil in the evil impulse does not always incite children to do wrong; rather, it simply fails to prevent them from doing wrong. When children mature, they know something they did not know before: they know right from wrong. The good impulse, what we would call "conscience," has emerged. It chides one when one is tempted to do wrong and therefore may be able to prevent wrongdoing.

I am reminded of the suggestion of Freud's protégé, Theodore Reik, that there is "an unconscious root of all temptations to break prohibitions." Reik tells the incident of a child who breaks some crockery. His mother asks him to promise not to do that in the future, and he says, "Bubi wants to be good, but Bubi can't be good." As the Sages said, the evil inclination is thirteen years older than the good inclination. Only with maturity do we develop the ability to regulate our drives and emotions and overcome the temptation to give in to impulses.

"Who is a hero?" asked the first-century Sage Ben Zoma. "He who conquers his impulse [*yetzer*]" (*Avot* 4:1).

Perhaps the evil inclination could more accurately be termed the inclination toward evil. It could refer to what today we might call human impulses, or in psychoanalytical terminology, the id. These impulses can lead to evil, but they can also be put to good use. As the midrash in Genesis Rabbah 9:7 put it, "Were it not for the evil impulse a man would not build a house, marry a woman, produce children or engage in business."

D'rash: Personal Reflection

HUMAN NATURE AT ITS WORST AND BEST

I visited the then USSR in the midseventies to meet and help Jews there who were being prevented from leaving. I was in Riga, a town in present-day Latvia, which had been part of the Soviet Union since the end of the Second World War. Nazi occupiers had decimated the once-flourishing Jewish community. A small number of Jews remained. There was still one synagogue at the center of whatever Jewish life still existed, severely curtailed as it was by the strictures of the Soviet regime. There I met a few dozen Jews who were studying Hebrew and trying to obtain exit visas, but without success.

This small group of young men and women in their late teens or early twenties had formed a very special bond as they studied and undertook important tasks together. On Sunday they asked my companion and me to accompany them on their usual Sunday endeavors. First they took us to the forest of Rumbele outside the town and showed us the mass graves of Jews whom the Nazis had murdered there by the hundreds. As usual in the Soviet Union, there was no official monument or signage to designate this graveyard of Jewish martyrs, nor were government officials doing anything to care for it. This extraordinary group of young Jews were taking it upon themselves to care for the graves, cleaning them every week and making sure they were not desecrated.

Then the young people guided us to a rather rundown farm, where we met an elderly woman and her son, a middle-aged man with severe mental disabilities. We learned that during the Nazi era this woman and her husband (now deceased), both devout Christians, had saved many Jewish lives at the peril of their own lives by hiding Jews in a secret spot under their barn. After the war, their neighbors scorned and isolated them for having saved Jews. Now that the husband was dead and the son incapable of real labor, the woman was in dire straits. So these young people came weekly to do chores and bring her food and supplies.

I asked the woman what had caused her to undertake that dangerous task. Her reply was very simple: "They were human beings. We had to help them."

Here I saw human nature at its best—a family compelled by the good impulse to save lives while their neighbors, impelled by the evil impulse, refused to do so and even punished those who did.

Human nature is what it is. We may carry within us "evil from youth," but we are also capable of great good. Our nature can thus lead us to become heroes or scoundrels or worse—purveyors of evil.

It is only when God comes to terms with this, as it were, that God is able to promise not to destroy all life again. Instead, God pledges to permit civilization to continue—to let human beings continue to struggle with their own natures so that good will overcome evil.

Lekh Lekha

Making Souls

GENESIS 12:1–17:27

*The Lord said to Abram, "Go forth from your native land and
from your father's house to the land that I will show you. I
will make of you a great nation, and I will bless you: I will
make your name great, and you shall be a blessing. I will
bless those who bless you and curse him who curses you; and
all the families of the earth shall bless themselves by you." . . .
Abram took his wife Sarai and his brother's son Lot, and all
the wealth that they had amassed and the souls that they had
made in Haran and they set out for the land of Canaan.*

—Genesis 12:1–5

P'shat: Explanation

Up until this point, the Torah has told us very little about Abram's life.
All we know is that he is married and that his wife is barren. Thus far,
Abram has lived very much in his father's shadow. Terah uprooted the
entire family, taking them from their home in Ur, the great Babylonian
city dedicated to worship of the moon goddess, and setting out for
Canaan. They stopped along the way in Haran, and there Terah died.

Now Terah's son Abram continues this journey at God's command.
God blesses him and promises to make him a great nation and to grant
his offspring the land of Canaan.

What, if anything, Abram had done to deserve this is not revealed.
Only after this will we begin to see Abram in action and to understand his character.

D'rash: Exposition of the Sages

Rabbi Elazar says in the name of Rabbi Yose son of Zimra: If the entire population were to come together to create even one gnat they would not be able to infuse it with a living soul and yet the text says, "the souls they had made!" Rather this refers to the proselytes they had converted. Should it then not have said, "they had converted" rather than "they had made"? This teaches you that if one persuades an idol worshipper to convert, it is as if he had made [created] him. Why does it say "they had made" rather than "he made"? Rabbi Huna said, "Abraham would convert the men and Sarah would convert the women."

—Genesis Rabbah 39:14

The Sages filled in the missing younger years of Abram's life with many stories indicating why he was worthy of God's blessing. In their writings we learn that the young Abram was an iconoclast—literally. According to the Sages, Terah was an idol maker, but Abram realized the idols were worthless and broke them in an effort to teach Terah that his religion was nonsense. Thus Abram becomes a pioneer: believing in a different kind of God and founding a new religion. His journey to Canaan, then, becomes a pilgrimage to a place where he can live and worship in a new way.

Rabbinic legends often spring from an interpretation of an unusual expression in a biblical verse. That is the case regarding the words "the souls that they had made" in the verse cited above. The new JPS translation renders this less literally as "the persons they had acquired." The midrash, however, seizes on the literal meaning of this strange expression and proclaims that it is impossible for anyone to create a soul.

Yose ben Zimra, a second-century Sage known for his creative legends, explains that no human being can infuse life, a soul, into any form he can create. Therefore, the phrase literally makes no sense. What, then, is the meaning of "making a soul"? His answer: when one converts a pagan into a Jew, one has created a new person, almost as if one has given him a new life. Therefore, he says, the verse is referring to the converts Abram and Sarai made while tarrying in Haran. They persuaded idol worshippers to worship the One God, so when they continued on their journey, they brought with them an entire congregation of believers.

Yose, of course, is transferring to Abram's time a practice that did not exist then but that was characteristic of the Judaism of the early Rabbinic period. The institution of conversion, a specific ceremony by which one moves from one religious group to another by means of certain actions or formal declarations, only came into being during the days of the Second Temple.

At the time, many more sophisticated citizens of the Roman Empire no longer found the stories of the gods and the worship of idols acceptable. They questioned the ancient stories of the lives of the gods and saw them as nothing more than colorful legends. Some then sought other definitions of the Divine. Judaism was then the only nonidolatrous religion in the Western world, the only one to teach the existence of One God who was subject to neither birth nor death and whose form could not be reproduced or worshipped. Thus Judaism was extremely appealing. Many religious seekers throughout the empire turned to it for answers.

Indeed, even earlier Judaism—with its deep belief that its God was the only God—envisioned a time when all humanity would give up the false gods and worship the Lord alone. Many of the great prophets had espoused this belief.

Thus in the centuries immediately before and after the Common Era, numerous men and women either embraced Judaism or became fellow travelers. Even after the Temple's destruction, this continued to some extent. It would cease completely only when Christianity assumed the role of the true Israel and became the official religion of the Roman Empire.

What the text really means by "the souls that they had made in Haran" is open to interpretation. Perhaps it simply indicates that

Abram and Sarai had prospered there and recruited or hired a large number of retainers, who went with them to Canaan.

The early Sages, however, give us a different picture. Because they looked favorably upon conversion, they read it back into the very beginnings of the religion of Israel. Because they wished to encourage conversion, they made Abram and Sarai into the patron saints of converts, anxious to spread God's word to others. They made Abraham and Sarah into the very exemplars of those who "made souls."

Therefore, thanks to Rabbi Yose ben Zimra, when someone converts to Judaism, he or she is said to be among the children of Abraham and Sarah, retroactively joining our earliest ancestors on an equal basis with those born as Jews.

D'rash: Personal Reflection

CREATING JEWISH SOULS

In 1959, fresh out of seminary, I was serving as a chaplain in the United States Air Force when one day a young airman I had not met before came to my office.

"Chaplain," he said, "I want to become a Jew."

I explained to him that military regulations forbade chaplains from conducting conversions, for obvious reasons. Therefore, I could not do what he wanted. He would have to find a civilian rabbi, enroll in a course, which would take a year or so, and then convert.

"But I can't wait a year," he said. "I need to convert right now!"

I asked him to explain the urgency of his need. Finally, he told me. "They want to post me to Saudi Arabia, but the air force doesn't send Jews there, so if you can make me a Jew, I won't have to go!"

Although I was sorely tempted to convert the young man in order to protest the government's policy concerning Jews and Saudi Arabia, I sent him away.

This first conversion experience was an anomaly. The many others convinced me that there is profound truth in the words of the

Sages: "If one persuades an idol worshipper to convert, it is as if he had made [created] him."

In London I created a large conversion program within the London Masorti (Conservative) movement, which provided a welcoming access to Judaism (in contrast to the very constricted program offered through the Orthodox London Bet Din). There I met, for example, a young Israeli man, a very talented scientist, who had fallen in love with an equally talented and intelligent young woman from Germany who was not Jewish. Since he was a *Kohen*, of direct patrilineal descent from Moses's brother Aaron the priest, no Orthodox authority would have been willing to prepare his proposed wife for conversion. The young couple joined our program. His knowledge of Judaism was already far beyond the usual; she absorbed whatever was taught and gladly took upon herself a religious way of life. She converted to Judaism, and afterward I had the honor of officiating at their marriage ceremony. On an ancient site—the steps leading up to the southern wall of the Temple ruins in Jerusalem—they pledged themselves to create a Jewish home and a Jewish family.

We have remained close ever since. Both of them are now teaching and doing research at one of the most prestigious universities in England. They are active in their local Jewish community. They also have two children who are being brought up to speak English, Hebrew, and German fluently and to proudly identify themselves as observant Jews.

It would be an act of hubris on my part to say that I "made a soul," but I have the feeling that at least I helped a new soul to emerge, adding a dedicated soul to the Jewish people's reservoir of energy and talent and creating a Jewish family where none had existed before.

Va-yera'

Loving One Another

GENESIS 18:1–22:24

*Now the Lord said, "Shall I hide from Abraham what I
am about to do, since Abraham is to become a great and
populous nation and all the nations of the earth are to bless
themselves by him? For I have singled him out, that he may
instruct his children and his posterity to keep the way of
the Lord by doing what is just and right, in order that the
Lord may bring about for Abraham what he has promised
him."... Abraham came forward and said, "Will You sweep
away the innocent along with the guilty? ... Far be it from
You! Shall not the judge of all the earth deal justly?"*
—Genesis 18:17–19,23,25

P'shat: Explanation

This portion contains two of the most famous events in the Torah—
the birth of Isaac, concluding with his binding, and the destruction
of Sodom and Gomorrah and the fate of Lot's family. The advent of
both events is conveyed as God's message to Abraham, delivered by
angels. Informing Abraham about his son Isaac's birth is understand-
ably crucial. However, why does Abraham have to know about the fate
of the wicked cities? What does it have to do with him?

Perhaps God wanted to involve Abraham in the punishment of
Sodom because his nephew Lot was living there. Yet the text conveys
that God *always* intended to save Lot and his family. They may not
have been the most righteous people in the world, as the story clearly
indicates, but neither were they truly wicked, as were the native inhab-

itants. Therefore, the most that might have been required was for God to inform Abraham that although the city was to be destroyed, his family would be saved.

On the contrary, in the entire account of Abraham's dispute with God, neither God nor Abraham ever mentions Lot. Abraham does not ask God to save Lot; his concern is for the innocent people, with whom he has no connection whatsoever. He wants God to deal justly. He has no personal familial interest in saving the city, purely a concern to see that justice is done.

The Torah explains that God feels that Abraham must be involved because Abraham's task is to teach his descendants "to do what is right and just." It seems that Abraham is being tried to see if he truly understands the importance of this mandate to pursue righteousness and justice. If so, Abraham passes the test brilliantly. He is so concerned about fairness and decency that he even dares to dispute with God and to challenge God to do justly. He becomes the first human exemplar to stand up to God (or to anyone in power) for justice and righteousness—a theme that continues in the works of the prophets, in the book of Job, and in the famous Hasidic *Kaddish* of Rabbi Levi of Berdetchev.

D'rash: Exposition of the Sages

Rabbi Levi said: "The judge of all the earth shall not deal justly!" If you want the world to exist, there cannot be strict justice. And if you want strict justice, the world cannot exist.
—Genesis Rabbah 49

One should love human beings and not hate human beings, for thus we find concerning the generation of the dispersion [i.e., the people who built the Tower and were then dispersed]— that since they loved one another, the Holy One decided not to destroy them but only to disperse them to the four corners of the globe. Concerning the people of Sodom, since

they hated one another, the Holy One eliminated them
totally from this world and from the world to come.
—*Avot de-Rabbi Natan A 12*

In discussing this story, Rabbi Levi, a third-generation *amora* (a Sage who lived after the completion of the Mishnah in ca. 200 CE) from the Land of Israel in the late third century CE who was famous as a great preacher and master of midrash, gives a novel interpretation to Abraham's plea to God. He claims that it is not a question but a statement. Abraham, he asserts, is not seeking justice but mercy. Therefore, he pleads with God *not* to do justly but to act mercifully.

This interpretation actually reflects the intent of the story, since in the Torah Abraham does not simply say to God, "Save the innocent," which would be an act of justice. Rather, he asks God to spare the guilty as well, to save the entire city, even if only a minority of the people there, as few as ten, are innocent. This is mercy, not justice.

Rabbi Levi sees Abraham as teaching God, as it were, an important truth: if the world were to be judged strictly, it could not continue to exist. If the Torah stresses the importance of justice, the Sages are more concerned with the importance of mercy.

The destruction of Sodom and Gomorrah is actually the third story in a series of stories showing God's displeasure with sinful human conduct and the punishment God then inflicts. The first was the story of the Flood. There the decision was that civilization—the world—could not continue to exist and would have to start over. The second was the story of the Tower of Babel. There the punishment was not destruction but dispersement. Now, this is the third.

In *The Fathers According to Rabbi Nathan*, the early expansion on the mishnaic order *The Fathers* (*Avot*), the Sages commented on the difference between the fate of the generation of the Tower and that of the people of Sodom. The anonymous Sage who created this interpretation makes a very definite value judgment here in which loving human beings takes precedence over reverence for God. Noting that in the case of the Tower, people worked with one another, he takes this as a sign of loving one another and concludes that as a result, even though they intended to defy God, their punishment was relatively mild. But there is no forgiveness for people who sin against one another, which is how he understands the word "wicked" in reference to the people of Sodom. That, above all their other misdeeds, was enough to seal their doom.

D'rash: Personal Reflection

THE GOD OF MERCY

On a visit to New York I saw an excellent play called *Indecent* that depicted the history of Shalom Asch's early twentieth-century Yiddish play *The God of Vengeance*. That play told the story of an overly strict and demagogic father who called down the wrath of an unforgiving God upon his own daughter. I'm not sure what Asch was trying to imply, but the very title seemed to play into the hands of antisemites who revile Judaism as a religion of vengeance governed by a cruel God.

The title was undoubtedly taken from the first line in Psalm 94 — *el nekamot hashem* — translated in JPS as "God of retribution" but by others as "God of vengeance." Actually, though, the psalm does not depict a cruel and unjust God but rather a God who is called upon to save the innocent, the helpless, the stranger, the widow, the orphan from evildoers who oppress and kill them. Nor is this the most common description of God in Judaism. Rather, when Moses asks to know God's qualities, he is told that God is "compassionate and gracious, slow to anger, abounding in kindness and faithfulness" (Exodus 34:6). This famous passage, teaching that God's quality of mercy outweighs God's quality of justice, has become the basis for our prayers on the Days of Awe. We recite it over and over, asking for forgiveness and atonement for our misdeeds.

As the Sages indicated, true justice would demand the destruction of too many unworthy civilizations and the punishment of too many individuals. When we look around our own world and read about the atrocities committed every day, do we not sometimes wonder why God puts up with this? Then we are brought to realize that the world exists only because there are good and decent people as well and because God is merciful and forgiving and does not demand strict justice. Given the choice between the world and justice, it seems that God has chosen the world.

Judaism is often thought of as a religion that places the strict observance of God-related rituals at the very center of its concerns, but that is not the case. The prophets are very clear about the fact that proper treatment of other human beings, love of one's fellow, love of one another are the very heart of God's requirements. That is why Rabbi Akiva chose the verse, "And you shall love your fellow as yourself" (Leviticus 19:18) as the most important general rule in the entire Torah (*Sifra* 89b), and that is why the Sages understood the punishment of the generation of the Tower to be so lenient. Whatever their sins, they loved one another.

For the Sages, God's merciful nature, choosing the world above strict justice is a given. Each human being has a choice—to hate others or to love them. God's mercy is not in our hands, but God's requirement that we love one another is within our power.

Ḥayyei Sarah

Sarah's Tent

GENESIS 23:1–25:18

*They called Rebekah and said to her, "Will you go with this
man [Abraham's servant]?" And she said, "I will." So they
sent their sister Rebekah and her nurse along with Abraham's
servant and his men.... Raising her eyes, Rebekah saw
Isaac. She alighted from the camel and said to the servant,
"Who is that man walking in the field toward us?" And
the servant said, "That is my master." So she took her veil
and covered herself. The servant told Isaac all the things
that he had done. Isaac then brought her into the tent of his
mother Sarah, and he took Rebekah as his wife. Isaac loved
her, and thus found comfort after his mother's death.*
—Genesis 24:57–59,63–67

P'shat: Explanation

This Torah portion emphasizes the important role the Matriarchs
played in the history of the Jewish people. It begins with the death
of the first Matriarch, Sarah, Abraham's mourning for her, and the
trouble Abraham took to find an appropriate burial place for her,
the cave of Machpelah. It then relates how Abraham, worried about
Isaac's future, sent his servant to find an appropriate wife for Isaac
among the members of his own family.

The question of who will be the next Matriarch is clearly important.
The question of who will succeed Sarah is treated with the utmost
seriousness and a very long narrative in the usually terse Torah.

The servant finds Rebekah, who seems to possess all the needed qualities. Interestingly, she is asked to consent to going with him to marry Isaac. She agrees. The description of what happens when they come back to the Negev in Canaan, Isaac's first sighting of her and then Rebekah's first sighting of him, speaks to a degree of mutuality in their upcoming marriage. The last verse quoted—"Isaac then brought her into the tent of his mother Sarah, and he took Rebekah as his wife. Isaac loved her, and thus found comfort after his mother's death"—emphasizes three points: that Isaac loved her, that she is the one who brings comfort to Isaac after his mother's death, and that she is Sarah's proper successor.

Love in a marriage is not to be taken for granted in the conditions of those times. Rather, it was unusual. We may assume that Abraham loved Sarah, but it is never stated. We know that Jacob loved Rachel. Society at the time was patriarchal; women were far from having equal legal status with men. Nevertheless, this section presents a very positive view of marriage and of the woman's role in it. Her consent to the marriage is required here; love and respect are seen, and mutuality is implied. It is significant that the Torah pays much attention to the Matriarchs and honors them so.

D'rash: Exposition of the Sages

As long as Sarah was alive the doors to her tent were open wide. When she died this ceased, but when Rebekah came they were open wide again. As long as Sarah was alive there was a blessing in the dough. When she died this ceased, but when Rebekah came the blessing returned. As long as Sarah was alive, a lamp was burning from one Sabbath night to the next in her tent. When she died this ceased, but when Rebekah came the burning lamp returned. When Isaac saw that her actions were like those of his mother he "brought her into the tent of his mother Sarah."

—Genesis Rabbah 60:16

For three years Isaac mourned his mother. Whenever he
would go into her tent and see that it was dark he would
tear out his hair. When he married Rebekah and brought
her into the tent the light returned as it had been, as it says,
". . . he brought her into the tent of his mother Sarah."
—Midrash ha-Gadol Hayyei Sarah 24:67

Both of these midrashim are concerned with the questions, Why was Isaac's marriage to Rebekah a comfort to him after his mother's death, and why did the verse mention that Isaac "brought her into the tent of his mother Sarah"? The latter seems to be a strange and unnecessary statement. The Sages then seize on the words "the tent of his mother Sarah," asking, What was unusual about that tent?

The legends followed: this tent was unusual because of Sarah's presence in it. She was a person of great virtues, to the extent that the cloud—always a symbol of the Divine Presence in the Torah and the writings of the Sages—hovered over her tent, and even the dough made in it had a special character. She was always hospitable, keeping the doors wide open for strangers, and industrious—her lamp was burning in the darkness because she was tending to the needs of her household. But after her death the tent was dark and desolate, with no cloud above it. All of this changed when Rebekah appeared and followed in Sarah's ways. This caused Isaac's mourning to cease, since a woman who represented everything that Sarah stood for was now the inhabitant of Sarah's tent, returning its light and its special features.

D'rash: Personal Reflection

ORDAINING WOMEN IN THE STATE OF ISRAEL

From these verses and legends it is apparent that our tradition has struggled with the question of women's proper roles and rights. Women are shown great respect here and throughout the Torah. Abraham obviously honors his wife. He shows the utmost concern about finding the proper wife for Isaac. Isaac misses his mother and will not cease his mourning, which has continued for three long years, until he finds a woman who is her equal, a woman he truly loves. Yet it is unquestionable that within this framework a woman is still not seen as truly equal to a man in her legal rights and status.

In modern times this problem has become ever more acute as women have struggled for greater rights and participation in Jewish religious life. While this struggle has taken different forms in Judaism's various streams, ways have been found to enable women in Orthodox, as well as Conservative and Reform, Judaism to participate more actively in religious life. Torah study for girls has become more widespread. Each group has grappled with the question of women serving as rabbis. Now there are many women serving as rabbis in both Reform and Conservative congregations throughout the world and women serving as spiritual leaders in Orthodox congregations even in Israel, although without the official title of rabbi.

When I was in charge of founding the first Israeli non-Orthodox rabbinical school to train native Israelis to be Masorti rabbis in the 1980s, I found myself in an uncomfortable position on this matter. Although the Rabbinical School of the Conservative Movement in New York had been ordaining women for several years, the founding board of the new Jerusalem school decided that it would solely ordain men. The reason was sociological and political rather than theological. None of the board members—women among them—objected to women rabbis, but they all felt that opening a Conservative/Masorti rabbinical school in Jerusalem was enough of a radical change and that adding women's ordination to the agenda would make it impossible for the school to be accepted as legitimate by the broader Israeli public. One step at a time.

When talented women came to me asking to apply to the school, I had no choice but to sadly turn them down. I advised them to apply to study in New York and then come back to Israel, and indeed some did, albeit reluctantly. Years later, after the first male Israeli rabbis had been ordained, the question was raised again. At that time I was no longer on the staff of the school, but I was a member of the Law Committee, which was asked to write an opinion on the matter. I did so, taking a strong stand justifying women's ordination according to Jewish law and urging that the rabbinical school accept them in Jerusalem for ordination. I was very pleased when the board accepted my opinion and changed the policy.

Since then, many women rabbis have graduated from the Israeli rabbinical school and served in various capacities, including as successful congregational rabbis in Israel. This has been generally accepted and is now taken for granted. In a sense, even in Israel women have now been taken into the tent of Jewish religious leadership to the benefit of all.

Toledot

GENESIS 25:19–28:9

He went to his father and said, "Father." And he said, "Yes, which of my sons are you?" Jacob said, "I am Esau, your first born; I have done as you told me. Pray sit up and eat of my game, that you may give me your innermost blessing." Isaac said to his son, "How did you succeed so quickly, my son?" And he said, "Because the Lord your God granted me good fortune." Isaac said to Jacob, "Come closer that I may feel you my son—whether you are really my son Esau or not." So Jacob drew close to his father Isaac who felt him and wondered. "The voice is the voice of Jacob, yet the hands are the hands of Esau." He did not recognize him, because his hands were hairy like those of his brother Esau; and so he blessed him.

—Genesis 27:18–23

P'shat: Explanation

Jacob's deception of his father, Isaac, at his mother's instruction is hardly an inspirational story. On the contrary, it is an example of what can happen in a family when open communication does not exist.

In the dialogue between father and son, we see that Jacob is forced to lie outright time and time again and does so easily. Isaac, on the other hand, seems skeptical. Since his eyesight is poor, he begins by asking which son has approached him. He then wonders how his son has managed to kill and prepare the game so quickly. Jacob's answer does not satisfy Isaac, probably because Jacob speaks of God in his explanation, something that would not have been expected of

Esau. Isaac says quite openly that he wants to make certain that the son before him is Esau. When he feels him and detects a hairy arm, which Jacob's is not, Isaac remarks on it in wonder: "The voice is the voice of Jacob, yet the hands are the hands of Esau." Nevertheless, he allows himself to be convinced. He cannot bring himself to believe that Jacob could or would deceive him like that, and so Isaac proceeds with the blessing he intended for Esau. It is a riveting and sad story with dire consequences.

D'rash: Exposition of the Sages

"The voice is the voice of Jacob, yet the hands are the hands of Esau." "The voice" is the cry [of Israel] heard when the Emperor Hadrian killed myriads of Jews in Alexandria of Egypt, twice as many as those who had left Egypt! "The voice" is the cry [of Israel] heard when the Emperor Vespasian killed four hundred thousand myriads in Beitar. "The hands of Esau" refers to the Roman government that destroyed our homeland, burnt the Temple and drove our people out of our land.
—Gittin 17b

Rabbi Abba bar Kahana said: There were no greater philosophers among the nations than Balaam ben Beor and Avnomos Ha-gardi. The nations gathered before Avnomos and asked, "Can we overcome this nation?" He said to them, "Go and see what is happening in their synagogues and houses of study. If you hear the sound of youngsters humming there, you cannot overcome them. If not, you can overcome them. That is what their Patriarch Isaac assured them when he said 'The voice is the voice of Jacob. Whenever the voice of Jacob is humming in synagogues and houses of study, the hands of Esau have no power.'"
Rabbi Shimon bar Yochai taught: If you see cities that are desolate in the Land of Israel, know that it is because they did

not support the schools there. How do we know this? "Why is the land in ruins, laid waste like a wilderness with none passing through? The Lord replied: Because they forsook My Torah that I had set before them" (Jeremiah 9:11–12). What did [the wicked] King Ahaz do when he wanted to drive God's presence from the world? He destroyed the synagogues and houses of study. He thought: . . . if there are no school-children, there are no adult students. If no adult students, no disciples. No disciples, no Sages. No Sages, no Torah. No Torah, no synagogues and houses of study. No synagogues and houses of study, the Divine Presence will depart from the world!
—Midrash ha-Gadol Genesis-Toledot 27:22

In the world of the Sages, verses or phrases often take on a life of their own quite different from their original meaning in the Torah. "The voice is the voice of Jacob, yet the hands are the hands of Esau" is a superb case in point. In context, Isaac is simply remarking with wonder over the fact that the person speaking to him sounds like Jacob, but his hands feel like Esau's. How can that be? The Sages transformed this into an easily quoted brief summary of Jewish history. Jacob—Israel—became the symbol of the Jewish people. During the Roman period the Sages used Esau as the symbol of Rome. The fact that Esau's other name was Edom, which means red, and red was the imperial Roman color made Esau an easy stand-in for Rome. If the Sages wanted to say something negative about Rome without using the word, they simply talked about Esau/Edom. Therefore, this verse could easily be made to mean that Jews (Jacob) are known for their voice, that is, studying texts and chanting Torah, while Esau/Rome has all the power, that is, physical strength.

In the first midrash, the Sages use this verse to convey that when the hands of Rome slaughtered Jews, the voice of Jacob—the Jews— cried out in pain. Examples are given of Rome quashing a rebellion of Egyptian Jews, Rome destroying the Temple and exiling Jews in 70 CE, and Rome executing victory over the Bar Kokhba rebellion in its last holdout fortress, Beitar, in 135 CE, a massacre of overwhelming proportions.

In the second interpretation, the Sages make the point that the voice, that is, the sound of study and prayer in houses of study and synagogues, is the true strength of the Jewish people. As long as these voices—the voice of Jacob—are heard, Judaism will live and overcome any enemies. This is expressed in a tale, undoubtedly apocryphal, of Avnomos, a famous gentile philosopher who lived in the Land of Israel and often engaged in discussions with Rabbi Meir (end of the first century to the beginning of the second century CE). Asked by enemies of the Jews if it is possible to defeat the Jews, Avnomos answers that as long as Jewish children—the voice of Jacob—are studying, the power of Rome—the hands of Esau—cannot defeat the Jews.

In the last interpretation (found as part of the discussion of *this* verse, although the verse itself is not cited), Rabbi Shimon bar Yohai, a disciple of Rabbi Akiva, takes this idea further, asserting that failing to support schools of Torah (where the voice of Jacob is heard) leads inevitably to ruin. The hands of Esau will then prevail. Having lived through the disastrous Bar Kokhba rebellion, bar Yohai blames the lack of support for educating children for the desolation and defeat that followed.

Jews, then, defined themselves as a people of words and study. Rome prided itself on the might of its arms. Unfortunately, the voice of Jacob was not always sufficient to defeat the hands of Esau, but it is true that without the voice of Jacob, without the study of Jewish tradition, without a good Jewish education for children, the future of the Jewish people and the continuity of Judaism cannot be assured.

D'rash: Personal Reflection

THE VOICE OF JACOB

When I became the rabbi of a young, small congregation, one of the delights of my work was the presence of a young boy, six or seven years old, who came to every service, asked questions, gave answers during my talks, and, in general, became my shadow. This was a child enamored of learning. He came alone, because his parents were members of a different congregation that was not traditional enough for him. When he reached the age when he could attend first grade in our afternoon school, Kitah Aleph, he asked to enroll. I was very pleased to think he would be studying with us and adding his voice to the voices of the children learning Torah. There was only one problem. His parents were not members of the congregation, and the synagogue rules stipulated that only children of members could attend our school. His parents, for whatever reason, refused to take out a membership, but they offered to pay the membership dues or even more so that he could attend our school. The synagogue board, which was generally rather reasonable, considered this offer, took a vote, and turned it down. No membership, no school!

The boy was devastated, and so was I. An emergency meeting of the board was called to discuss the problem. The board remained adamant. It had become a matter of principle. They argued that if we admitted this child without membership, our whole membership program would collapse.

As I listened to the discussion, I could not believe what I was hearing. No child in our school was more anxious to learn. No one else was so devoted and regular in attendance at the synagogue. Were we really going to turn him away?

Finally, it was my turn to speak. Very quietly I said, "I don't think I would really want to be the rabbi of a synagogue that denied a child the opportunity to go to school and study Torah." There was total silence. A vote was taken, and he was admitted to our school. I breathed a sigh of relief.

After a few years I moved on to another synagogue and lost touch with the youngster. Some fifteen years later, when I was in charge of the rabbinical school program in Israel for the seminary students who spent a year studying in Jerusalem, I would go to New York to interview the students who would be coming the following year. Once a young man came into my room in New York to be interviewed. I did not know who he was. He said to me, "Do you remember the youngster who used to follow you around and answer all your questions?" I said, "Yes, of course!" and said the boy's name. "Well, that's me!" he said, and we had a joyful reunion.

He continued his studies and became a rabbi, a very successful one, beloved by the congregation he served faithfully for many years. When he invited me to speak there, the members came up to thank me for having risked my position so that he could go to school, because without that, he had often told them, he would never have become a rabbi, and they would never have had the privilege of his teaching and guidance. His was indeed the voice of Jacob, helping to assure the Jewish future. I could not have been prouder.

Va-yetse'

The Place

GENESIS 28:10–32:3

Jacob left Beer-sheba, and set out for Haran. He came upon a certain place and stopped there for the night, for the sun had set. Taking one of the stones of that place, he put it under his head and lay down in that place. He had a dream; a stairway was set on the ground and the top reached to the sky, and angels of God were going up and down on it. And the Lord was standing beside him and He said, "I am the Lord, the God of your father Abraham and the God of Isaac: the ground on which you are lying I will assign to you and your offspring."

—Genesis 28:10–13

P'shat: Explanation

Faced with the threat of death at the hands of the brother he has outwitted, Jacob leaves the land of Canaan for his ancestral home in Paddan-Aram. This entire section is filled with echoes of previous journeys filled and unfulfilled. His father, Isaac, had wanted to go down to Egypt because of a famine; God forbade Isaac to leave the land but promised him the land of Canaan and heirs great in number. This is the same promise God made earlier to Abraham (Genesis 26:1–4).

Now God tells Jacob the very opposite ("Remember, I am with you: I will protect you wherever you go") while continuing to give him the same promise of land and posterity. This is the blessing Jacob received from Isaac before he left, but now it comes from God, the source of all blessing.

34

This meeting also echoes Abraham's servant's journey to the same ancestral home in order to find a wife for Isaac. That is exactly what will happen here as well; Jacob too will find a wife from within the family. But unlike the servant, who went with an entire caravan, gold, and jewels and came back immediately with the bride, Jacob goes with nothing, no prospects, and no hope of a speedy return. Yet he has one important thing: God's promise that he will return and that he will be protected and blessed.

D'rash: Exposition of the Sages

"He came upon a certain place [makom] . . ." Rabbi Huna said in the name of Rabbi Ami: Why is the Holy One called by the name "Makom — Place"? Because God is the place of His world, but His world is not His place. Another interpretation. "He came upon a certain place . . ." "Came upon" means prayer. He [Jacob] prayed there. Rabbi Shmuel bar Nahman said, "The three daily prayers were created to reflect the three times a day when the day changes."
—Genesis Rabbah 68:9

"He came upon a certain place . . ." Rabbi Joshua ben Levi said: The daily prayers were created by the Patriarchs. Abraham created the Morning Prayer, as it says "Next morning, Abraham hurried to the place where he had stood before the Lord . . ." (Genesis 19:27). "Standing" always means praying, as in "Phinehas stood and prayed . . ." (Psalm 106:30). Isaac created the afternoon prayer, as it says, "And Isaac went out to meditate in the field toward evening" (Genesis 24:63). "Meditate" always means praying, as in "A prayer of the lowly man when he is faint and pours out his meditation before the Lord" (Psalm 102:1). Jacob created the evening prayer, as it says, "He came upon a certain place and stopped there for the night, for the sun had set." "Came upon" always means

praying, as in ". . . As for you, do not pray for this people, do
not raise a cry of prayer on their behalf, do not come upon
Me . . ." (Jeremiah 7:16). The Rabbis said, "They established the
daily prayers according to the Tamid offering in the Temple."
—Jerusalem Talmud *Berachot* 4,7a

The first two Hebrew words in the verse, *va-ifga ba-makom*, translated as "He came upon a certain place," seemed unusual to the Sages, who gave them various interpretations. The root of *va-ifga* means "to come close," "to approach," or "to appeal to someone." Therefore, it could easily mean "to pray." *Makom*—a place—is used in later Hebrew as a name of God— "the place of His world." This phrase might mean that Jacob prayed in that place or that he prayed to God. Calling God "the place" is explained as meaning both that God is all that exists (God is the place in which the universe exists, a rather mystical approach to the Creation) and that God is not to be identified with the physical world. God is unique, the Other.

Once the Sages determined that *va-ifga* means that Jacob prayed (either in that place or to God), they began a discussion on the origin of the three daily prayers. The crucial point is that Jacob created what has become the daily evening prayer. The Sages then demonstrate that each of the other two Patriarchs also created a daily prayer, Abraham for the morning and Isaac for the afternoon.

Three different explanations are given to the question, Why do we have three daily prayers? First, they reflect the three different parts of the day: morning, afternoon, and evening. Second, we Jews follow the precedent established by Abraham, Isaac, and Jacob. Third, the prayers were established to be recited in synagogues at the same times as the required daily *Tamid* sacrifices: they were brought in the morning and again in the afternoon, and the remaining parts were burnt in the evening.

The third reason is most probably closest to the historical reality. Attaching the prayers to the Patriarchs, however, establishes a connection to our early history and to the lives of our ancestors, giving an extra dimension to them.

D'rash: Personal Reflection

PRAYING WHEN GOD IS ABSENT

Prayer, especially fixed, required prayer, is a difficult art. Reciting a certain predetermined set of words at specified times every day, whether one feels the need and the inclination or not, is not easy. According to Jewish tradition, true prayer requires *kavannah*, usually translated as "intention" or "concentration." The Hebrew comes from a word meaning "direction." It is similar to the idea of "hitting the mark." The mark, in this case, is communication with God. Can one really have such intention day after day?

While delivering a talk to seminary students on the subject of prayer, Prof. Louis Finkelstein, then chancellor of the Jewish Theological Seminary, was asked if meaningful daily prescribed prayer, as opposed to spontaneous prayer, was really possible. He responded that it was not only possible but necessary, because only continual daily prayer would enable one to reach true *kavannah*. He was then asked if he always had *kavannah* when he prayed, to which he replied, "Only sometimes, but unless I pray routinely daily I would never have it."

I know what he meant. I have taught liturgy and written extensively about it, but understanding prayer and achieving true prayer are two different things.

Perhaps the closest experience I have ever had of true prayer with *kavannah* was also the time when I could not pray at all. It occurred during a study tour to Poland. The trip took us to Warsaw, Lublin, Krakow, and many small towns along the way, as well as to Treblinka and Majdanek. The last stop was Auschwitz. I must admit that I had always been reluctant to go to Poland. Why would anyone want to visit places in which such terrible atrocities had been perpetrated? Yet I had come to the conclusion that it was important for me to see the Nazi camps in Poland. I had always felt a certain guilt over the fact that I lived through the years of the Shoah as a child and teenager in peace and happiness when my fellow Jews of the same age were being tortured and slaughtered in Europe. Had my grandparents not immigrated to the United States, my family and I would have been there as well. Later in life I made very close friends who were Shoah survivors, including some who had survived Auschwitz. Now I felt it only right to go to the place they had been. Obviously, my experience would not in any way re-create what they had suffered, but just being there would somehow be a tribute to them and to all those who endured that martyrdom.

We began each day with the morning service in a different synagogue, usually one that was no longer a house of prayer but either a ruin or a museum of Polish Jewish history. The day we went to "tour" Auschwitz, we arose very early and traveled in the dark through dense fog. Remembering the 1956 film *Night and Fog*, I had the strangest feeling: "I am on the way to Auschwitz!"

Stopping first in the town of Oswiecim just outside the camp, we recited *Shacharit*—the morning service—in the restored synagogue that is part of the museum there. It was at the same time both the most meaningful *Shacharit* I have ever experienced and the only time I felt I could not pray at all. How could one reach God, experience true prayer, at the entrance to Auschwitz? If there is any place—*makom*—in the world where God—*ha-Makom*—was not to be found, it was surely there. Yet in a strange paradox that I cannot truly explain or understand, out of the total absence of the Divine, I suddenly prayed with more *kavannah* than ever before and experienced the deepest emotion one could imagine. It is as if only when in total despair can one begin to feel a glimmer of hope. The only words that can express it are from the story of Jacob as understood by the midrash, *va-ifga ba-makom*, "He approached the place—he approached God in prayer."

Va-yishlah

Jacob's Dilemma

GENESIS 32:4–36:43

*Jacob was greatly frightened and troubled, and he divided
the people with him, and the flocks and herds and camels,
into two camps, thinking, "If Esau comes to the one camp
and attacks it, the other camp may yet escape." Then Jacob
said, "O God of my father Abraham and God of my father
Isaac, O Lord, who said to me, 'Return to your native land
and I will deal bountifully with you!' I am unworthy of all the
kindness that You have so steadfastly shown Your servant"*
—Genesis 32:8–11

P'shat: Explanation

Of the three Patriarchs, Jacob is the most complex and the only one
who really changes as time goes on. The Jacob who returns to Canaan
after so many years in exile is not the Jacob who fled from his home.
Not only has he become wealthy when before he was poor, not only
does he now have a huge family when before he was alone, but his
character has changed. He left as a schemer and returns as a humble
man who begins his plea to God with the words, "I am unworthy."

The change is marked with the change in name, from Jacob, a word
that connotes something curved or crooked, to Israel, which implies
the word *yashar*—straight and upright. He is frightened and troubled
by the coming encounter with his brother, Esau, who had threatened
to kill him. Does Esau still harbor those thoughts? The information
Jacob receives that Esau "is coming to meet you, and there are four

hundred men with him" (Genesis 32:7) is quite sufficient to cause him concern.

Yet even though he is frightened and troubled, Jacob is not primarily concerned for himself. His first thought is of his family, his wives and his children. He divides his group into two so that in case of a catastrophic attack, at least some will survive (Genesis 32:8). He asks God to deliver him and to care for "mothers and children alike" (Genesis 32:11). He does his best to move them all out of harm's way. He prepares for the meeting as best he can and at the same time begs God for protection.

D'rash: Exposition of the Sages

Rabbi Pinhas said in the name of Rabbi Reuven: Two people received assurance from the Holy One and yet were afraid—the chosen one among the Patriarchs and the chosen one among the prophets.... To [Jacob] the Holy One had said, "Remember, I am with you: I will protect you wherever you go..." (Genesis 28:15) but nevertheless he was frightened, as it says, "Jacob was greatly frightened."... To [Moses] the Holy One had said, "...I will be with you..." (Exodus 3:12) but nevertheless he was frightened, as it says, "But the Lord said to Moses, 'Do not fear him...'" (Numbers 21:34) and it would not say "Do not fear him" unless he was afraid.... From this we learn that the righteous are never at ease in this world. "Jacob was greatly frightened and troubled..." Rabbi Judah b'reb Elai said, "Are not 'frightened' and 'troubled' the same thing? Rather it means: he 'was greatly frightened' that he might kill and 'troubled' that he might be killed." [Jacob] thought, "If he overpowers me he will kill me and if I overpower him, I will kill him!" Therefore he "was greatly frightened" that he might kill and "troubled" that he might be killed.

—Genesis Rabbah 76:1–2

The verse stating that Jacob was afraid seems to have bothered the Sages. First of all, they wondered why he should have been afraid when he had God's assurance that God would protect him. In fact, he had been so awestruck by his vision of the stairway to heaven that he had proclaimed he was in the very abode of God and in the gateway to heaven. And he had indeed come safely through all the events in Laban's house, difficult as they may have been.

The Sages noticed that Moses also had been afraid. They concluded that the righteous are never truly at ease in this world. Are they justifying these fears? After all, if one sees someone else's army on the way, is it not normal to have fear, even if one believes that God will help? Or are the Sages saying that no one—not even the most righteous— should ever feel totally assured of not facing any troubles?

The other matter that bothered Rabbi Judah, a second-century *tanna* (the early Sages prior to 200 CE) who lived in the Land of Israel, was the Torah's use of two similar words to describe Jacob's fear: one from the root "to be afraid" (*vayira*) and the other from the word for "trouble" (*vayetzer*). Assuming that each word has significance, he explains that two different things worry Jacob. There can be only two outcomes to his conflict with Esau—either Jacob kills Esau or Jacob is killed by Esau—and he is terrified by either one.

One might have thought that, given their history, Jacob would be happy to be rid of Esau. Defeating him, that is, killing him, might seem a good solution to his problems, but Rabbi Judah does not see it that way. Of course, Jacob does not want to die—who does? But he also does not want to kill, even if it is in self-defense. Was Jacob a pacifist? Hardly. Nor can one find justification for pacifism within Jewish teachings. Pacifism in such a context would imply surrendering one's very life to evil. Judaism, rather, teaches that you must kill the one who is trying to kill you. But that does not mean that you have to make killing your goal. There should be some restraint, some hope that killing can be avoided. Rabbi Judah's interpretation of Jacob's fears and troubles makes this point.

D'rash: Personal Reflection

FEAR OF KILLING OR BEING KILLED

Although I have served in two armies, I have never been in combat. As a chaplain in the US Air Force I was prohibited from even learning how to fire a weapon, much less carry one. Later, at a more mature age, I served in the Israeli army reserves, but not in a fighting unit. Therefore, I have no firsthand knowledge of what it means to be engaged in an endeavor where killing another human being, the enemy, is the goal.

Some of my children and grandchildren have faced this in their service in the Israel Defense Forces (IDF), and I do not envy them. I am glad that the Israeli army has a code of ethics that limits unnecessary killing. The existence of cases in which soldiers have been convicted for killing terrorists when the terrorists were no longer threats is to the IDF's credit.

I did have one experience, however, that helped me to appreciate Jacob's dilemma. As a rabbinical student, I was one of a group of ten Americans who spent a year studying in Israel in 1955–56. At the time, there were many incursions of Palestinian terrorists into Israel, resulting in the deaths of innocent civilians. In the spring our group volunteered to go to a kibbutz on the border with Jordan and help build needed defenses against possible incursions. During the day we dug trenches and erected barbed-wire fences. At night from time to time we had guard duty.

The first time I was to guard, I was given a rifle. I had no training in shooting and had not the slightest idea of how to handle it. I was given a very rudimentary introduction and sent off to patrol a certain section of the kibbutz.

Late at night I suddenly saw a figure coming toward me, holding something and saying something I could not understand. As he came closer, I could see by his clothing that he was an Arab. I held up my rifle and was totally frozen. I think I told him to stand still, but he didn't, and I thought, Should I shoot? Shoot into the air? Had I been trained, I might have known what to do and how to use that rifle. If he had a gun or even a knife, I could be killed. I hesitated.

And just then a member of the kibbutz came running to me. "It's OK," he said. "He's a friend, someone from the area we know." The kibbutznik explained that they had given this fellow a place to sleep for the night, and he was asking me for some kerosene for the lantern he was holding. They had simply neglected to tell me that he would be arriving. That neglect could have ended in catastrophe. Even untrained as I was, I might have shot an innocent man. I put down the rifle and could breathe again. But I returned to my room, and I was as pale as a ghost.

Then I really understood Jacob's dilemma: what it means to feel fear—fear of killing and fear of being killed.

Va-yeshev

Joseph the Youth

GENESIS 37:1–40:23

At seventeen years of age, Joseph tended the flocks as a young
helper to his brothers, the sons of his father's wives Bilhah and
Zilpah. And Joseph brought bad reports of them to their father.
Now Israel loved Joseph best of all his sons, for he was the child
of his old age; and he had made him a coat of many colors.
And when his brothers saw that their father loved him more
than any of his brothers, they hated him so that they could
not speak a friendly word to him. Once Joseph had a dream
which he told to his brothers; and they hated him even more.

—Genesis 37:1–5

P'shat: Explanation

This is the first of three biblical portions devoted to the saga of Joseph.
From here until the end of the book of Genesis, Joseph is the central character. His life story is told in greater detail than that of any
other figure in Genesis, and it is a fascinating story, perhaps the finest novella in ancient Hebrew literature. No wonder, then, that the
great German writer Thomas Mann created the long tetralogy *Joseph*
and His Brothers.

Although it seems that this is one of those stories in which "all's well
that ends well," that is not quite the case. There is more than a bit of
tragedy here, especially in the subsequent portions, and the central
elements of the tragedy are contained in this portion's few introductory verses. To put it mildly, there is no love lost between Joseph and
his brothers—or, more accurately, his half-brothers. He has only one

full sibling, the young Benjamin. We see immediately why the brothers detest Joseph: he is what we would today call "an informer." Given the task of assisting his older siblings in tending sheep, he takes the opportunity to bring back evil reports of their conduct to their father, Israel. We are not told what Joseph said they did or even if Joseph reported the truth, but it does not matter. What did he expect would happen if he spied and told on his brothers? Did it never occur to him that there was any cause for concern? After all, he knew his father favored him, and that was all that mattered, or so he thought.

Later, when Joseph has dreams predicting that he will lord it over his brothers and parents, just as he did not hesitate to tell tales to his father, so he does not hesitate to reveal these dreams to his brothers. Silence in both cases would have been the better part of discretion.

Nor is his father, Israel, without blame. A parent who openly favors one child over another is only asking for trouble, and in this case troubles came in myriads. Did Israel think that a coat of many colors wouldn't be noticed or that his other sons wouldn't resent such a lavish gift to this young lad who habitually acted as if he were their superior?

D'rash: Exposition of the Sages

"At seventeen years of age, Joseph tended the flocks as a young helper." He was seventeen years old and you call him "young"? Rather, "young" here means that he acted young and foolish! He would make-up his eyes, adorn his hair and walk on high heels. What bad reports did he bring? Rabbi Meir says, "Your sons are under suspicion of eating a limb from a living animal." . . . Rabbi Shimon says, "They are lusting after the native women." He was punished for these false reports. Resh Lakish says in the name of Rabbi Elazar ben Azarya, "A parent should not treat one child better than another, for it was the coat of many colors that caused Joseph's brothers to hate him so."

—Exodus Rabbah 44:7,8

The Sages had no problem finding fault with the actions of biblical figures, even exalted ones. Although it became common parlance for Joseph to be called "Joseph the righteous," and although Jacob is one of the three Patriarchs lauded time and time again in Jewish liturgy, whenever the Sages looked at Joseph's and Jacob's deeds and found them unacceptable, the Sages said so loudly and clearly.

In this case, verse 37:1 contained a word the Sages found puzzling. The Hebrew word *na-ar* is translated here as "young helper." Usually, the word simply means a "young person," not a child, yet not quite an adult man. At times, however, it seems to connote an aide to someone else. That seems to be the usage here. Since Joseph was much younger than his brothers, he was not assigned to them as an equal but as an assistant. In this sense, the word is not pejorative but simply descriptive.

The Sages, however, did not see it that way. They defined *na-ar* by its more common meaning, "youngster," and therefore found the text problematic, because at age seventeen, as specified here, Joseph would be too old to be called a youngster. At seventeen one is considered to have outlived early youth.

Yet in Rabbinic times, being a *na-ar* sometimes had another meaning: acting childishly, foolishly, even in a ridiculous manner. (Later this evolved into the Yiddish word *naarishkeit*, "nonsensical actions.") Therefore, the Sages said that this verse could only mean that although Joseph was already seventeen, he acted in a much less mature manner, outlandishly, as only a foolish child would. He painted his eyes, he curled his hair, he walked strangely. He called attention to himself in an unseemly manner—perhaps akin in our own time to how some teenagers dress and display body piercings to emphasize their rebelliousness and independence. Perhaps the over-the-top coat Jacob gave him encouraged Joseph to adopt these somewhat repulsive practices.

The Sages also understood the expression "bad reports" to mean not simply that Joseph related the bad things his brothers had done but that the reports themselves were bad in being untrue and intended to cast aspersions on innocent people. For these reasons Joseph was punished.

Furthermore, the Sages concluded that Jacob had acted wrongly. He had violated one of the basic principles of good parenting: he did not treat his children equally. Jacob was therefore the cause of the hatred Joseph's brothers felt for him that brought tragedy in its wake.

In sum, the Sages were very clear here that the events to come that caused Joseph and Jacob to suffer were largely the result of their own foolish actions.

D'rash: Personal Reflection

NO HUMAN BEING IS BLAMELESS

To me, one of the finest things about the way the people in the Torah are depicted is that none of them — absolutely none — is without fault. And the recognition of their imperfections is found in both the Torah and the explanations and legends the Sages created. If the Torah could relate the sins of Moses, Aaron, Miriam, and Joseph, it surely could relate them of anyone else. After all, no one in Judaism is without sin, and we do not believe that any human being is perfectly blameless.

That is why I was upset when attempts were made to force prominent authors in the Orthodox world to recall books they wrote that dared to portray biblical figures as less than perfect. An extremely well known authority in Israel had to withdraw some of his books, and another in Great Britain was compelled to rewrite some sections of his book due to the protests of extremist groups. If the Sages could say of Joseph that he acted foolishly and of Jacob that giving Joseph a coat of many colors was the cause of his son's being sold, why can't scholars today say similar things?

Some people are also inclined to castigate anyone who finds fault with their rabbinical leaders, leading to situations in which certain religious authorities are perceived as perfect, placed on a pedestal above ordinary human beings, and become cult figures worshipped by their followers. This distortion of Jewish belief and Jewish tradition should be resisted at all costs. We worship God alone, and not human beings, exalted and learned as they may be.

Mikkets

The Dangers of Power

GENESIS 41:1–44:17

*Pharaoh then gave Joseph the name Zaphenath-paneah; and
he gave him for a wife Asenath daughter of Poti-phera, priest
of On. Thus Joseph emerged in charge of the land of Egypt. . . .
Before the years of famine came, Joseph became the father
of two sons, whom Asenath daughter of Poti-phera, priest
of On, bore to him. Joseph named the first-born Manasseh,
meaning, "God has made me forget completely my hardship
and my parental home." And the second he named Ephraim,
meaning, "God has made me fertile in the land of my affliction."*
—Genesis 41:45,50–52

P'shat: Explanation

This is the high point of the original "rags to riches" story. Earlier,
Joseph descended to the depths of the pit, to the land of Egypt, to
slavery and to imprisonment. Now he rises in one fell swoop to the
heights of power, second in command in the world's greatest kingdom, Egypt. He is robed in splendor, adorned with jewels, and given
a chariot. The lad whose fabulous coat had been ripped from him so
that he was dressed in rags now bears the robes of a prince.

Pharaoh also gives Joseph a name or perhaps a title in Egyptian
whose meaning is uncertain. It may mean "God speaks; he lives." The
Greek translation of the Torah understands it as "the sustainer of life."

Pharaoh, incidentally, continues to refer to him as "Joseph" (Genesis 41:55). He also gives Joseph a wife of high status: the daughter
of an important priest of the Egyptian religion.

In what way, if any, does Joseph remain a "Hebrew"? Wouldn't the daughter of the priest raise her children as Egyptians, worshippers of On? Joseph certainly dresses and acts like an Egyptian. When his brothers come down to Egypt they do not recognize him. He speaks to them in Egyptian and uses a translator. When they report back to Jacob they refer to him as "the man who is lord of the land" (Genesis 42:30,33). He does not eat with them, because he follows the Egyptian practice of "not dining with the Hebrews, since that would be abhorrent to the Egyptians" (Genesis 43:32).

For all that, when his sons are born he gives them Hebrew names! (Did he circumcise them as well? Circumcision was practiced in Egypt, although not on the eighth day.) The names Joseph chose are descriptive not of the children but of Joseph's circumstances. The first, Mannaseh, means "to forget"; Joseph says that he has forgotten his troubles "and my parental home." Does that mean that he has cut himself off completely from his origins—or is intending to do so? That might explain the fact that in all the years of reigning as second in command in Egypt, he never attempted to contact his family. This would have been easy enough. More than that, he never attempted to inform his father that he was alive—and when the opportunity came to do so upon his brothers' appearance he postponed acting upon it, keeping his father still in the dark while Joseph played out his plan to test his brothers.

The second son's name, Ephraim, comes from the Hebrew for "fertility"; Joseph says that he has been made fertile "in the land of my affliction." It seems strange to call Egypt, which he now effectively rules, the land of his affliction. If anything, it is the land of his prosperity. Perhaps he is referring to what he suffered at the beginning when he was a slave. Or is this a Freudian slip, indicating that he is still not really at home here? Perhaps he has not forgotten his parents' home so completely after all.

Yet for all that, where is his concern for his father, Jacob, all this time? Carrying out his elaborate plan with his brothers when they come down to Egypt, did Joseph not stop to think about his father's feelings? What kind of a person acts like that?

D'rash: Exposition of the Sages

Joseph earned merit by tending to his father's burial
himself, even though he was the greatest of the brothers,
as it is said, "So Joseph went up to bury his father . . ."
(Genesis 50:7). And whom have we greater than
Joseph, since Moses himself attended to his burial?
—Mishnah *Sotah* 1:9

Rav Judah said in the name of Rav: Why was Joseph
referred to as "bones" when he was still alive? ["So Joseph
made the sons of Israel swear, saying, 'When God has
taken notice of you, you shall carry up my bones from
here'" (Genesis 50:25).] Because he did not attempt to
safeguard his father's honor when they [his brothers]
said to him, ". . . your servant, our father . . ." (Genesis
44:31). He did not reprimand them. . . . Why did Joseph die
before his brothers? It was because he acted haughtily.
—*Sotah* 13b

The Mishnah, which Rabbi Judah the Prince had edited in its final
form by ca. 200 CE, is usually devoted to discussions of Jewish law.
From time to time, however, it discusses legends and interpretations of biblical stories. In this section it comments on Joseph's
merits and praises him in exaggerated terms. The Sages notice that
for the great burial cortege of Jacob, Joseph himself gathers all
the entourage of Pharaoh's court to honor his father. His brothers
are not mentioned at all. In other words, Joseph personally under-
takes what might be considered a task too trivial for a person as
great as he. And Joseph's merit is demonstrated afterward by the
fact that no less a personage than Moses personally takes care of
finding Joseph's body and carrying it out with the Israelites when
they leave Egypt (Exodus 13:19). Thus, this Mishnah sees Joseph as
a man of great integrity.

In the discussion in the Talmud, however, Rav, a third-century Babylonian *amora* who had studied with Rabbi Judah in the Land of Israel before founding the great academy in Sura, seems to take a completely different stance concerning Joseph. According to Rav, Joseph does not defend his father's honor. When his brothers refer to Jacob as "your servant," not yet knowing that this Egyptian overlord is actually their brother, Joseph should not have allowed them to call Jacob "your servant." That was not proper respect. Furthermore, Rav noted, Joseph is on his deathbed before his older brothers and makes them promise to carry out his bones from Egypt. Why does Joseph die before them? Because "he acted haughtily." His exalted position went to his head.

Rav was not alone in criticizing Joseph. Another midrash, for example, contends that he was punished for "causing his brothers to rend their garments" when the golden cup was found among Benjamin's possessions (Genesis Rabbah 92:13).

D'rash: Personal Reflection

THE RABBINICAL EGO

Calling Joseph "haughty" is not a light matter. It reflects a serious criticism, since "haughty" is the exact opposite of "humble," a virtue highly praised in Jewish tradition and in fact the highest compliment in the Torah. Of Moses the Torah says, "Now Moses was a very humble man, more so than any other man on earth" (Numbers 12:3).

Haughtiness comes easily to those in positions of power and influence. Considering the position into which Joseph was catapulted, one can understand how he came to be haughty. It is always difficult to be the person in charge, like Moses and Joseph, or otherwise attain a high position and title—king, president, pope, or even just rabbi—and still remain humble. Yet understanding and condoning haughtiness are not the same thing. Somehow Moses resisted and Joseph did not. Other leaders have done so as well—and some have not.

When my wife and I became engaged to be married, I was still a rabbinical student. The teacher who inspired me and encouraged me to become a rabbi told my then fiancée that the most important thing she could do as my wife would be to see to it that I did not develop a swelled head. It would be her job to keep me from becoming self-important—haughty. He felt that the rabbinate led to that all too easily.

That may be why, when my alma mater, the Jewish Theological Seminary, asked me to present a paper at a conference entitled "Moral and Ethical Dilemmas in the Rabbinate," I spoke about the rabbinical ego, calling it the most dangerous character-destroying factor rabbis face. Anytime one is put in a position of representing the Torah, of standing for Jewish law, of having a title that automatically grants one respect, even if only outwardly, while exactly the opposite feelings may lie behind the scenes, it is all too easy to develop an inflated ego and believe the nice things people say to your face. Standing on a platform and giving advice to hundreds of people week after week can have a devastating effect on one's attempts to remain humble.

I made several suggestions to help reduce the feeling of superiority, to bring the rabbi closer to the congregants and lessen any feeling of arrogance and superiority. Mainly, I suggested that a rabbi should try to see himself (this was before there were women rabbis) as a teacher. "A teacher is not a cleric, a functionary, a prophet, or a dogmatist; he is a guide to Jewish living," I wrote, recalling that the ancient title for rabbis was ḥakhamim—Sages, meaning "teachers."

Working with rabbis in training for many years, I always assigned that paper for their reading and discussion, hoping that it would help them to avoid this pitfall in their careers as I tried to avoid it myself—with the constant help of my wife.

Va-yiggash

GENESIS 44:18–47:27

*Then Judah went up to him and said, "Please, my lord, let
your servant appeal to my lord, and do not be impatient
with your servant, you who are the equal of Pharaoh. . . .
Now, if I come to your servant my father and the boy is
not with us—since his own life is so bound up with his—
when he sees that the boy is not with us, he will die, and
your servants will send the white head of your servant
our father down to Sheol in grief. Now your servant has
pledged himself to the boy to my father, saying, 'If I do not
bring him back to you, I shall stand guilty before my father
forever.' Therefore, please let your servant remain as a slave
to my lord instead of the boy, and let him go back with his
brothers. For how can I go back to my father unless the boy
is with me? Let me not be witness to the woe that would
overtake my father!" Joseph could no longer control himself.*
—Genesis 44:18,30–45:1

P'shat: Explanation

The long and fascinating saga of Joseph and his brothers comes to a
climax when Judah speaks to him so eloquently and with such heart-
rending pathos. Joseph has maneuvered his brothers into a situation
where they have to make decisions similar to those they made years
before concerning Joseph. When his brothers first come to him, he
does not immediately reveal who he is. From there, he could have
either castigate them for what they have done (while promising

to care for them nevertheless, for his father's sake) or forgiven and embraced them on the spot. Instead, Joseph acts in a very calculated fashion. He intends to cause them anguish and see if they will repeat their callousness shown to him years ago or act differently when confronted with leaving Benjamin with him in Egypt. Perhaps this is his revenge. Perhaps it is simply his way of making certain that his brothers repent and change their ways. Or perhaps it is a bit of both.

Judah's beautiful speech (only its end is reproduced above) shows without doubt that the brothers have changed. They would no longer do what they had done, and those, like Judah, who had shown some concern for Joseph but had not acted bravely enough were now committed to save Benjamin at all costs.

The speech does something else as well. By the continuous references to Jacob and the description of what Jacob would feel, the references to Jacob's frailty and possible death, Judah breaks through Joseph's outward coldness and causes him to simply lose control: he weeps and reveals himself as their forgiving brother. It is as if suddenly the dam has burst and all Joseph's pent-up emotions are released. The Egyptian viceroy has now simply become Joseph their brother. The rest is reconciliation and reunion with Jacob.

D'rash: Exposition of the Sages

His students said to Rabbi Tarfon, "Our Master—teach us by what merit did Judah warrant receiving the kingship?" He said to them, "What do you say?" They replied, "Because he said, 'What do we gain by killing our brother and covering up his blood? Come let us sell him to the Ishmaelites, but let us not do away with him ourselves. After all, he is our brother, our own flesh'" (Genesis 37:26). He said to them, "Saving Joseph's life was only sufficient to atone for selling him!" "If so, it was because he said, 'She [Tamar] is more in the right than I...'" (Genesis 38:26). He said to them, "His confession was only sufficient to atone for his having relations with her!" "If

so it was because [of his humility when] he said, 'Therefore
please let your servant remain as a slave to my lord instead of
the boy, and let the boy go back with his brothers'" (Genesis
44:33). He said, "But in every case one who makes a guarantee
is required to fulfill it." They said to him, "Our Master—teach
us by what merit did Judah warrant receiving the kingship?"
He said to them, "When the tribes of Israel stood at the sea
each one contended, 'I will plunge in first!'. . . While they were
arguing, Nahshon son of Aminadav, followed by the entire
tribe of Judah, jumped into the waves of the sea. Therefore the
tribe of Judah merited receiving the kingship. Said God, 'He
who sanctified My Name at the sea shall rule over Israel.'"
—Mekhilta Be-Shallah 6

This dialogue between the first-century Sage Rabbi Tarfon and his students demonstrates that the Sages of Israel preferred to involve their
students in discussing matters of interpretation and religious values.
This is similar to the Greek philosophers' use of the Socratic method
of give-and-take to arrive at the truth. Their discussions did not always
concern matters of Jewish law or observance but also included understanding Torah texts and questions of morals and ethics.

Here the discussion begins with a simple question. The students
want to know why the tribe of Judah received the honor of kingship.
The discussion then centers on Judah's personality and actions. He
was one of two brothers who attempted to prevent Joseph's murder,
the other being Reuven, the firstborn. Perhaps the kingship should
have gone to the firstborn.

Rabbi Tarfon elicits from his students that Judah had merit because
of his words and actions. He stopped his brothers from killing Joseph.
He volunteered to become Joseph's slave in Egypt so that Benjamin
could be free. In the incident with his daughter-in-law Tamar, he
confessed his sin. All of these are praiseworthy actions, but in each
instance Tarfon forces the students to see that none was sufficient
to earn Judah the great privilege of having the kings of Israel be his

descendants. In each case, whatever good he did was sufficient only for balancing out his transgressions and nothing more.

In the end, Rabbi Tarfon answers that this honor came to the tribe not because of anything Judah did but because of the actions of his descendant Nahshon and the entire tribe of Judah when they plunged into the sea before anyone else, trusting that God would save them and bring Israel through the sea in safety. This act of *kiddush ha-Shem* — sanctifying God's name — warranted their becoming the head of all the tribes. Rabbi Tarfon thus teaches his students that sanctifying God's name is a matter of supreme importance.

D'rash: Personal Reflection

MY UNCLE'S SACRED ACT

The Rabbinic value-concept of *kiddush ha-Shem* that Rabbi Tarfon emphasized is usually thought of as connoting martyrdom, and indeed that is the most extreme case. One gives up one's life rather than abandon Judaism and the worship of the One God. In Judaism, however, martyrdom is not an ideal to be pursued. Whenever possible one is to save one's life. We would rather live for the sake of God than die for it. Therefore, the same concept, *kiddush ha-Shem*, is applied to the way in which we live. Anything we do that brings honor to Judaism and God is an act of *kiddush ha-Shem*.

My uncle was not a particularly religious man, although late in life he did become active in a synagogue. But shortly before his death he told me of an incident that I think qualifies as a sacred act bringing honor to Jews.

In World War II he was part of the American force that invaded Normandy. At the very conclusion of the war, when he was with troops advancing into Germany, he and a companion were driving an army vehicle on the road when they saw a man walking on the roadside. From his appearance and clothing it was apparent that he was a concentration camp survivor. By this time the camps had been liberated, and survivors would sometimes be seen wandering from place to place. My uncle stopped the vehicle, and the man joined them. It turned out that he was indeed a Jew, even though they had no language in common.

After a while they came across a country tavern and stopped to eat and drink there. A German woman was standing at the bar in front of shelves filled with bottles of beer and other drinks. My uncle asked her to serve food to the three of them. Looking at them, the woman indicated plainly enough that she would serve the two soldiers but not him, pointing to the survivor—not the Jew. Startled, my uncle asked her to repeat that, which she did. He then calmly took his gun and shot up the bottles on the shelf behind her. Still holding the gun, he asked, "Will you serve the Jew now—and me as well, since I too am a Jew—Jude?" She said nothing but hurried to bring them food. My uncle laughed when he told the story. He was rightly proud of what he had done, and so was I.

Va-yeḥi

No Unworthy Children

GENESIS 47:28–50:26

*And Jacob called his sons and said, "Come together that I may
tell you what is to befall you in days to come. . . ." When Jacob
finished his instructions to his sons, he drew his feet into the
bed and, breathing his last, he was gathered to his people.*
—Genesis 49:1,33

P'shat: Explanation

The last portion of the book of Genesis recounts at some length the
story surrounding the death of the last of the Patriarchs, Jacob, also
known as Israel. Of all the life stories of the Patriarchs, Jacob's story
is the most complete. Of him alone are we told the complete saga of
his life, beginning with his birth and concluding with his death and
burial. We know what happened to him at every stage and his emotions as well. On his deathbed, he calls his sons together and speaks
individually to each, describing their strengths or weaknesses and
predicting their futures. He gives instructions concerning his burial
in the ancestral burial cave, and then he breathes his last.

D'rash: Exposition of the Sages

*All of his life our father Jacob was troubled, thinking, "Woe
unto me! Perhaps unworthy children will be born to me as
they were to my ancestors. Ishmael was born unto Abraham,
Esau was born unto Isaac—let no unworthy children be
born unto me as they were to my ancestors!" Thus it is that*

when our father Jacob was about to depart from this world,
he called his children to him and chastised them one by one.
When he finished speaking to them individually he called
them all together and said to them, "Do you have any doubts
in your hearts concerning your belief in He Who Spoke
and the world came into being?" They said to him, "Hear O
Israel our father—just as you have no doubt in your heart
concerning your belief in He Who Spoke and the world came
into being, so we have no doubts in our hearts concerning our
belief in He Who Spoke and the world came into being, rather
the Lord is our God, the Lord is One." Thus it is said, "Then
Israel bowed at the head of the bed" (Genesis 47:31). Did he
actually bow down upon the head of the bed? Rather it means
that he gave thanks and praise to God that no unworthy
children had been born unto him and he said, "Blessed be
the Name of His glorious Majesty for ever and ever!"
— Sifre Deuteronomy 31

In Sifre Deuteronomy, an ancient Rabbinic commentary to the book of Deuteronomy, the Sages enlarged upon the biblical story, creating a legend connecting this last scene in Jacob's life to the verse: "Hear O Israel! The Lord is our God, the Lord is One" (Deuteronomy 6:4).

This may well be the most famous verse in the Torah. Almost every Jew, learned or not, religious or not, knows these words—and can usually recite them in the original Hebrew as well: "Sh'ma Yisrael Adonai Eloheinu Adonai Ehad." The verse also became famous as the words to be recited by martyrs after Rabbi Akiva uttered it at the time of his death in the second century CE.

More than any other single verse, this verse contains the essence of Moses's teaching to the people Israel about God: the identification of the Lord—Adonai—as the one and only God. It is the essence of monotheistic belief. God's name, which we no longer know how to pronounce and for which we substitute the word Adonai, meaning "my Lord," stems from the Hebrew root meaning "existence." This

God is the very essence of existence, the source of all that exists. The word "one" asserts uniqueness. It also negates the common belief in Moses's day in the existence of a multiplicity of gods or even of two gods—a god of light and a god of darkness. There is only one.

According to this Rabbinic legend, however, the verse was first said long before the time of Moses. It was uttered by the sons of Jacob/Israel and addressed to him. Since Jacob's name was Israel, the Sages read this verse as if Jacob/Israel's sons were addressing him ("Listen, O Israel our father") and reassuring him that they too believed in the One God just as he did. This verse thus becomes Jacob's children's response to that which had troubled him all his life: his fear that his children would stray from the belief Jacob held so dear and abandon the heritage he sought to bequeath to them. He knew the history of his family. Abraham and Isaac had wayward children who did not follow their father's ways and beliefs, so it was possible that his children might go astray as well. Only when assured that all of them intended to continue in his path could Jacob die in peace. The legend then places in his mouth—as a response to their affirmation—the words that appear in the prayer book following the *Sh'ma*: "Blessed be the Name of His glorious Majesty for ever and ever!"

Was something happening in Jewish life at that time—the first and second centuries—that would have caused the Sages to read such a concern into Jacob's deathbed story? Were Jews leaving their ancestral faith? We know that paganism was no longer the threat it once had been, but perhaps the newly emerging Christian faith was a temptation to some Jews. After all, it had originated as a Jewish messianic sect.

Be that as it may, Jacob's concern as described here is very common. Most parents worry about their children's futures. What will they do, what will they believe, what will their values be? Will those things that mean the most to us continue in the lives of our children, or will our children stray in ways that bring us pain? If both Abraham and Isaac could have children who abandoned their father's beliefs, why couldn't it happen to any one of us?

In a narrow sense, this can be seen as describing the concern of every Jewish parent for whom Judaism is important about the future of his or her family. As has often been said, in the modern world, where assimilation is so easy and tempting, the question is not were our ancestors Jews, but will our descendants be Jews?

If we keep this legend created by the Sages in mind when we recite the *Sh'ma*, it makes the recitation into more than an affirmation of faith. It puts us in the place of Jacob's sons, facing Jacob, the personification of all our ancestors. In a sense we are turning to all those who have come before us—parents, grandparents, great-grandparents, and so forth, to the very beginning of the existence of Jewish identity—and assuring them that their efforts at preserving Judaism and all that it stands for were not in vain, for we are here to carry on the tradition.

D'rash: Personal Reflection

FOLLOWING MY GRANDFATHER'S WAY

My maternal grandfather passed away a year or so before my bar mitzvah. He had come to America from Lithuania at the end of the nineteenth century with the mass emigration of Eastern European Jews. In Lithuania he had had a traditional religious upbringing, studied in a yeshivah, and lived an observant life. Somehow in America all that changed.

The story in our family was that when he first arrived in New York and wanted to attend a synagogue on the High Holy Days, he was turned away because he had not been able to buy a ticket. It was said that this turned him off to Judaism. Although his home was kosher and there was some observance of Jewish holidays, these were mostly because of the influence of his wife, my grandmother. As a result, their children did not receive any Jewish education, and though, with one exception, they all married Jews, religious observance was not part of their lives.

My grandfather's life changed, however, when his daughter, my mother, married my father. He came from an observant family. My father's parents were Shabbat observers and active participants in a small Orthodox congregation. All their children had received a Jewish education and were identified Jews. Somehow my grandfather was influenced by his new *machatonim* (my father's parents) to return to the Judaism of his youth. He joined the synagogue and became very active in it. He had a lovely voice and began to lead prayers there. He was a *Kohen* (a descendant of the priestly family of Aaron), and one of my fondest memories is hearing his voice as he chanted the Blessings of the Priests during the services on the High Holy Days.

When the congregation purchased an old house and remodeled it to turn it into a synagogue, my grandfather, who was then a house painter, painted the inside of the building so that it looked like marble. He took me to watch how he did it.

At times I accompanied him to the synagogue on Shabbat and walked home with him. From our conversations it was very clear that he regretted that his children were not more concerned with their Jewishness. When we all came together for the Passover seder, for example, they could not really participate and left the table without finishing the Haggadah reading. A few others and I sat with him to conclude it.

What made him happy was that I was attending Hebrew school, was interested, and came to pray with him. At least one of his descendants could tell him that he shared his renewed beliefs and Jewish way of life. Fortunately, there were others as well.

I have always been glad that I was able to give him that assurance before he passed away. I only wish he could have lived to see that I was not the only one of his descendants to follow in his way.

II

Exodus (Shemot)

Shemot

Where Was God?

EXODUS 1:1–6:1

A new king arose over Egypt who did not know Joseph.
And he said to his people, "Look, the Israelite people are
much too numerous for us. Let us deal shrewdly with
them, so that they may not increase; otherwise in the event
of war they may join our enemies in fighting against us
and rise from the ground." So they set taskmasters over
them to oppress them with forced labor; and they built
garrison cities for Pharaoh: Pithom and Raamses.
—Exodus 1:8–11

P'shat: Explanation

The children of Jacob—now beginning to be known as an ethnic group, "the Israelites"—find themselves ensconced in Egypt. And although Jacob only intends to sojourn there in order to escape a famine, it will be some four hundred years before his descendants leave, not a small period of time by any means.

They come as honored guests, the family of the Grand Vizier Joseph, but all of that changes in this Torah portion. They become slaves, living in danger and forced to engage in backbreaking labor. An attempt is even made to kill all the male children. A long time ago, God had told Abraham this would happen and assured him that eventually the Israelites would leave as free people (Genesis 15:13–14). But "eventually" is a long time away.

In our own day, as we collectively exalt in the triumph of the Exodus, we tend to diminish the great suffering and sorrow that preceded our people's redemption.

D'rash: Exposition of the Sages

Whenever Israel is enslaved, the Divine Presence—as it were—is enslaved with them, as it is said, "And they saw the God of Israel and under His feet the likeness of bricks . . ." (Exodus 24:10). But after they were redeemed, what does it say? ". . . like the very sky for purity" (ibid.). As it says, "In all their troubles He was troubled" (Isaiah 63:9) . . . and it says, ". . . Your people whom You redeemed for Yourself from Egypt, the nation and its God!" (2 Samuel 7:23). . . . Rabbi Akiva said, "Were it not written explicitly in Scripture, it would be impossible to say it. . . . [I]t is as if Israel said to God, 'You redeemed Yourself!' Thus we find that wherever Israel was exiled, the Divine Presence—as it were—was exiled with them, as it is said, 'I was exiled to your father's house when they were in Egypt' (1 Samuel 2:27). . . . And when they will return in the future, the Divine Presence—as it were—will return with them, as it is said, 'Then the Lord your God will return with you . . .'" (Deuteronomy 30:3).
—*Mekhilta Pisha 14*

When the Sages interpreted the story of the enslavement in Egypt over a thousand years later, they did not forget the suffering. Living after the trauma of the Babylonian exile and during the period of Roman subjugation following the destruction of the Second Temple, they were keenly aware of the trial those hundreds of years of slavery must have been.

Moreover, the Sages added a dimension to the story that is missing in the original account. Knowing full well of God's promise, they nevertheless wondered at God's willingness to keep silent during this long period of affliction. Where, they wondered, was God?

Rabbi Akiva and his followers developed a daring theory: God was actually suffering along with Israel. They went so far as to picture God as enslaved together with Israel and subsequently redeemed together with Israel. According to this interpretation, at a time of human tragedy God is not passive or remote. He certainly is not on the side of the oppressors. Rather, God suffers with us and is in need of redemption, too.

According to this midrash, during the period of Israel's slavery, God appears to the people together with bricks, the symbol of slavery. (Other midrashim even specify the appearance of tools the slaves used for building.) Later, when the Israelites are redeemed, God reappears without those bricks, signifying that God is no longer enslaved.

The contention that whenever Israel suffers, God suffers as well is based on the prophet Isaiah's statement, "In all their troubles He was troubled." And, by rather complicated and daring methods of interpretation, the Sages offer as proof texts other biblical verses that say that when Israel was redeemed from Egypt, God was also redeemed.

Akiva enlarges this conception to teach that in every exile, including the current one of his time, God's Presence, the *Shekhinah*, accompanies Israel into exile and returns only when Israel returns. Thus, with no explanation of how this can be, and with the caveat that this can be said only because it is written in the Bible, Akiva contends that God is a suffering God, God is enslaved and in exile, and when we celebrate our redemption, as we do at Passover, we are actually celebrating God's redemption as well. "Said Rabbi Meir: The redemption is Mine and yours. As it were I was freed together with you!" (Exodus Rabbah 15:12).

To speak of God as a slave seems almost blasphemous. If there is anything certain about the Jewish concept of God, it is that God is not human. Unlike paganism, Judaism has no story of God's birth, death, or physical needs. For Judaism, Christianity's story of God assuming human form, dying, and coming to life again can only be seen as an alien intrusion of pagan ideas into Judaism's pure monotheism. Surely Rabbi Akiva, a dedicated monotheist and opponent of the Judeo-Christianity of his day, would not have believed in a God who becomes human. Indeed, Akiva continually uses the word *kivyachol*—"as it were"—to distance himself from a too literal interpretation of these ideas. Rather, by God's suffering he means that God identifies so closely with those who suffer that it is *as if* God were suffering. God feels our pain and is relieved and redeemed only when we are.

From Akiva's understanding, when suffering comes upon us, we need not believe that it is God's doing or that it represents God's will. We may not be able to explain why the good suffer and we may not be able to answer the question, Why did God permit this? but we can assert that God identifies with those who suffer.

D'rash: Personal Reflection

LIBERATING GOD

Akiva's intriguing idea keeps coming to mind whenever I consider our understanding of the Holocaust. How do we deal with the presence or the absence of God during that catastrophic event? Does Akiva's concept seem appropriate for our understanding of the Shoah as well?

Frequently, the Shoah is compared to the destruction of the Temple on Tisha b'Av, another catastrophic event in Jewish history. Some have even suggested that there is no need for Yom ha-Shoah (Holocaust Memorial Day) because the Shoah should be commemorated on Tisha b'Av. Fortunately, that suggestion has not been adopted. Theologically, Tisha b'Av has a very different answer to the question, Why did this happen to the Jewish people? The destruction of the Temple was God's punishment for the sins of the people. The prophetic teachings and even sections of the Torah that speak of God's forthcoming punishment as a result of disobedience are completely clear on the matter. And so, to merge the Jewish people's commemoration of the Shoah with Tisha b'Av would be to say that the Shoah too was a punishment that reflected God's will. This idea is in fact still found in the writings of certain extremist groups who point the finger at Zionism, secularism, or even non-Orthodox forms of Judaism as inducing God to punish European Jewry. I find the idea repulsive and insulting—insulting to God and insulting to the millions who perished.

The image of God enslaved in Egypt offers an alternative. When I visited concentration camps, Akiva's teaching that God appeared as a slave became for me an image of God appearing in the striped clothing of the prisoners, in the emaciated figures of the starving inmates, in the pictures of the suffering ghetto children. Only with the liberation was God freed as well—"a nation and its God."

As my teacher Prof. Abraham Joshua Heschel once said, "History is the arena in which the will of God is defied." The Holocaust was not God's punishment of the Jews; it was the result of human beings defying God's rules and God's will. Indeed, "in all their troubles He was troubled."

Va-'era'

Steeped in Idolatry

EXODUS 6:2–9:35

"Say, therefore, to the Israelite people: I am the Lord. I will free you from the labors of the Egyptians and deliver you from their bondage. I will redeem you with an outstretched arm and through extraordinary chastisements. And I will take you to be My people, and I will be your God. And you shall know that I, the Lord, am your God who freed you from the labors of the Egyptians. I will bring you unto the land which I swore to give to Abraham, Isaac, and Jacob, and I will give it to you for a possession, I the Lord." But when Moses told this to the Israelites, they would not listen to Moses because their spirits were crushed and because of hard labor.

—Exodus 6:6–9

P'shat: Explanation

These are the words that God instructs Moses to say to the people of Israel when he introduces himself to them and tells them of his mission to free them. It is an extraordinary speech, summarizing in just three verses what God has promised to do for them and why. It describes—exactly—the broad outline of what will happen to them as related later in the Torah.

It begins with the solemn proclamation of the name of the God who is making this pledge: the Lord, later identified as the God of Israel. The Lord promises to free the Israelites, deliver them, and redeem them through delivering great punishments upon the Egyptians. God then foretells what will happen at Sinai: there the Israelites will become God's people, and the Lord will become their God. After this, God assures the people that God's promise to their ancestors will be fulfilled: they will possess the land of Canaan. And then God's message concludes as it began: with the proclamation of the name of the Lord. What a wonderful, concise recitation of the Exodus story.

The verse that follows God's message, however, is unexpected. Instead of rejoicing at this news, the Israelites reject it and will not listen to it. Furthermore, the reported rebuff is very strange, since it contradicts what was related earlier (in verse 4:31), where we are told that after Aaron conveyed the message and demonstrated the miraculous signs, "the people were convinced. When they heard that the Lord had taken note of the Israelites and that He had seen their plight, they bowed down in homage."

It may be that this section depicts a later incident evoking disappointment, possibly the failure of the first attempt to influence Pharaoh. Many scholars believe, however, that this is an alternative account of the beginning of Moses's mission. While according to the first account it was greeted with enthusiasm, in this second account it was met with skepticism and rejection.

D'rash: Exposition of the Sages

Rabbi Judah ben Bateira says: It is stated that "they would not listen to Moses because their spirits were crushed and because of hard labor." Is there anyone who would not rejoice when receiving good news? If one is told, "A son is born to you!" would one not rejoice? "Your master has emancipated you!" would one not rejoice? If so, what does it mean when it states "they would not listen to Moses because their spirits were crushed and because of hard labor"? Rather it means that it was hard for them to contemplate giving up idol worship. [The Hebrew word avodah, translated as "labor," also means "worship."] As it is written, "I also said to them, 'Cast away, every one of you, the detestable things that you were drawn to, and do not defile

yourselves with the fetishes of Egypt. But they defied me and refused to listen to Me. They did not cast away the detestable things that they were drawn to, nor did they give up the fetishes of Egypt'" (Ezekiel 20:7–8). Thus it is written thereafter, "So the Lord spoke to both Moses and Aaron and commanded them regarding the Israelites . . ." (Exodus 6:13)—commanding them to separate themselves from idol worship.
Israel was steeped in idol worship in Egypt and idol worship is equivalent to all of the commandments of the Torah. . . . [F]or one who worships idols breaks off the yoke (of Torah), annuls the covenant and falsifies the Torah.
—Mekhilta Pisha 5

Rabbi Judah ben Bateira, an early *tanna*, reads the verse as if it is referring to idol worship. In Hebrew, idol worship is called *avodah zarah*, and the word *avodah* itself can mean either "hard work" or "worship." By interpreting the word *avodah* to mean "worship" rather than "hard work," Rabbi Judah thus finds an answer to the problem of why the Israelites did not react with joy and enthusiasm to Moses when he brought them good tidings of freedom and salvation. While the Torah's answer seems to be that they were simply worn down by their enslavement, he asserts that the people did not listen to Moses because it was hard for them to abandon idol worship. They were disturbed by God's new requirement that they relinquish their idols and worship God alone.

Rabbi Judah ben Bateira derives proof for this from verses in the book of Ezekiel that specifically state that Israel was drawn to Egyptian idol worship. Ezekiel says exactly that. God is quoted as remembering that at this point in time God commanded the Israelites to abandon those fetishes, and they refused. What better proof could one have that the people were indeed steeped in idol worship?

Although idolatry had largely vanished among Jews by the Second Temple period, it was a major concern in biblical days. The prophets of Israel harshly condemned it: "How can you say, 'I am not defiled,

I have not gone after the Baalim?' Look at your deeds in the Valley, consider what you have done! . . . Where are those gods you have made for yourself? Let them arise and save you if they can, in your hour of calamity. For your gods have become, O Judah, as many as your towns!" (Jeremiah 2:23,28).

It is quite understandable, therefore, that the Sages generally believed that the Israelites had become idol worshippers while in Egypt—and, in fact, that they had been "steeped" in idolatry. This account appears in many Rabbinic legends. When interpreting the command given to them just before the Exodus to take a lamb on the 10th of Nisan and slaughter it on the 14th—the original paschal Lamb that became an integral part of the Passover celebration and is still recalled on seder plates to this day (Exodus 12:3-10)—the Sages noted that worshipping the lamb had been part of Egyptian idol worship adopted by the Israelites, and the sacrificial act was meant to wean them away from idolatry. "Withdraw your hands from idol worship and take the lamb and slaughter the god of Egypt, making it the Pascal offering" (Exodus Rabbah 16:2).

D'rash: Personal Reflection

SPECTACULAR RUINS

After wanting to visit Egypt for many years, my wife and I finally went there to see the ancient monuments in the Nile Valley. We took the famous boat trip down the Nile to Luxor and other such sites, visiting the spectacular ruins of ancient temples and exploring the magnificent tombs in the Valley of the Kings.

We were overwhelmed by the sheer size, complexity, and beauty of what we saw. Even though I was familiar with these places from having seen so many photographs of them, the reality was far more impressive than the pictures. Standing in the shadow of giant pillars, gazing at the remnants of depictions of the myths of the Egyptian gods, viewing statues that were simply immense in scope, one could not but be awestruck by these ruins. I began to also consider how much more impressive they must have been when experienced at their full glory.

Right then this ancient Rabbinic text asserting that the Israelites in Egypt had been steeped in idolatry and that "they did not listen to Moses because it was hard for them to contemplate giving up the worship of idols" came to my mind. For the first time I felt that I truly understood that midrash because I could see before me how tempting it must have been to experience the spectacular pagan rites that had taken place within these magnificent idolatrous temples. How did these ancestors of ours, rather plain and simple shepherds and farmers, absorb the splendor of Egypt? Did they manage to resist it and remain true to the stark worship of One God whose likeness was never allowed to be depicted, or did they succumb to the temptations placed before them? The Sages were convinced that the people gave in, and perhaps they were correct.

But before we condemn the enslaved Israelites and think ourselves superior because we no longer are inveigled by these pagan rites and myths, let us remember that we have our own forms of idol worship, false gods we find difficult to resist: the pursuit of wealth at the expense of honesty, the worship of power, the addiction to drugs and gambling, the temptations of hatred of others and neglect of the needy. All of these and more are still part of our lives.

Our ancestors had their addictions, and we have ours. Do we also have the will to overcome them?

Bo'

Divine Protection

EXODUS 10:1–13:16

"They shall take some of the blood and put it on the two
doorposts and the lintel of the houses in which they are to
eat it. . . . For that night I will go through the land of Egypt
and strike down every first-born in the land of Egypt, both
man and beast; and I will mete out punishments to all
the gods of Egypt, I the Lord. And the blood on the houses
where you are staying shall be a sign for you: when I see
the blood [u-fasaḥti] I will protect you, so that no plague
will destroy you when I strike the land of Egypt."
Moses then summoned all the elders of Israel and said to them,
"Go, pick out lambs for your families, and slaughter [ha-pesaḥ]
the Pesach offering. Take a bunch of hyssop, dip it into the blood
that is in the basin, and apply some of the blood that is in the
basin to the lintel and to the two doorposts. None of you shall
go outside the door of his house until morning. For when the
Lord goes through to smite the Egyptians, He will see the blood
on the lintel and the two doorposts, and the Lord [u-fasaḥ] will
protect the door and not let the Destroyer enter and smite your
home. . . . And when your children ask you, 'What do you mean
by this rite?' You shall say, 'It is the Pesach sacrifice to the Lord,
because He protected [pasaḥ] the houses of the Israelites in
Egypt when He smote the Egyptians, but saved our houses.'"
—Exodus 12:7,12–13,21–23,25

P'shat: Explanation

The last and most terrible plague — the death of the firstborn — is about to be inflicted on the Egyptians. Afterward the Israelites will depart.

This impending plague is understood as a fitting retribution for Pharaoh's early decree to kill every boy born to the Israelites (Exodus 1:16). The verses emphasize again and again that God is the Israelites' savior and protector. Tonight the Israelites are to offer a sacrifice known as the Pesach, the paschal Lamb, marking the doors of their dwellings with lambs' blood. When God sees this sign, God will protect the people "and not let the Destroyer enter."

In the future the Israelites will observe the rite of the paschal Lamb, though not the placing of blood on the doorposts; there is no need for that. They will explain to their children that, as the very name Pesach signifies, this was done in order to remember the way in which God saved and protected them on the night of that terrible plague.

In actuality, two holidays are observed in Nisan in remembrance of the Exodus. Both have agricultural origins that extend back far beyond the actual Exodus. The Pesach, the holiday of the birth of the new lambs, is observed by the Pesach sacrifice of the evening of the 14th of Nisan. Matzot, the feast of unleavened bread, the holiday of the new wheat harvest, is observed for seven days, from the 15th through the 22nd.

Both holidays were given historical significance connected to the Exodus. Matzot reminds us of the Exodus itself; the Israelites ate matzot in their hurry to leave Egypt (see Exodus 12:17–19,39). Pesach reminds us of God's protection of Israel at the critical moment before the Exodus. In the verses cited above, the recurring repetition of the Hebrew root p-s-ḥ is meant to explain the symbolic meaning of the sacrificial lamb by informing us why it is called the Pesach. What that meaning is, then, depends on the meaning of the root p-s-ḥ, and that is a matter of conjecture. Translators have used either "to pass over" or "to protect." If it means "to pass over," it implies that God went from house to house killing the Egyptian firstborn while skipping over the houses of the Israelites. If it means "to protect," it implies that God had released a destructive force but protected the homes of the Israelites so that the force could not enter them. By extension, the paschal Lamb would therefore represent God's protection of Israel during the years of the people's slavery.

D'rash: Exposition of the Sages

". . . shall be a sign for you . . ." A sign for you and
not for Me! A sign for you and not for others.
". . . when I see the blood . . ." Rabbi Ishmael would say, "Is
not everything revealed before God? What then can be the
meaning of 'when I see the blood'? 'As a reward for your
performance of the commandment [of slaughtering the lamb
and applying the blood] I will reveal Myself and care for you,'
as it is said: u-fasaḥti aleihem and fasaḥti means to care for
and protect, as we see in the verse: Like the birds that fly,
even so will the Lord of Hosts shield Jerusalem, shielding and
saving [pasoaḥ], protecting and rescuing" (Isaiah 31:5).
". . . when I see the blood . . ." I see the blood of the binding
of Isaac, as it is said, "And Abraham named the site
Adonai-yireh—the Lord will see" (Genesis 22:14).
"I will protect . . ." Rabbi Joshua said, "Read not u-fasaḥti
but u-fasa'ti (step over), for the Lord skipped over the
houses of the Israelites in Egypt, as it is said, 'Hark!
My beloved! Here he comes, skipping over mountains,
bounding over hills'" (Song of Songs 2:8).
Rabbi Jonathan says, "'I will protect you.'. . . You will I
[God] protect, but I will not protect the Egyptians."
—Mekhilta Pisha 7

The early Sages were troubled by two aspects of these verses. The first was the very idea of God telling Israel to place a sign on the houses so that God would see it and not smite the Israelites. Therefore, they stressed the words "for you." The sign meant something to the Israelites; it was intended for their benefit. By following God's instruction, they would earn merit. It was not there to convey information to God.

Rabbi Ishmael, a great first-century Sage who created a set of classic midrashim on the books of the Torah, interpreted the Torah in a very rational fashion. How could God, who sees all and knows all, ever say that God needed to see a sign in order to know which houses were Israelite and which were Egyptian? That is obviously absurd. Therefore, he taught, the Israelites had to place such a sign in order to demonstrate their adherence to God's command and merit a reward for doing so. The reward will be God's care and protection of them when the plague is spreading throughout the land.

An unnamed Sage who is also bothered by the verse suggests that "I will see the blood" does not refer to the blood of the lamb but to something else altogether. At Mount Moriah, when Abraham was willing to shed the blood of his beloved son, Isaac, Abraham proclaimed that "the Lord would see" — that is, that there would be a time in the future when God would take into consideration what he, Abraham, had done and therefore protect Isaac's descendants at their time of need. That time was now, during the plague of the firstborn.

Rabbi Joshua is troubled by something else. He wonders at the very meaning of *u-fasaḥti*. What does that word actually mean? What does the Pesach sacrifice stand for? What did God really do? While all the other Sages interpret *u-fasaḥti* to mean "protect," Rabbi Joshua suggests that the text should be read as *u-fasa'ti*, with the third root letter being an *ayin* rather than a *het*. This root means "to take a step" or "to skip over." He cites a verse from Song of Songs, a book the Sages interpreted as telling of the love between God and Israel, in which the lover, God, is depicted as "skipping over" mountains in order to reach the beloved more quickly. Similarly, according to Rabbi Joshua, as God goes from house to house destroying the firstborn, God skips over the Israelites' homes.

This interpretation, which supports the other common translation of the word, "passing over," in turn became the usual English name for Pesach: Passover.

D'rash: Personal Reflection

A MODERN EXODUS

Given a choice, I would certainly side with those who understand Pesach as indicating "protecting" rather than "passing over." Protecting is a positive action—saving a life. Passing over is passive—not doing harm. I would rather think of God as protecting and assuring the people's survival in difficult circumstances.

In general, the story of the Exodus reminds me of the saga of Soviet Jewry. It is no accident that the slogan of the free Soviet Jewry movement was taken from God's message to Pharaoh, "Let My people go!" The Kremlin rulers were no more attentive to that message than was Pharaoh of old. For decades they refused to listen, but neither the refuseniks in the USSR nor their compatriots throughout the Jewish world would desist from that demand until finally it was achieved and millions left, the majority moving to Israel, the others to the United States or Europe.

It was my privilege to participate in that struggle, if only in a minor way. In the midseventies, a time when Israelis were not allowed to travel to the Soviet Union, the Israeli government sent me on a mission there. Having an American passport (as I was born and resided in the United States for many years until I made *aliyah*), I was able to establish a false identity as if I lived in America. Over a period of two weeks, a partner from New York and I met with dozens of refuseniks and others in the USSR. We lectured about Judaism in homes where our conversations were bugged. We also spoke secretly to many about their problems and needs, brought them critical information, and relayed their messages to the proper Israeli authorities who could help them. The KGB followed us everywhere we went. We were fortunate not to have been stopped or imprisoned.

When we finally left, I felt a mixture of relief at having come back safely and guilt at leaving behind so many people who had become dear to me, people who had sacrificed everything for the right to leave the USSR and live freely as Jews. Why could I leave when they could not?

Thankfully, many, probably most, of the Jews I met were eventually able to leave, and there was no greater joy than meeting them in Jerusalem rather than in Moscow or Leningrad. I felt I was witnessing a modern retelling of the Exodus. Once again, the symbolic meaning of Pesach had been realized.

Be-shallaḥ

A Surfeit of Prayer

> *But Moses said to the people, "Have no fear! Stand by, and*
> *witness the deliverance which the Lord will work for you*
> *today; for the Egyptians whom you see today you will never*
> *see again. The Lord will battle for you; you hold your peace!"*
> *Then the Lord said to Moses, "Why do you cry out to Me?*
> *Tell the Israelites to go forward. And you lift up your rod."*
> —Exodus 14:13–16

P'shat: Explanation

The Israelites have escaped from Egypt. At first, paralyzed by the death of their firstborn, the Egyptians, headed by Pharaoh, want only to rid themselves of the Hebrews, who have brought death and destruction upon them. But it doesn't take long for Pharaoh to realize what he has done: he has let this huge group of slaves go free. He rallies his army in pursuit (Exodus 14:5–9).

Freedom had seemed so near, but now the Hebrews fear for their lives. Standing at the sea, they are so afraid that they plead with Moses to turn back to the safety of Egyptian servitude. Moses attempts to reassure them: you need not fear; God will destroy our enemies.

Although the text does not report it, from God's reply it seems clear that Moses then pleaded with God to help the people. God then rebukes him. Why? Since when is it improper to cry out to God for help? Isn't that what prayer is all about?

81

D'rash: Exposition of the Sages

Rabbi Joshua says, "The Holy One said to Moses,
'Moses — all Israel has to do is go forward!'"
Rabbi Eliezer ben Hyrcanus says, "The Holy One said to
Moses, 'Moses — My children are in deep distress — the sea is
a barrier in front of them and the enemy is pursuing them —
and you are standing around and engaging in lengthy prayer?!
Why do you cry out to Me?" As [Rabbi Eliezer] used to say,
"There is a time to be brief and there is a time to be lengthy."
Rabbi Judah says, "When the Israelites stood at the sea,
this one said, 'I will not be the first to jump into the sea,'
and this one said, 'I will not be the first to jump into the
sea.' While they were arguing about it, Nahshon son of
Amminadav jumped into the sea [and was drowning in
its waters]. At that very moment Moses was engaging in
lengthy prayer.... Said the Holy One to him, 'My dear one
[Nahshon] is drowning in the sea — the sea is a barrier in
front and the enemy is pursuing — and you are standing
around and engaging in lengthy prayer?!' Moses asked, 'What
can I do?' God said to him, 'And you lift up your rod.'"
—*Mekhilta Be-Shallah 4,6*

The editor of an ancient collection of midrash, the *Mekhilta*, collected several of the early Sages' comments concerning this passage. They want to know why Moses was praying, why God tells him to stop, and what God wants him and Israel to do at this critical juncture.

Emphasizing the last part of the verse ("Tell the Israelites to go forward"), Rabbi Joshua believes God is indicating that this is the time for action. Words are not sufficient; something has to be done. If the Israelites stay where they are while you, Moses, turn to God for help, they will perish. If you tell them to move forward, they will be able to proceed and be saved.

Rabbi Eliezer (first century CE), Rabbi Akiva's teacher at the famous academy at Yavneh after the Great War, has a similar message, but he emphasizes the first part of the verse ("Why do you cry out to me?"). There are many different Hebrew words for prayer and many ways to pray. Prayer can be praise; prayer can be a request. The particular Hebrew word used here, from the root meaning "to cry out," to scream in desperation, is seen as indicating prolonged, almost uncontrolled pleading. There is no time for that. The situation is too critical; immediate action is required. Short prayer, Rabbi Eliezer says, is just as efficacious as long prayer.

Rabbi Eliezer then cites an example of each. The shortest prayer in the Torah, found in Numbers 12:13, is Moses's prayer for Miriam's healing: five very brief Hebrew words, "el na r'fa na lah" (O God, pray heal her!). As for the longest prayer, recorded in Deuteronomy 9:18, the same Moses prays and fasts for forty days and nights asking God to forgive Israel for the sin of the Golden Calf.

Going further, Rabbi Judah adds a legend. He indicates that God's words come after an otherwise unrecorded incident. As the Hebrews find themselves in this terrible situation, it is obvious that someone has to muster the courage to risk plunging into the water. Turning back is not a realistic option. While the people stand about arguing over the matter, Nahshon takes the plunge—but almost loses his life. While Nahshon struggles in the water, Moses is busy pleading with God. It is then that God tells him to stop praying and do what God has commanded: Moses should lift up his staff and smite the waters, thus saving Nahshon and the entire people of Israel. According to Rabbi Judah, then, two events occurred that are not recorded in the Torah: Nahshon's dangerous plunge into the sea and Moses's overly long prayer.

What all of these interpretations have in common is the emphasis on deeds over *words*. Moses has to turn to the people (rather than to God) and tell them to go forward; an individual has to plunge ahead; Moses has to initiate lifting the rod. Passivity, the wringing of hands and utterances of despair, will not solve the problem.

D'rash: Personal Reflection

PRAYING WITH YOUR FEET

One of my most distinguished teachers was Prof. Abraham Joshua Heschel, of blessed memory. The scion of a distinguished Hassidic family, Heschel was a fervent advocate of heartfelt prayer. He was in turn appalled by the formality, rigidity, and coldness of the prayer services he perceived in many American synagogues. All too often he felt they were performances rather than acts of true participatory prayer. People were spectators in a well-rehearsed show rather than participants pouring out their hearts. To him, prayer was not to be measured by its length in words or time but by how moving it was, by the soul that was poured into that prayer. One came to the synagogue not to be entertained but to be moved: to recognize the wonder of life and to be overwhelmed by the awesomeness of the world God created and the life God bequeathed to us.

At the same time that Heschel emphasized the need for true prayer, he also recognized that the worship of God extended beyond prayer into deeds—acts of moral and ethical living. Doing was more important than words. Fighting injustice was more important than praising God.

He set an example of moral courage. He demonstrated on behalf of Soviet Jewry and raised funds on behalf of the State of Israel when it was in peril. He became a leading figure in protesting the Vietnam War and supporting the struggle for civil rights. He was not afraid to take unpopular positions or to be seen as "un-American" even if he might be jailed or beaten. When he participated in the march at Selma, Alabama, with Martin Luther King Jr., an act preserved forever in the iconic photograph of him in the front row of the marchers, he said that he felt then that he was praying with his feet. Literally moving forward was more important than verbal prayer at that moment in time.

Heschel became a model for many rabbis, including myself. He encouraged and inspired me to speak out against injustice even when it was not a popular thing to do—and not only to speak but to act. Following his example, I became active in Clergy Against the Vietnam War, participating in public rallies and speaking strongly on that subject in a Kol Nidre sermon, although I knew that many in the congregation would not agree with me. Many years later, a young man who was a teenager at the time told me that he had been inspired by my actions and my sermons to make the cause of social justice the focus of his life's work.

When I became the rabbi of a Chicago congregation at the time of the infamous Democratic National Convention there in 1968, I denounced the police and Mayor Daley for their violence against demonstrators, even though to Chicago Jewry Daley was second only to God. Later in my life, when living in Israel, I took stands in Israeli newspapers in favor of peace and against Israeli government actions I believed were unfair and undemocratic—the confiscation of Arab land, the establishment of new settlements, and the discrimination against Arab students seeking to rent rooms near universities, among them—even when these positions were unpopular. I also wrote a responsum that declared that any laws in Judaism that discriminated against non-Jews were to be declared no longer valid. Issued in both English and Hebrew, it stirred up controversy when it called upon our school system to make certain that any discriminatory passages not be presented as authentic Jewish teaching.

By his example, Heschel truly taught me the meaning of Rabbi Eliezer's phrase, "My children are in deep distress—the sea is a barrier in front of them and the enemy is pursuing them—and you are standing around and engaging in lengthy prayer?!"

Yitro

Diminishing the Image

EXODUS 18:1–20:23

God spoke all these words, saying: I the Lord am your God who brought you out of the land of Egypt, the house of bondage.
—Exodus 20:1–2

P'shat: Explanation

With this passage we come to the very heart of the Torah: the words spoken by God at Sinai to the assembled people of Israel. This section through verse 14 is known as the Decalogue, meaning the Ten Words, the Ten Pronouncements, or, popularly, the Ten Commandments. In Hebrew they are called either *Aseret ha-D'varim* (the Ten Words) or *Aseret ha-Dibberot* (the Ten Pronouncements) because they are spoken by God. Although God speaks often in the Torah, from God's first words, creating light (Genesis 1:3), to God's final words, telling Moses he will not cross over the Jordan to reach the Promised Land (Deuteronomy 34:4), God otherwise only talks to one individual or possibly two, whereas here God speaks directly to the entire people of Israel.

The words are the terms of the covenant that the people have agreed to accept, making them God's treasured people, while God becomes their Sovereign. At first the words are delivered orally. Only later are they inscribed upon two tablets of stone: "When [God] finished speaking with [Moses] on Mount Sinai, He gave Moses the two tablets of the Pact, stone tablets inscribed with the finger of God" (Exodus 31:18).

Both traditional texts and modern commentaries address the question of how the Decalogue is broken up into ten pronouncements. Some scholars believe that "I the Lord am your God" is the beginning of the First Commandment. Others think this is only the prologue introducing God as the author of the commandments that follow. In that case, verse 3 — "You shall have no other gods besides Me" — would be the First Commandment. This would make sense if we consider the Pronouncements to be literal "commandments" — telling us what to do. "I the Lord" does not tell us what to do; it merely identifies the One who is commanding. On the other hand, if we define the Pronouncements as do the Hebrew terms, Ten Words or Ten Pronouncements, "I the Lord" is undoubtedly the first.

D'rash: Exposition of the Sages

How were the Ten Pronouncements arranged? There were five on one tablet and five on the other. Thus on one tablet was written "I the Lord am your God who brought you out of the land of Egypt, the house of bondage." Opposite it on the other was written "You shall not murder" (Exodus 20:13). This informs us that if one sheds blood it is accounted as if one had diminished the Image [of God]. This can be likened to a human king. When he enters a city they erect portraits and images and mint coins in his likeness. After a while they upset his portraits, break his images and deface his coins thus diminishing the likeness of the king. Thus if one sheds blood it is accounted as if one had diminished the Image [of God], as it is said, "Whoever sheds the blood of man, by man shall his blood be shed. For in His image did God make man" (Genesis 9:6).
—Mekhilta Ba-Hodesh 8

This midrash, which accepts the usual position of Jewish tradition that "I the Lord" is actually the First Commandment, attempts to answer the question of how the Decalogue was written on these two tablets. And why two tablets? Would not one have been sufficient? The first answer here is that there were five pronouncements on one and five on the other. The second answer is that this was not done because of aesthetics or insufficient space but in order to show a connection between the commandments on the first tablet and those on the second. The First Commandment is related to the Sixth, the Second to the Seventh, and so forth. Indeed, the entire midrash expounds on each of these pairs and shows the connections.

Interestingly, this arrangement of five and five has become the standard way of depicting the two tablets of the Decalogue, even though at the end of the midrash we learn that this was the opinion of only one Sage, Rabbi Hananiah son of Gamliel. All the other Sages say: "All ten were written on each of the two tablets." The latter opinion is also notably shared by most modern scholars, who point to the common practice in ancient times of creating two identical copies of a given covenant, one for each of the two parties entering into the agreement.

Yet Rabbi Hananiah's connection of Commandments One and Six is very important from the point of Jewish doctrine. The Torah's statement that God created human beings in God's image thus provides a theological basis for the concept that all human life is sacred. Why should murder be outlawed? Why should human life be valued over other forms of life? Why should we treat human beings in a special way? It is because of the doctrine of the Divine Image.

This idea cannot be verified by science. It is a truth that in fact needs no proof because it is grounded in a self-evident belief. It means that human beings—*all* human beings—are to be treated with dignity, and human life is to be considered not only valuable but sacred. Humans are the very Image of the Divine.

D'rash: Personal Reflection

WHAT I LEARNED IN POLAND

That Jews were the victims of a belief in racial superiority that placed them in the category of subhumans is a tragic historical irony, since it was Jewish thought that had taught the ultimate value of all human life. I was struck by this during a visit I undertook not long ago to Holocaust sites in Poland, the Warsaw Ghetto, the death camps, and mass graves.

This visit felt a thousand times more intense than my visiting the graves of loved ones, because these were not normal deaths. They were deliberate murders undertaken in the cruelest possible way—a veritable industry of death. A calculated policy of dehumanization, undertaken by a nation that was supposedly the epitome of culture and knowledge, had made this possible. Nazi doctrine professed bogus racial purity theories in which humankind could be divided into categories: the pure race and the inferior races. Pseudoscientific teachings were promulgated to demonstrate the racial inferiority of non-Aryans, most particularly of Jews. They were different. They were subhuman. They were rodents. Once that was established firmly as fact, not fantasy, there was no impediment to slaughtering them as one might slay animals or stamp out vermin.

There are no words that can describe what happened in the camps and forests in Poland. Seeing those mass graves, including those of eight hundred children near Tarnow, visiting town after town where huge numbers of Jews were marched out and brutally shot, viewing synagogue after synagogue now either in ruins or preserved as a museum because there are no longer any Jews there, standing in silence next to the enormous mound of human ashes preserved in a monument in Majdanek, I was confronted by the question, How could human beings do this to other human beings? It is simply incomprehensible. Yet it happened. In the terminology of the Sages, millions of times the Divine Image was diminished—yet "diminished" is too mild a word. The Image was smashed and destroyed over and over.

I realized then that there are two important lessons to be learned from the Shoah. First, we must never let this happen to us again. Second, we must always fight against the concept that humans can be divided into superior and inferior races. This also means that we must never permit Judaism to teach anything that even faintly resembles that doctrine. Any such belief will inevitably lead to acts of violence and the taking of life by extremists who believe that they are acting in the name of God. As a people that has experienced the Shoah, we must reject such beliefs and reaffirm the sacredness of all human life. We must never permit the Image to be diminished.

Mishpatim

Mitzvot with Meaning

EXODUS 21:1–24:18

These are the rules that you shall set before them. . . .
Moses went and repeated to the people all the commands
of the Lord and all the rules; and all the people answered
with one voice, saying, "All the things that the Lord has
commanded we will do!" Moses then wrote down all the
commands of the Lord. . . . Then he took the record of the
covenant and read it aloud to the people. And they said,
"All that the Lord has spoken we will faithfully do!"
—Exodus 21:1, 24:1–4,7

P'shat: Explanation

In this Torah portion, which follows immediately after the Decalogue, God conveys to Moses a predominantly civil code of law. Moses recites it aloud and writes it down in a scroll, the people accept these regulations, and they become part of the covenant ceremony held between God and Israel at Mount Sinai. In other words, these laws are no less a part of the covenant than the Decalogue itself. They are the very foundation of the system of Jewish law and Jewish practice.

Here these laws are called *mishpatim*, translated as "rules." Elsewhere in the Torah, though, all laws, whether civil or ritual, are called *mitzvot*, usually translated as "commandments." Whereas the word *mishpatim* emphasizes that these are civil norms regulating human interaction, the word *mitzvot* shows that they are of divine origin, reflecting moral and ethical values.

This latter term became the norm in Rabbinic literature. In all of the Jewish liturgical blessings, we refer to God as having sanctified us through God's mitzvot and commanded us to perform them.

Eventually, it was determined that there were 613 mitzvot, even though there was never universal agreement as to exactly what constituted the 613. They were divided into positive and negative ones and into mitzvot between God and human beings, that is, rituals, and mitzvot between one human and another, that is, civil or ethical commands.

D'rash: Exposition of the Sages

Rabbi Simlai said: Moses was given 613 commandments, 365 negative ones corresponding to the number of the days of the year, 248 positive ones corresponding to the parts of the body. David came and reduced them to eleven: Who may live on Your holy mountain? i He who lives without blame, ii who does what is right, iii and in his heart acknowledges the truth, iv whose tongue is not given to evil, v who has never done harm to his fellow, vi or borne reproach for his neighbor, vii for whom a contemptible man is abhorrent, viii but who honors those who fear the Lord, ix who stands by his oath even to his hurt, x who has never lent money at interest, xi or accepted a bribe against the innocent. The man who acts thus shall never be shaken (Psalm 15:1–5). Isaiah came and condensed them into six: i He who walks in righteousness, ii speaks uprightly, iii spurns profit from fraudulent dealings, iv waves away a bribe instead of grasping it, v stops his ears against listening to infamy, vi shuts his eyes against looking at evil. Such a one shall dwell on high (Isaiah 33:15–16). Micah reduces them to three "What does the Lord require of you? Only to do justice and to love mercy and walk modestly with your God" (Micah 6:8), Isaiah to two "Observe what is right

*and do what is just" (Isaiah 56:1). Amos reduces them to one,
"Seek Me and you will live" (Amos 5:4) as does Habakkuk "The
righteous will live according to his faith" (Habakkuk 2:4).*
—Makkot 23b

The great number of mitzvot in Judaism can indeed be off-putting.
Who can possibly observe that many commandments?

It helps to recognize that many of the 613 mitzvot apply only to
one specific group, such as priests or Levites, or to special situations
most people are unlikely to encounter. Furthermore, a great many
apply solely to the Temple or to the monarchy, both of which no longer exist. In addition, many apply only to the Land of Israel and not
to Jews living elsewhere.

In talmudic times, the enormous number of demands may have
underlain the famous story of a potential convert who came to Shammai and said, "Convert me—on condition that you teach me the entire
Torah while standing on one foot." Shammai, whose impatience and
quick temper became legendary, drove him away instead of finding a
way to provide an answer. When the man then came to Hillel with the
same question, Hillel responded, "What is hateful to you, do not do
to your fellow. That is the entire Torah. The rest is commentary. Now
go—learn" (Shabbat 31a). In his reply, Hillel was citing an Aramaic
interpretation of the verse "Love your fellow as yourself" (Leviticus
18:19). Hillel was not denying the importance of all the commandments
but demonstrating that all of them had the same purpose: to enable
us to live lives in which we demonstrate love and care for one another.

There were many such attempts to explain the ethical and moral
principles underlying the code of 613 mitzvot. The teaching by Rabbi
Simlai, a third-century *amora*, is one of the most extensive. Rabbi Simlai is certainly not implying that any of the prophets cited intended
to eliminate commandments. He is saying, rather, that all of the
commandments are meant to induce us to become people who will
always act according to the principles of ethical and moral living
enunciated in these teachings. He further asserts that regardless of

how many observances a person may uphold, anyone who does not follow these particular principles cannot be said to be an observant Jew. It cannot be accidental that Rabbi Simlai, who taught elsewhere that the Torah begins and ends with acts of loving-kindness (*Sotah* 14a), does not mention any of the important ritual demands of the Torah but confines himself solely to morality and adherence to God. Even the rituals are intended to lead to ethical living.

It could be said with some justification that Judaism is basically a system of mitzvot, of commands that determine what we should and should not do, and that these mitzvot, rather than beliefs or dogmas, are the basis of Jewish life. The danger with this conception is that Judaism could become a series of actions that are blindly performed without understanding or meaning—mere religious behaviorism. This was certainly not the intent of the Sages, who taught that all of these actions were intended to shape the character of the person performing them. The common formulation was "Mitzvot were given in order to purify human beings."

D'rash: Personal Reflection

PRAYING AT THE KOTEL

In the 1990s I was one of the delegates who negotiated with the Israeli government for the right to conduct egalitarian services at the Robinson's Arch area of the Western Wall. The negotiation was successful. Since then, thousands of Jews from Israel and the entire world have been able to pray there according to their own customs.

We were somewhat apprehensive, however, that this site could turn into what has been called "Kotalatry," that is, a place of superstitious actions and beliefs rather than religious and historical inspiration. Therefore, I was asked to prepare a special prayer to be recited when visiting the site, one that would direct people to the true meaning of the place, remind them of what Judaism required of them, and suggest what a visit to this spot might inspire them to do.

Inspired by Rabbi Simlai's use of Psalm 24, I concluded my prayer with the recitation of the verses in that psalm to indicate that from ancient days to our own times, only those who conducted themselves according to those ethical norms were fit to stand in this place. "It was here," I wrote, "that the prophets came to teach us that God is not to be placated with offerings, but demands righteousness and loving-kindness, justice and mercy of those who would worship Him."

Yes, a multitude of mitzvot detail the outlines of a Jewish life, and ultimately these specific actions concretize basic concepts and ways of improving our characters so we will become the kinds of individuals Judaism wants us to be.

Terumah

Creating the Sanctuary

EXODUS 25:1–27:19

*And let them make Me a sanctuary that I may dwell
among them. Exactly as I show you—the pattern of the
Tabernacle and the pattern of all its furnishings—so shall
you make it. Of the planks of the Tabernacle, make twenty
planks on the south side: making forty silver sockets under
the twenty planks . . . and for the other side wall of the
Tabernacle, on the north side, twenty planks. . . . And for
the rear of the Tabernacle, to the west, make six planks.*
—Exodus 25:8–9, 26:19–20,22

P'shat: Explanation

At Sinai, first the Ten Commandments are proclaimed (Exodus 20:1–
14). Then God gives Moses a series of laws to convey to the Israelites
(Exodus 21:1–23:19). Now, while still on the mountain, Moses receives
detailed instructions on how to build a portable sanctuary for the
Israelites to use when they leave Sinai and journey to Canaan. The
architect, as it were, is the Lord. God even states here that God will
show Moses the precise plans of the building and all the furnishings
to be assembled within it.

The purpose of this sanctuary, referred to as the Tabernacle, is made
clear: so that God "may dwell among them." In pagan religions the
Temples were considered to be homes for the gods on earth—even if
those gods also had other dwellings in heaven. Although the God of
Israel is never depicted in the Torah as having physical needs, there is

still a requirement for a physical place where God can be worshipped by Israel and so the people can feel that God dwells in their midst. This Tabernacle will also contain a place to house the Tables of the Law and from which God will speak to Moses (Exodus 29:42, 30:6).

In a sense, this sanctuary is a portable Sinai. Just as God descended on Mount Sinai to speak with Israel, so will God be present in the sanctuary with the people, wherever they may be.

D'rash: Exposition of the Sages

*When the Holy One said to Moses, ". . . Make Me a sanctuary,
. . ." [Moses] was shocked and said, "The glory of God fills
the heavens and the earth and yet He tells me 'Make Me a
sanctuary?!'" Furthermore he looked into the future and
saw that Solomon was going to build the Holy Temple which
was so much greater than the sanctuary, and would say to
the Holy One, "But will God really dwell on earth? Even
the heavens to their uttermost reaches cannot contain You,
how much less this House that I have built!" (1 Kings 8:27).
Said Moses, "If that is what Solomon says concerning the
Holy Temple which is so much greater than the sanctuary,
how much more is that true of the sanctuary!" The Holy One
said [to Moses], "My thoughts are not your thoughts—just
put twenty planks on the north side and twenty planks on
the south and eight on the west. Furthermore, I will descend
and contract My Shekhinah into one amah by one amah."*
—Exodus Rabbah 34:1

The Sages wondered, "What must have Moses thought when he received this command?" Was he not startled by being given such a difficult—perhaps impossible—task? After all, knowing the greatness of God, whose glory filled the world, how could any human being possibly create a physical space that could contain God? No one could do that.

The Sages also ascribed to Moses prophetic powers that allow him to see into the future. Hence Moses knows that the building he is asked to create is much smaller than the Temple King Solomon will build, and Solomon himself will even acknowledge that his great structure is incapable of containing God. How much more would this be true of the modest place Moses can create! God is indeed asking the impossible of Moses.

According to the midrash, God's response to Moses's quandary is quite simple: It's not what you think. It's not nearly so complicated. I'm only asking you to follow these simple instructions. As it says in the verses from chapter 26, put this number of planks here and this number there. That's all I ask, and you are capable of doing this. I will see to the rest.

The midrash also uses a well-known mystical concept to explain how the infinite God can possibly dwell therein: *tzimtzum*, "contraction." God has the power to contract the Divine Presence so that it can enter the world and reside in the sanctuary, thus defying human logic. Jewish mysticism had also used this concept to explain how the universe itself could exist if God is truly everything and everywhere. God contracted to make room for the world.

By contrast, there is nothing supernatural and nothing magical about the Tabernacle. It is a human creation built by the hands of human beings following the instructions of God. It is by no means an impossible task. Just put the pieces together, and God will find a way in.

D'rash: Personal Reflection

WHERE DOES GOD DWELL?

The tentlike sanctuary Moses was commanded to construct was eventually supplanted by the Jerusalem Temple King Solomon built around 960 BCE. The Babylonians destroyed that building in 586 BCE, the returning exiles rebuilt it in 520 BCE, Herod enlarged it around 20 CE, and then the Romans destroyed it in 70 CE, only half a century later.

Jews have not had a Temple—a place of sacrificial worship—since. Synagogues, often called "small sanctuaries," *mikdash m'at*, have been our only houses of worship for nearly two thousand years.

During this period of time, however, Jews have hoped and prayed for the rebuilding of the Temple and the restoration of its rituals. They have also visited its ruins, although remnants of the actual Temple itself disappeared within a century of the destruction. All that has remained in sight are the retaining walls Herod created to enlarge the top of the mountain, where a huge, newly built edifice would stand.

Since the Western Wall of that retaining wall was the sole remnant Jews could reach, it became the place of pilgrimage for those seeking connection with the ancient Temple. Since the Six-Day War, however, when the entire area came into Israeli control, archaeologists have been able to reveal other parts of Herod's structure, such as the southern entrance to the actual Temple.

During my first visit to Israel in 1955 with my wife and during a subsequent visit in 1965 with my three daughters, the Western Wall was not within our reach, since the entire Old City of Jerusalem was then under Jordanian control. I remember how we would seek out various high places, such as buildings on Mount Zion, from which a tiny part of that wall was visible, and we would strain to see it.

The first time we actually got to the site was on an Israel trip my congregation took immediately after the 1967 Six-Day War. There was as yet no plaza or other permanent arrangements near the Wall as there are today. It was just a dusty open area, but for our group, reaching and touching the Wall and praying there were emotional experiences. The place touched us deeply because it seemed to embody and represent not only all the tragedies of Jewish history but also the feeling of ultimate triumph that having it in Jewish hands and open freely to Jewish visitation again signified.

As I have mentioned before, years later, a negotiated arrangement between the Masorti movement and the government of Israel led to free (albeit limited) access for egalitarian prayer at the section of the Wall near the Robinson's Arch area—and to countless Movement prayers and bar/bat mitzvah ceremonies there. Some people feel that since this area is not the old section where Jews have prayed for centuries, it is not as important a place. To my mind, though, this section is more authentic than the other part because more layers of the Wall have been revealed even farther down so that one has a more accurate picture of what this structure really was. In addition, here one walks on pavement that actually existed when the Temple stood. These are the same stones that people trod upon when going to the Temple two thousand years ago. What is more, one sees there a tremendous pile of stones lying exactly where they landed when the Romans hurled them down from the top in 70 CE. One really steps back into history at this site.

For all that, I find it important to remember what the Sages taught. These structures are not divine; nor were they constructed by magical means. As God tells Moses, to create them all you have to do is put this and that together properly. Nor is this the only place I or anyone else needs to go in order to feel God's Presence. Each synagogue is a miniature sanctuary where God's Presence can be felt by each of us. As a matter of fact, as a Hasidic saying has it, "God dwells wherever you let Him in."

Tetsavveh

For Whom the Light Burns

EXODUS 27:20–30:10

*You shall further instruct the Israelites to bring you clear oil
of beaten olives for lighting, for kindling lamps regularly.
Aaron and his sons shall set them up in the Tent of Meeting
outside the curtain which is over [the ark of] the pact [to
burn] from evening to morning before the Lord. It shall be
a due from the Israelites for all time, throughout the ages.*
—Exodus 27:20–21

P'shat: Explanation

This is the second Torah portion to discuss the portable sanctuary the
Israelites were commanded to build. The first described the structure
itself. This one is concerned with the priests who are to serve in it,
the special garments they are to wear, and their consecration rituals.

Prior to this is a command concerning the oil the priests are to use
to kindle a lamp in the sanctuary. It is to burn in front of the Holy of
Holies throughout the night. This oil lampstand is known as the Ner
Tamid, frequently translated as an "eternal light." "Eternal," however,
implies that the lights the priests kindled burned at all times, but they
did not; they burned only at night. The new JPS translation, however,
offers a more exact meaning: lamps that burned "regularly," that is,
every single night.

Although this command only concerned the lampstand in the sanctuary, in later times it became customary for all synagogues to have
a Ner Tamid that, unlike the Temple candelabrum, is kept burning at
all times in front of the Holy Ark. It represents the light of the Torah,

the light of God's instruction, which illuminates us at all times. In this way as well, synagogues remind us of what existed in the sanctuary and later in the Temple.

D'rash: Exposition of the Sages

"You shall further instruct the Israelites to bring you clear oil of beaten olives for lighting. . . ." Rabbi Samuel ben Nahmani said: ". . . to bring you — but not Me, for I [God] do not need light." The table was on the north side and the menorah was on the south side. Said Rabbi Zerika in the name of Rabbi Eleazar: "I [God] do not need food and I do not need light." "And he [Solomon] made the windows of the House broad and narrow" (1 Kings 6:4) — broad without and narrow within, "for I am not in need of light." . . . How could you possibly think that He is in need of light when for the forty years that the Israelites traveled in the wilderness, they journeyed only by His light!
— *Menachot 86b*

According to the Sages, the light that burned at night in Moses's sanctuary and later in Solomon's Temple was there to give us an opportunity to serve God, or to demonstrate Israel's closeness to God and the ways in which God and God's commands illuminate the world. Most importantly, they emphasized what the light was *not*. It was not kindled for God's benefit. God did not need the light. God has no such needs.

Shmuel ben Nahmani and Rabbi Zerika, both third-century *amoraim*, stressed this by showing that although the sanctuary contained many of the same things housed in pagan temples to satisfy those gods' needs, these objects did not play the same roles in Israel's Temple. There were indeed a table and a lamp, for example, but they were placed far from each other. If the table was intended for eating, as it would be in a normal house, the lamp would be near it. In the sanctuary the extensive distance from the lamp to the table emphasized that God has no need of either a table for food or a lamp for light. The pagan gods have physical needs. The God of Israel has none.

The Sages also discussed the windows in Solomon's Temple. The biblical verse describing them is ambiguous and has been interpreted in different ways, but the Talmud clearly understands the verse to mean that they were designed the opposite way from common windows. Windows are usually either the same inside as out or broader inside, where the light needs to be spread. Here they were narrow inside, because God does not need light, and wider outside, so that the divine light in the Temple would spread outside to illuminate the world. When the light of God—the pillar of fire—had guided the people Israel throughout their long journeys, how could one possibly think that God requires any light that we humans can provide?

It is clear that the Sages were not fundamentalists when they interpreted the Torah. Fundamentalists take the words of the Bible literally and will not deviate from what they perceive to be the basic meaning of the texts, even if they contradict logic or nature. Fortunately, that has not been the accepted way of Jewish biblical exegesis. When the Sages came upon a text that they felt might contradict their beliefs, as in this case of the light, they interpreted it in a way that brought it into line with what they believed was true. This flexibility of interpretation has served Judaism well, enabling us to liberate the text from the strictures of literalism and broaden the scope of our beliefs to keep them in accord with the times.

D'rash: Personal Reflection

UNCOMFORTABLE TRUTHS CANNOT BE DENIED

One of the most distinguished scholars of Judaism in modern times was also one of the most controversial. I am referring to Louis Jacobs, who has often been referred to as "the greatest Chief Rabbi that England never had."

Ordained as an Orthodox rabbi, he first served a United Synagogue (Orthodox) congregation and taught at the flagship school Jews College. There was absolutely no one in the British rabbinate who came close to him in erudition and in the ability to teach and interpret Jewish tradition and law. His knowledge of both Jewish and general subjects was phenomenal. He could speak and quote chapter and verse spontaneously without notes on any subject until the very time of his death.

In 1956 his book *We Have Reason to Believe* was published. It explained why he could not believe that every word in the Torah had been written by God. His reason and scholarship had convinced him that although inspired by God, the Torah reflected the concepts of the people who wrote it—and in fact it may have come from more than one author and one time. This truth, he said, had to be accepted; a way had to be found to incorporate it into Jewish belief. Truth could not simply be denied because it was uncomfortable.

Jacobs did not think that this stance would remove him from the ranks of British Orthodox Jewry, which at that time was rather liberal. As he used to say, he did not leave Orthodoxy; Orthodoxy left him.

Jacobs had been slated to become the principal of Jews College, but the post was denied him. In the 1960s he was denied permission to serve as a congregational rabbi in any Orthodox synagogue. Everyone knew he was also the obvious candidate to become the next chief rabbi, but his rejection of a fundamentalist approach to the Torah—his attempt instead to demonstrate how one could accept the Divinity of the Torah while simultaneously accepting that the Torah was written and edited by human beings—cost him that post, too.

In 1964 Rabbi Jacobs founded the independent New London Synagogue, which later on became the flagship of the Masorti/Conservative movement in Great Britain. When he retired from his rabbinical position some forty years later, I was asked to temporarily fill that position while congregation officials conducted a search for a permanent rabbi.

Unfortunately, he passed away at the end of the first year I was there. Nevertheless, that year gave me the privilege to get to know him better, to appreciate his work, and to admire his courageous stance regarding how one is to understand the Torah today in the light of modern scholarship.

That year, British Jewry's weekly newspaper, the *Jewish Chronicle*, usually known simply as JC, ran a contest in which readers voted on "who has been the greatest British Jew of all time?" Louis Jacobs won hands down, well ahead of Chief Rabbi Joseph Hertz, Benjamin Disraeli, and Moses Montefiore, among others. However, when I suggested to the JC that it cosponsor an event to celebrate Jacobs's receiving that title, the editors declined, saying that only their readers—not the JC itself—had proclaimed him the greatest British Jew.

Our congregation therefore went ahead and hosted the celebratory evening. The synagogue was packed as I interviewed Jacobs about his teachings and his life. Whatever question I asked, he answered with his usual candor. He took the straightforward position that truth was the seal of God and could not be denied. He reiterated his position that one could no longer accept the position that every word in the Torah was written by God; it was written by human beings, based upon Moses's teachings. To his mind, those who ostracized him were the ones who were deviating from true Judaism.

It is important to remember that Louis Jacobs was devoted to encouraging Jewish belief and observance. He believed that a synthesis is possible between permanent values and truth of tradition and the best thought of the day. He was attempting to make people think seriously about what they believe so that Judaism could withstand the challenges of the age. What he was doing for his time, controversial as it may have been, was not different from what the Sages did for theirs: interpreting the Torah honestly and showing how it can be understood and applied today.

Ki Tissa'

Sin and Reconciliation

EXODUS 30:11–34:35

He [Moses] said, "Oh, let me behold Your Presence!" And He
answered, "I will make all My goodness pass before you, and
I will proclaim before you the name Lord, and the grace that
I grant and the compassion that I show. . . ." The Lord came
down in a cloud; He stood with him there, and proclaimed
the name Lord. The Lord passed before him and proclaimed:
"The Lord! the Lord! a God compassionate and gracious,
slow to anger, abounding in kindness and faithfulness,
extending kindness to the thousandth generation, forgiving
iniquity, transgression, and sin; yet He does not remit all
punishment, but visits the iniquity of parents upon children
and children's children, upon the third and fourth generations."
—Exodus 33:18–19, 34:5–7

P'shat: Explanation

The narrative of the events at Sinai—interrupted by commands concerning the construction of the sanctuary—now continues with a description of the sin of the Golden Calf and its aftermath. While Moses is on the mountain, the Israelites, feeling helpless, build and proceed to worship a golden calf. Furious at the people's faithlessness, God is on the brink of destroying the Israelites. God turns to Moses, offering to create a new nation from his descendants (Exodus 32:10). Demurring and instead following Abraham's example at Sodom and Gomorrah, Moses argues with God. He protests that God had promised the Patriarchs to bring their progeny to their own land, so it would be wrong to destroy them.

Moses is successful: God forgives Israel. God also gives him a physical symbol of this forgiveness: the second set of tablets, which replace those Moses had shattered in his own anger at the people.

Nevertheless, Moses still feels the need to be reassured of God's willingness to forgive and to be present with the people as they continue on their journey. He asks no less than to see the Presence of God and to understand God's ways. Although God tells him that no man may "see Me and live" (Exodus 33:21), God nevertheless agrees to grant Moses a vision and to reveal to him the knowledge of God's qualities, thus assuring Moses that the Lord is indeed a forgiving God. It is this vision, accompanied by the proclamation of the merciful qualities of God, that brings the saga of the sin of the Golden Calf to a close.

What God reveals to Moses (as quoted above) is no less than an expansion of the first of the Ten Commandments (Exodus 20:5–6). Now, however, the order of punishment for sin and kindness for love of God is reversed, so that kindness comes before punishment and is especially emphasized.

This new version becomes the basis of Judaism's concept of God as "the Merciful One," a God of forgiveness and compassion.

D'rash: Exposition of the Sages

"The Lord passed before him and proclaimed. . . ." Rabbi
Yohanan said, "Were it not written in the text, it would be
impossible to say—but the verse actually teaches us that
the Holy One wrapped himself in His shawl as does the
leader of the congregation and demonstrated to Moses what
should be said in prayerful petition before Him. He [God]
said to him, 'Whenever [the people of] Israel sin, let them
recite this service before Me and I will pardon them.'"
"The Lord! the Lord!" I am "the Lord" before one sins
and I am "the Lord" after one has sinned—"a God

compassionate and gracious." Rav Judah said, "A covenant
has been made that if they recite these Thirteen Attributes
they will not be turned away, as it says thereafter, 'He
said, I hereby make a covenant'" (Exodus 34:10).
—Rosh Hashanah 17b

Rabbi Yohanan, a third-century *amora* born in Tzipori in the upper
Galilee, depicts the synagogue practices then followed during the
recitation of these verses describing God. This recitation of what
were called the Thirteen Attributes of God, emphasizing God's merciful and forgiving nature, had become a central feature on the High
Holy Days, as it still is today.

According to Rabbi Yohanan, this practice originated from God's
personal example and instruction to Moses that when asking for forgiveness from sin, one should put on a tallit and recite the Thirteen
Attributes; then forgiveness will be attained.

Interestingly, in traditional Jewish liturgy these verses are always
curtailed so that they conclude with "and remits all punishment"
rather than "does not remit all punishment." This is accomplished by
eliminating two Hebrew words, *lo yinakeh*, "does not remit all punishment," and ignoring the text that follows—"but visits the iniquity
of parents upon children and children's children, upon the third and
fourth generations." Thus, by eliminating all references to punishment, the Sages have gone one step further than the Torah text in
depicting God's attribute of mercy as not only dominant but absolute.

Rav Judah goes even further. Basing his claims on the fact that
"covenant" is mentioned following these verses, he teaches that God
has given us an absolute covenantal promise: whenever we recite
these verses, God will always accept our prayers and forgive our sins.

The Talmud then remarks on the fact that God's Name, the Lord—
the four-letter name YHVH, which is not pronounced today but was
used in Second Temple times—appears twice in a row in the verse. It
interprets this repetition to mean that YHVH—a name that according
to the Sages is always associated with God's attribute of mercy—is

merciful both before one sins and after one has transgressed. God's mercy never changes.

For the Sages, this remarkable passage served as proof that the name YHVH—the Lord—epitomized the God of mercy, kindness, and forgiveness. Whatever else the Torah might say about God's attributes, these are the qualities that count. They can be used to invoke God's forgiveness when we transgress. They are as close as we will ever come to understanding the nature of the God we worship. They assure us of the possibility of atonement.

D'rash: Personal Reflection

ATONEMENT WITHOUT BLOOD

For several years I taught a class called Understanding Judaism in the Jerusalem branch of a college sponsored by an American fundamentalist Christian group. My students were college-age men and women enrolled in that college in America who were spending a year at the Jerusalem branch. They were believing Christians, steeped in the Bible, which they knew well, chapter and verse. They were favorably inclined toward Zionism and toward Jews but extremely devout in their belief in Jesus as the Messiah and in his divinity. My task was to help them understand Jewish teachings and beliefs and the meaning of Jewish observances.

A devoted group, these students took their studies seriously. Usually, they accepted what I had to say or asked respectful questions intended to clarify what they could not understand. Occasionally, however, they found a Jewish teaching so opposed to what they believed that they could not resist questioning it.

This happened once when the discussion concerned Judaism's approach to atonement. How does one achieve atonement for sin? Explaining the Jewish concept of *teshuvah*, "repentance," I discussed the ways in which we confess our sins, commit to changing our ways, and invoke God's mercy through recitation of the Thirteen Attributes and other prayers for forgiveness. After the session, a few of the students approached me. They were clearly quite agitated by what I had taught. "But there can be no atonement without blood!" they said. "And without atonement, your sins are not forgiven."

At first I was somewhat confused. What does blood have to do with it? Then I remembered the description in Leviticus 16 of the High Priest's cleansing of the sanctuary. The text states that atoning for the sins of Israel on Yom Kippur requires not only a sacrifice of a goat but also the sprinkling of blood on the cover of the Ark and on the altar. The students obviously knew that section and deduced from it that blood was an essential component of attaining atonement. But more than that, their Christian belief was that the blood of their messiah, whom they term the "sacrificial lamb," was now the blood needed for atonement, the blood that "atones for the sins of the world." Essentially, they were telling me that unless we Jews adopt the students' Christian belief, there is no hope for the cleansing of our sins. Therefore, we Jews are doomed. They found this deeply upsetting.

They were not antisemitic. On the contrary. But their fundamentalist beliefs were so strong that they could not accept the validity of any belief that contradicted them. They were truly distressed that I would not be saved, and I'm afraid nothing I said could convince them otherwise.

Our God is a forgiving God. God makes that very clear to Moses, and the Sages assure us that, blood or no blood, atonement is achievable by our own actions and by invoking the Thirteen Attributes in our prayers.

Va-yak'hel

Enough Gold

EXODUS 35:1–38:20

*Take from among you gifts to the Lord; everyone whose heart
so moves him shall bring them — gifts for the Lord: gold,
silver, and copper; blue, purple, and crimson yarns, fine
linen, and goats' hair. . . . [They] said to Moses, "The people
are bringing more than is needed for the tasks entailed in
the work that the Lord has commanded to be done." Moses
thereupon had this proclamation made throughout the camp:
"Let no man or woman make further effort toward gifts for
the sanctuary!" So the people stopped bringing: their efforts
had been more than enough for the tasks to be done.*
—Exodus 35:5–6, 36:5–6

P'shat: Explanation

Immediately after the incident of the sin of the Golden Calf, the Torah
reports that the actual work of creating a sanctuary for the worship
of God begins. The people are told what materials are needed and
are asked to bring them. The Torah then relates that the people give
their contributions so generously that they actually have to be commanded to stop. There is more than enough.

A feeling of exuberance is conveyed by this description. We have
the impression of a people undertaking this sacred task with great
devotion and zeal. If the story of the Golden Calf described in the
last Torah portion left us with the negative impression of an undisciplined, wild mob creating an abomination and worshipping it madly,

in this portion we have exactly the opposite picture: discipline and enthusiastic dedication to God.

D'rash: Exposition of the Sages

He [God] said to them [Israel], "I would have overlooked everything that you have done, but the incident of the golden calf is worse to Me than all the rest put together!" Rabbi Shimon says, "A parable: This may be likened to one who welcomed and entertained scholars and students and was praised for it. Heathens came and he welcomed them. Robbers came and he entertained them as well! Finally people said, 'It is simply his nature to entertain anyone at all!' Thus it was that Moses said, 'Enough gold! (Deuteronomy 1:1). Enough gold for the Sanctuary. Enough gold for the calf!'" R. Benaiah says, "Because of their worship of idols [the Golden Calf] they were deserving of annihilation. However the gold of the Sanctuary atones for the gold of the calf."
—Sifre Deuteronomy 1

When they made the calf, the Holy One said to Moses, "Now let Me be that My anger may blaze forth against them and that I may destroy them . . ." (Exodus 33:10). [Moses] said to Him, "[Look ahead and] investigate what those who will build the Sanctuary will do." What is written concerning that terrible deed? "Take off the gold rings . . ." (Exodus 33:2) and what did they bring? Gold rings. And when they make the Sanctuary they will bring the same thing, as it is written, "Men and women and all those whose hearts moved them, all . . . came bringing brooches, earrings, rings, and pendants—gold objects of all kinds" (Exodus 35:22). They sinned with gold rings and they make up for it with gold rings.
—Exodus Rabbah 48:6

The Sages were sensitive to every nuance in the Torah. When the same word or phrase appears in different places, they tried to discern the reason and to identify what the various verses have in common. In the text describing the building of the sanctuary, gold plays a prominent role. Gold is the first contribution God asks of the people. And when, as the text later relates, the people were so generous that they had to be told to stop giving, their contributions of "gold rings" and "gold objects of all kinds" are singled out for mention.

But gold plays a similar role in the story of the creation of the Golden Calf, which immediately precedes this one. And there too the people are told (now by Aaron) to contribute gold rings, which they do.

The two incidents are polar opposites. The worship of a calf is the most serious violation of God's commandments—idolatry. The building of a sanctuary in which the presence of God will dwell and be worshipped is the most sacred task imaginable. The Sages therefore discussed the question, How are these two related?

An early tannaitic work, Sifre Deuteronomy, interprets the name of a place mentioned in Deuteronomy 1:1, Di Zahav, as a reference to the sin of the Golden Calf, since Zahav means "gold" and Di could be read as *dai*, meaning "enough." Thus, even though God is willing to overlook other things the people have done, the sin of the Golden Calf by itself is enough to establish their guilt.

Rabbi Shimon makes the connection between the building of the calf and the construction of the sanctuary. In both cases, the people are willing to contribute abundant amounts of gold. He thus criticizes them for not discriminating between a good and an evil cause.

Rabbi Benaiah, however, takes a more positive view. On the contrary, he says, the people's considerable contributions to the sanctuary are intended to compensate and atone for their earlier contributions to the Golden Calf. Indeed, Rabbi Benaiah argues, the people's very generosity cancels the sentence for their extinction.

A later midrashic work, Exodus Rabbah, carries this idea even further. It teaches that when Moses was attempting to convince God not to destroy Israel for worshipping the Golden Calf, he asked the all-

knowing God to gaze into the future and see the Israelites enthusiastically contributing gold to build the sanctuary, thus consciously
attempting to compensate and atone for their sins. This is what causes
God to cancel the severe decree. The gold for the sanctuary is atonement for the gold for the calf.

Rabbinic exegesis thus not only connected these two central events;
it also provided an explanation for the Israelites' extraordinary generosity and deepened the meaning of building a sanctuary in which
God's Presence forever dwells.

D'rash: Personal Reflection

A GENEROUS DONATION

The sanctuary whose plan and creation have occupied so many chapters of Exodus was the first house of worship for the people Israel.
Although the exact plan, including material and size, is said to have
come directly from God, the Jerusalem Temple, built by Solomon
around 690 BCE, followed it only in its general outline. The divine
blueprint was never utilized again.

In later times, a different structure was created for the worship of
God: the synagogue. It differed greatly from the sanctuary both in
purpose and in design. Nonetheless, just as the Israelites built their
sanctuary with generosity, enthusiasm, and love, so too throughout
the centuries Jews have given greatly of their currencies, skills, and
passion to create their synagogues—often called "small sanctuaries."

Having seen many of these buildings in my travels throughout
the world, I remain inspired by the care that went into them. Often
reflecting the local architecture, they are distinctive and vastly different from one another, their only commonalities the presence of
an Ark of the Torah and the eternal light. In Israel there are ancient
stone buildings dating to the first centuries of the Common Era with
Roman pillars, beautiful mosaics, and stone carvings. In Dura-Europos,
in present-day Syria, there is a simple synagogue building adorned

with magnificent wall paintings. In Toledo, Spain, there are handsome synagogues with a Moorish tinge that were turned into churches after the expulsion. Some synagogues are grandiose, such as the huge edifices built by Hungarian Jewry in modern times. To me, the most beautiful of these is the synagogue in Szeged, a symphony in blue and gold, with each detail representing a Jewish symbol. Visiting Poland, I was impressed by the magnificently decorated wooden synagogues, filled with paintings, colorful designs, and letterings on all the walls. Many of these are in ruins, reflecting the fate of Polish Jewry, but some have been lovingly restored and turned into museums. Just standing in them gives one an understanding of the greatness of Polish Jewish civilization that has been destroyed. The history of our people can be traced in these attempts to build sanctuaries in which the presence of God can be felt.

I was personally involved in raising the funds needed to build a synagogue in Jerusalem. As usual, the fund-raising was done in the United States. I had been introduced to a potential donor who had the ability to contribute the rather large amount that was needed to finance the project. Although he was interested, he had never before given a sum of that nature and was hesitant to do so. I met with him several times over a period of months and then had the opportunity to see him weekly for about six weeks. When I was about to return to Israel and still had not received his agreement, I told him how nice it would be if he could give me his answer—positive, of course—before I left.

When the day of my return came, I still had not heard from him.

I literally was going out the door, suitcases in hand, to the airport when the phone rang. I stepped back inside the room to answer it. "Rabbi," my donor friend said, "you can go back and tell them you have the funds to build the synagogue."

At that moment I believed I understood how Moses must have felt when he was told there was enough gold and the people could stop bringing donations. "Enough gold," I said to myself while thanking him for his generosity.

Pekudei

A Symbol to the Nations of Forgiveness

EXODUS 38:21–40:38

These are the records of the Tabernacle, the Tabernacle of
Testimony. . . . When Moses had finished the work, the cloud
covered the Tent of Meeting, and the Presence of the Lord filled
the Tabernacle. Moses could not enter the Tent of Meeting
because the cloud had settled upon it and the Presence of
the Lord filled the Tabernacle. When the cloud lifted from
the Tabernacle the Israelites would set out, on their various
journeys; but if the cloud did not lift, they would not set out
until such time as it did lift. For over the Tabernacle a cloud of
the Lord rested by day, and fire would appear in it by night, in
the view of all the house of Israel throughout their journeys.
—Exodus 38:21, 40:33–38

P'shat: Explanation

After offering a detailed account of everything that went into the
creation of the Tabernacle, the book of Exodus concludes with this
unusual passage, which serves as a bridge between what has been
completed and an anticipation of what is to come. The first word,
vay'hal, "and he finished," seems to echo the word *vay'hulu*, "and they
were finished," in Genesis 2:1, summarizing the conclusion of God's
creation of the world. The heaven and the earth and all their array
were finished. I assume that the Torah uses this word deliberately
in order to connect the two events. God finished creating the world,
and Moses finished making the Tabernacle in which the Creator of
the world will now be present.

Erecting the Tabernacle also finishes a chapter in the history of the people Israel. With the construction of the Tabernacle, Israel has completed the passage from a slave people to a covenant people, a holy nation pledged to follow the ways of God in this world. This journey began with the exodus from Egypt, continued with the final rescue at the sea, and then proceeded with the events at Sinai, where the people accept God's covenant and receive the Ten Commandments and the accompanying laws. God's appearance at Sinai, the revelation, is then institutionalized and concretized in the creation of the Tabernacle. God's covenant is enshrined in the Ark (the "Testimony" probably refers to the tablets of the covenant being housed in the Ark), and God's presence in the Tabernacle will accompany the people onward to their homeland.

What is conspicuous by its absence is even a hint that this generation will not complete the journey—that it will take forty years for the people to enter the Land of Israel. Is this omission telling us that it did not have to happen this way? The people could have chosen to act otherwise and thereby could have avoided the calamity to come. To paraphrase Shakespeare, "The fault . . . is not in our stars but in ourselves."

D'rash: Exposition of the Sages

The Holy One loved Israel and brought them to Mount Sinai,
gave them the Torah and called them "a kingdom of priests"
(Exodus 19:6). Forty days later they sinned, at which time the
pagans said, "God no longer desires them." Once Moses begged
God to be merciful toward Israel, the Holy One immediately
forgave them. . . . Moses said, "Master of the universe, I am
satisfied that You have forgiven Israel, but let the nations
of the world know that You have nothing against them."
The Holy One said, "By your life! I shall make My Presence
dwell in their midst," as it is said, "And let them make Me
a sanctuary that I may dwell among them" (Exodus 25:8).
"Thus they shall know that I have forgiven them." Therefore

it is called "the Tabernacle of Testimony" (Exodus 38:21)
since it testifies that the Holy One has forgiven Israel.
— Exodus Rabbah 51:4

When was Moses told about making the sanctuary? On Yom
Kippur. . . . Even though . . . this chapter commanding creating
the sanctuary appears in the Torah before the story of the
golden calf . . . there is no chronological order in the Torah
and this actually occurred later, on Yom Kippur when Israel
was forgiven for the sin of the calf. That is when the Holy One
said, "And let them make Me a sanctuary that I may dwell
among them" so that all the nations would know that God had
forgiven them for their sin of the golden calf. That is why it is
called "The Tabernacle of testimony" since it testifies to all the
nations that the Holy One dwells in their Tabernacle. . . . And
on the very day when the Tabernacle was erected His Presence
descended and entered into it, as it is said: Moses could
not enter the Tent of Meeting because the cloud had settled
upon it and the Presence of the Lord filled the Tabernacle.
— Tanhuma Terumah 8, Pekudei 11

The Sages wondered why the Tabernacle was called the Tabernacle of Testimony. They felt the name held a greater meaning than merely referring to the contents of the Ark. The answer given in Midrash Exodus Rabbah is that the existence of this structure in which the *Shekhinah*, the Presence of God, dwells in the midst of the Israelites testifies to all the nations of the world that God has indeed forgiven the Israelites for their sin and is willing to dwell among them. Otherwise, God's forgiveness would not be apparent to the other nations.

Furthermore, that name reassures Israel that the people are in God's good graces once more. In fact, the midrash goes so far as to make this the very reason for the creation of the Tabernacle. For the Sages, the idea of God as a forgiving God could never be emphasized enough.

The unstated assumption behind this Rabbinic teaching is that had the people not sinned, it would not have been necessary to build such a structure. God certainly did not need it. The problem with this idea, though, is that according to the order of the stories in the Torah, God gives the command to build the sanctuary while Moses is still on Mount Sinai, *before* the Golden Calf is made.

A later midrash, the Tanhuma, deals with this by invoking the Rabbinic principle that the chapters in the Torah are not necessarily in chronological order, so that something told earlier might actually have taken place later. That, the Sages say, is the case regarding the command to build the sanctuary. It appears earlier but actually happened later, *after* the sin of the calf. Computing the dates of these events, the Tanhuma concludes that Moses obtains God's forgiveness for Israel's idolatry on Yom Kippur—the very same day on which God commands Israel to build the sanctuary—thus providing an outward sign to the people and to all the world that God has forgiven Israel.

Consequently, this adds a historical event to Yom Kippur, which otherwise would have none. It is not an arbitrary date but the day when God first said, I forgive Israel. We can expect to be forgiven on this day as well.

D'rash: Personal Reflection

RIGHT VERSUS RITE

I find something very refreshing about the Sages' reasoning as to why God commanded Israel to build the Tabernacle (a rationale that applied to the Temple as well, the later reincarnation of that structure). In their view, the Tabernacle was a sign of God's forgiveness and of God's love for us. God did not need the structure; only Israel did. And it had no magical properties. Above all, its presence in Israel's midst did not confer automatic protection upon the people.

There is always the danger that an object designated as sacred can be imbued with magical properties and become a substitute for the practices of justice and mercy, which are the true demands of God.

When, for example, did the stones of the remnants of the Temple turn into objects of worship that can answer our prayers? Where did the idea come from that a note written and placed in the stones of the Western Wall is a particularly efficacious act of piety?

The Sages of Israel were not the first ones to understand that the sanctuary and the Temple were not endowed with extrahuman powers but were simply aids to bringing us closer to God and to inspiring us to live moral lives in accordance with divine teachings. The prophets of Israel vehemently preached against endowing the Temple with magical powers and forgetting God's moral demands.

I learned this forcefully from my studies of the writings of Jeremiah with Prof. Shalom Spiegel, a great pedagogue who brought the words of this prophet to life. To this day I can never read them without hearing how he declaimed them in class. This is particularly so of chapter 7, where Jeremiah speaks to people who have come to the Temple seeking protection. "Do not put your trust in illusions and say, 'The Temple of the Lord, the Temple of the Lord, the Temple of the Lord are these buildings'" (7:4). Instead of ascribing magical powers to these structures because they are sacred, Jeremiah says, "Mend your ways and your actions; if you execute justice between one man and another; if you do not oppress the stranger, the orphan and the widow" (7:5). That—and that alone—will make a difference. Otherwise, you are simply making this Temple into "a den of thieves" (7:11), a place that is worthy of destruction.

In 1957, when I was still a rabbinical student, I was also privileged to hear Professor Spiegel deliver a magnificent (and now legendary) lecture in the presence of Chief Justice Earl Warren, subsequently published under the title "Amos versus Amaziah." In it Spiegel demonstrated that the prophet Amos had set the pattern for Jeremiah and others, establishing that while formal rituals were important, the demand for justice should always take precedence over rituals. Amos had dared to prophesy that the Shrine to God would be destroyed because of the lack of justice in the kingdom. For Amaziah the priest, this was not only blasphemy but also rebellion against the state. He therefore brought charges of treason against Amos (Amos 7:10–17).

Both in his Jeremiah class and in his lecture about Amos, Spiegel demonstrated that the ancient lessons of the prophets are no less revolutionary today than they were thousands of years ago. True religion is not the handmaiden of government but must stand above it, preaching truth to power. True religion must never become a mere set of standardized rituals that blind us to eternal truths. The fact that our tradition justified the teachings of Amos and Jeremiah, placing right above rite, has made Judaism into a powerful force for justice as relevant today as it ever was.

III

Leviticus (Va-yikra')

Va-yikra'

Sacrifices Then and Now

LEVITICUS 1:1–5:26

The Lord called to Moses and spoke to him from the Tent of Meeting, saying: Speak to the Israelite people, and say to them: When any one of you presents an offering of cattle to the Lord, you shall offer your offering from the herd or from the flock.

—Leviticus 1:1–2

P'shat: Explanation

These opening lines from the book of Leviticus introduce a series of lists of sacrifices and instructions for offering them that sets the tone for the entire book. In Hebrew, Leviticus is known as *torat Kohanim*, the Instruction of the Priests or the Instruction for the Priests. Yet *torat Kohanim* first instructs the people, teaching them what to bring as offerings to God and for what reasons. Then it explains to the Priests how to offer the sacrifices.

The instructions for building the Tabernacle had been recorded in the book of Exodus, although at this point the structure has not been completed and dedicated. Now comes the nitty-gritty of what is to be done there—the offerings brought to God.

The central role that sacrifices played in the religion of Israel in ancient days and up until the destruction of the Second Temple in 70 CE should not be underestimated. It is not incidental that so much space in the Torah is devoted to this one theme.

The concept of offering sacrifices, however, was not new. It dated back to the earliest times of human worship and was appropriated from the major religions that preceded Judaism. There was, however, a profound difference between pagan and Israelite sacrifice, a difference that reflected the revolutionary concept of God introduced by the religion of Israel. Whereas pagan sacrifice answered a need of the gods for either physical sustenance or magical renewal, the God of Israel had no need for the sacrifices for either nourishment or anything else. The sacrifices were not meant for God but for human beings. Sacrifices allowed them to feel close to the Divinity, to offer thanksgiving, and/or to assuage feelings of guilt and attain forgiveness.

Although Moses certainly could have decreed a way of worshipping God that did not require sacrifices, this would have been completely against what everyone expected. In early times, worship without sacrifices was unimaginable because sacrifices were so deeply embedded in human consciousness. In a sense, then, sacrifices were a concession to human need.

Beyond this, it was radical enough at the time to teach the people that they could not worship a physical image of their God. To also eliminate sacrifices would have been beyond the pale.

Still, sacrifices had to be limited. Therefore, the text makes it very clear that they were not actually consumed by God. For example, there was the showbread—twelve loaves that were placed "before the Lord" on a special table, representing the twelve tribes, but the loaves were simply left there all week and then replaced by new ones and eaten by the Priests (Leviticus 24:5–9). God did not eat them or need them.

Taking this idea further, the prophets made it plain that sacrifices were actually displeasing to God unless they were accompanied by observance of Judaism's ethical teachings. Jeremiah went so far as to declare that God had not commanded the sacrifices "when he freed your fathers from the land of Egypt" (7:22). Amos proclaimed: "If you offer me burnt offerings—or your meal offerings—I will not accept them . . . but let justice well up like water, righteousness like an unfailing stream" (5:22,24).

D'rash: Exposition of the Sages

Whenever Temple worship exists the world is blessed for
its inhabitants and rain comes at its proper time, as it
says (Deuteronomy 11:13). And whenever Temple worship
does not exist, the world is not blessed for its inhabitants
and the rain does not come at its proper time, as it says
(11:16). . . . Thus you learn that there is no worship beloved
more by the Holy One than the worship of the Temple.
—*Avot de-Rabbi Natan A 4*

Once Rabban Yohanan ben Zakkai was leaving Jerusalem
followed by Rabbi Joshua and saw the ruins of the Temple.
Rabbi Joshua said, "Woe unto us that this place is destroyed,
the place in which the sins of Israel were atoned." Rabban
Yohanan said to him, "Do not be so troubled. We have another
atonement no less effective. What is it? Acts of lovingkindness,
as it is said, 'For I desire lovingkindness, not sacrifice . . .'
(Hosea 6:6). So too do we find that Daniel the greatly beloved
man busied himself with acts of lovingkindness. . . . And
what were those acts? . . . He cannot have offered sacrifices
in Babylon—rather, he would adorn the bride and make her
rejoice, accompany the dead, and give a coin to the needy,
pray three times a day and his prayer would be accepted."
—*Avot de-Rabbi Natan A 3*

After the Romans destroyed the Temple in 70 CE and sacrifices were
no longer possible, Jews were cast into despair. The very central pillar of their religious ritual life had been shattered. The selections
from *Avot de-Rabbi Natan* (*The Fathers According to Rabbi Nathan*), a
very early tannaitic work likely compiled a few hundred years or so
later, speaks of the Jews' great distress and feelings of helplessness.
With these words, the Sages communicated that sacrificial worship

in the Temple was a prime value to both the common people and the Sages. For this reason, prayers for the restoration of sacrifices have been central to Jewish liturgy.

Still, because of the idea found in the Torah and prophets that sacrifices were not God's main requirement, one famous Sage, Rabban Yohanan ben Zakkai, found a way to help the people overcome their despair at their loss.

Rabban Yohanan ben Zakkai was the outstanding Sage of the period before and immediately after the destruction of the Temple. It is said that he attempted to prevent the revolt against Rome, counselling its leaders to give in to Emperor Vespasian's demands rather than see the Temple and Jerusalem destroyed. When he did not succeed, his students smuggled him out of Jerusalem in a coffin. Afterward, Vespasian granted him permission to establish a center of learning in Yavneh. This became the new Sanhedrin, guiding Jews on how to live under conditions of total surrender to Rome.

His love for Jerusalem and the Temple cannot be denied. Legend has him trembling while watching the ensuing destruction and tearing his garments and crying aloud in mourning when it was a finality. Yet he had the presence of mind to counsel his student Joshua not to despair and to know that the Temple, for all its splendor and importance, was not irreplaceable. He seized upon a particular verse from Hosea, one of many prophetic verses denoting that sacrifices were not the most important part of God's demands. In God's eyes, Hosea said, *hesed* was more important than sacrifices.

In Hosea's time *hesed* meant loyalty to God, but by Rabbinic times the word had come to mean much more than that: acts of kindness toward others, acts of love. The particular actions mentioned in the passage—adorning the bride, burying the dead, giving charity to the poor—were examples of deeds in which the individual goes beyond the requirements of the law to help those in need. Rabbinic Judaism would constantly praise such acts of loving-kindness.

In seeking to console the people, ben Zakkai could simply have said that prayer will substitute for sacrifice (and, indeed, to some extent that is what happened; the synagogue service replaced Temple offerings as the heart of Jewish ritual). Instead, Rabban Yohanan ben Zakkai directed his followers toward charitable acts. These, he insisted, would make human beings acceptable before God. These would achieve the people's desired atonement from sin. And these deeds do not require a Temple or elaborate sacrificial ritual.

D'rash: Personal Reflection

A TEMPLE WITHOUT SACRIFICES

In recent times, it has become acceptable to assume that sacrifices are no longer needed in Judaism. Secular Jews certainly see no need for them, and Reform Judaism has eliminated them entirely from its liturgy. Conservative Judaism's prayer books have turned prayers for sacrifices into historical references on the ways our ancestors offered sacrifices—and while these books may still contain prayers for the eventual restoration of the Temple, it is for a Temple without sacrifice.

On the other hand, the 1967 restoration of the Temple Mount by Jewish hands has led to renewed interest in restoration of the Temple and the sacrificial service in some circles (even though that would not be possible as of this writing). Each year, a group holds a Passover sacrifice somewhere in Jerusalem, as close to the Temple area as possible. Is this the direction we wish to go, or should we view the rejection of sacrifices as a necessary next step in Judaism's development?

My own view coincides with something an Israeli Orthodox rabbi, Shmuel Reiner, once wrote: "When prayer replaced sacrifice, a different spiritual world was created. In place of the active, physical worship of the Temple came the inwardness of prayer. The consciousness of the person who stands before God is no longer that of someone in the time the Temple stood. A man or woman now worships God through inner intent and direction."

Another earlier rabbi and Zionist thinker, Rabbi Haim Hirschensohn, stated that a culture cannot go backward. Therefore, it is unimaginable that Jews could return to sacrifices. Indeed, Judaism has always taught that God did not need sacrifices. Maimonides saw them as a concession to human feelings, Rabbi Yohanan ben Zakkai said that acts of loving-kindness were an adequate substitute, and the prophets viewed them as less important than the pursuit of justice.

Perhaps, then, we can appreciate the vital role sacrifices played in Judaism two thousand years ago without desiring to see them return.

Tsav

Concern for Our Welfare

LEVITICUS 6:1–8:36

*This is the offering that Aaron and his sons shall offer to the
Lord on the occasion of his anointment: a tenth of an ephah
of choice flour as a regular meal offering, half of it on the
morning and half of it in the evening. It shall be prepared
with oil on a griddle. You shall bring it well soaked, and offer
it as a meal offering of baked slices, of pleasing odor to the
Lord. And so shall the priest, anointed from among his sons to
succeed him, prepare it; it is the Lord's — a law for all time — to
be turned entirely into smoke. So too, every meal offering
of a priest shall be a whole offering: it shall not be eaten.*

—Leviticus 6:13–16

P'shat: Explanation

The first portion of Leviticus outlined the various types of sacrifices
and explained why each was to be brought. Leviticus now moves on
to instruct the Priests on exactly how to offer these sacrifices and
describes the offerings the Priests are to bring, both now, when they
are to be anointed to their sacred task, and in the future.

The Torah offers no explanation as to these details. We do not
know why a specific animal or food was to be brought, why a particular quantity was required, or why different methods were called for.
Some sacrifices, for example, were to be totally consumed by fire, "a
whole offering"; others were to be eaten in part by the Priests.

The one aspect that remains very clear is that in the religion of Israel, none of the sacrifices were intended for God's consumption. Note the phrase used here: pleasing odor to the Lord. When describing Noah's offering to the Lord after the Flood a similar phrase is used: "The Lord smelled the pleasing odor" (Genesis 8:21). By contrast, in the earlier Mesopotamian versions of the Flood story, when the first sacrifice is given after the Flood, the gods are said to swarm down like flies to devour it. After not having any sacrifices to eat for such a long time, they are starving.

In other words, the most the Torah allows itself to say is that God smelled the sacrifice. This is a way of indicating that God found it pleasing, even though God did not need it.

D'rash: Exposition of the Sages

"A regular meal offering . . ." Rabbi Joshua of Sikhnin said in the name of Rabbi Levi: Come and see how concerned the Holy One is for Israel's wealth. He says to them, "Someone who has to bring a sacrifice shall bring it from cattle — 'If his offering is a burnt offering from the herd . . .' (Leviticus 1:3). But if he does not have cattle, he can bring a lamb — 'If his offering is from the flock . . .' (Leviticus 3:6). And if he does not have a lamb, he can bring a goat — 'And if his offering is a goat . . .' (Leviticus 3:12). And if he does not have a goat, he can bring it from birds —
'If his offering to the Lord is a burnt offering of birds . . .'
(Leviticus 1:14) — and if he does not have a bird, he can bring flour — '. . . a tenth of an ephah of choice flour as a regular meal offering . . .' (Leviticus 6:13). . . . And not only that, but whoever brings that [meal offering] is considered by Scripture as if he had offered sacrifices from one end of the world to another, as it is said, 'For from where the sun rises to where it sets, My name is honored among the nations, and everywhere incense and pure meal-offering are offered to My name'" (Malachi 1:11).
—Leviticus Rabbah 8:4

Rabbi Levi ben Sisi, a prominent *amora* living at the end of the second century and a close associate and student of Rabbi Judah the Prince, has cleverly combined various verses from Leviticus describing the sacrifices to make the point that the most humble offering is as valuable as the most expensive. Each verse he chooses mentions a different animal that can be offered, proceeding from the most to the least costly—cattle, sheep, goats, birds—and, finally, a meal offering made of flour. He assumes that the order in the text is meant to assist the people in selecting the sacrificial animal they can afford. If you cannot afford to sacrifice something from the herd, bring a sheep. If you cannot manage that, a goat will suffice. If a goat is not within your means, offer a bird. Finally, it is perfectly all right if you bring a meal offering. Capping off his teaching, Rabbi Levi cites a verse from the prophet Malachi mentioning this least expensive offering that seems to indicate that it is to be valued from where the sun rises to where it sets, that is, throughout the entire world.

In other words, Rabbi Levi asserts, God doesn't want you to eat up all of your funds for the sacrifice. God is concerned for Israel's wealth. God will be pleased with whatever you can afford. God has compassion for the people.

The Sages cite the principle Rabbi Levi invokes, that is, that God does not make excessive demands that will reduce the people to poverty, with regard to many other matters as well. This was a basic concept in their thinking. For example, when the first fruits were brought as an offering to the Temple, the Mishnah specifies that although the wealthy brought them in silver or gold baskets, others less fortunate would bring them in simple woven baskets (Bikkurim 3:8).

This concern is not to be taken for granted. Monarchs expect their subjects to bring them offerings of great value, and the same is true of divine monarchs, "gods" who expect only the finest gifts. Yet the God of Israel is not like that. God's love and concern for the people extend to worrying about their financial welfare.

Throughout the ages, this principle has also been cited in decisions of Jewish law as a reason to permit something to be used or eaten when doubt exists as to whether it is kosher or not. If the loss is truly great, the inclination is to accept it as kosher rather than to declare it unusable.

D'rash: Personal Reflection

SAVING A WEDDING FEAST

I am reminded of a well-known tale told of Jerusalem in the early days of the twentieth century that may or may not be true. There was to be a wedding in Mea Shearim to which hundreds of people had been invited. Weddings of that size were to be expected in those circles. It was, as usual, a meat meal, and on that very day, as the food was being prepared, somehow some milk was accidentally spilled into the huge pot. The worried family hurried to the rabbi, a very prominent and revered authority. What should they do?

He could have easily said that the food was *treif*—not kosher—and could not be served. Instead, he asked question after question and finally told the family to send the milkman to meet him privately in his study.

After the milkman finally emerged from the rabbi's study, the rabbi told the family (much to their relief) that the food was kosher and could be served. He refused to give an explanation for his ruling.

Many years later, when the milkman was no longer alive, the rabbi was finally willing to answer the family's questions about his ruling. What had he asked the milkman? "I asked him how much water he put into his milk. The amount was so large that I could rule that the quantity of actual milk in the pot was not enough to render it unusable." And, concerned about the family's finances, he had investigated the matter thoroughly and ruled as leniently as possible. In order to not harm the milkman's reputation, however, the rabbi did not reveal what he had learned until the man had passed from this world.

I believe it is vital that all Jews have the opportunity to live Jewish lives. Regardless of their financial means, they should be able to participate fully in synagogue, education, and many other Jewish functions. This premise encompasses death as well as life. My late friend and colleague Rabbi Samuel Dresner led a movement to keep Jewish funeral expenses in line by establishing a policy by which only plain wooden caskets could be used for burial. Many Jewish communities adopted these practices, much to the relief of many families.

By these acts, I believe, we follow God's ways. We can—and, I affirm, we should—be as concerned as God for the needs of all: rich and poor alike.

Shemini

Alien Fire

LEVITICUS 9:1–11:47

*Now Aaron's sons Nadab and Abihu each took his fire
pan, put fire in it, and laid incense on it; and they offered
before the Lord alien fire, which He had not enjoined upon
them. And fire came forth from the Lord and consumed
them; thus they died before the Lord. Then Moses said
to Aaron, "This is what the Lord meant when He said:
Through those near to Me I show Myself holy, and gain
glory before all the people." And Aaron was silent.*
—Leviticus 10:1–3

P'shat: Explanation

Tragedy strikes at the very moment when joy should reign. The sanctuary has been erected at great cost in time and effort as well as precious materials. It is intended to be the place in which the Presence of the Lord will dwell and accompany the people on their journey: it is the Holy of Holies, a portable Mount Sinai. Aaron has offered appropriate dedicatory sacrifices and then blessed the people, as did Moses. God's acceptance of this is demonstrated by the "fire [that] came forth from before the Lord and consumed the burnt offering" (Leviticus 9:24).

Ironically, though, once again, immediately thereafter, "fire came forth from the Lord" (Leviticus 10:2)—and this time it does not consume the sacrifice but the sacrificers! Aaron's two sons, Nadab and Abihu, both Priests like their father, have performed an "alien" ritual in the sanctuary, bringing "alien fire" that was not commanded. As punishment, they too perish by fire.

The narrative does not explain what was wrong with Nadab and Abihu's fire, but the obvious implication is that instead of heeding God's commandments concerning ritual practices, the two Priests acted according to their own ideas and thus violated the sanctity of the place. Thus, even if we never know all the whys, we can easily understand what the story is meant to teach us. Leviticus is the manual telling the Priests what to do and how to do it. This story warns them in the strongest possible terms to follow those instructions to the letter. Anything else is forbidden and carries deadly consequences. As Moses says to Aaron, those who are closest to God must sanctify God by demonstrating complete obedience. Any deviation becomes *avodah zarah*, literally, "alien worship," that is, idolatry.

For his part, Aaron does not respond to the death of his sons. He remains silent. Some see this as a sign of his acquiescence. But perhaps, as a grieving father who has experienced the greatest of all tragedies, he is simply struck dumb.

D'rash: Exposition of the Sages

Said Rabbi Elazar HaModai: How difficult for the Lord was the death of the two sons of Aaron, for in four different places the death of the sons of Aaron is mentioned and in each place the reason for their death is mentioned. Why? To teach that alien fire was their only sin. And so that people should not say that they had committed dissolute practices in secret and were killed because of that. . . . Rabbi Simon said, "Here the expression 'before the Lord' is found twice while 'before their father Aaron' is said elsewhere only once (Numbers 3:4). Why? To teach that their deaths were twice as difficult for the Holy One to bear as for their father."

—Numbers Rabbah 20:24

Rabbi Eliezer taught: The sons of Aaron died because they
determined legal matters in the presence of their Master Moses.
Bar Kappara said in the name of Rabbi Jeremiah son of
Elazar: The sons of Aaron died because of four things: they
approached God's Presence, they brought an unnecessary
offering, they brought alien fire, and they did not take council
with one another as it is said, "each took his fire pan"—each
did so independently, not taking council with the other.
Rabbi Levi said: They were arrogant. There were many
women waiting for them to deal with their problems
because they could not remarry, having the status of
agunot [chained women]. What did they say? "Our
father's brother is the sovereign, our mother's brother is
a prince, our father is the High Priest, and we are both
vice-priests. What woman is worthy of our attention?"
Furthermore—note this: "Then He said to Moses, 'Come
up to the Lord, with Aaron, Nadab and Abihu'" (Exodus
24:1). This indicates that Moses and Aaron walked at the
front but that Nadab and Abihu followed closely while all
the rest of Israel went behind and they [Nadab and Anihu]
said, "These two old men will die soon and we will take their
place as leaders of the community!" The Holy One said to
them, "Do not boast of tomorrow, for you do not know what
the day will bring" (Prov. 27:1). Many a young donkey
has died and became a saddle on the back of its mother!
—Leviticus Rabbah 20:6,8,10

The death of these two Priests was so shocking that the Sages frequently discussed what had happened. Two different approaches
emerged.

One indicated that these two young men were guilty of just one
misdeed, and it was not a terrible one at that. Nevertheless, God
had no choice but to punish them, since they had transgressed the
holiness of the ritual and thus the sacredness of God. Their deaths,

however, weighed heavily upon the Holy One. Therefore, God made certain that everyone knew that they were not guilty of an egregious moral failure.

From this approach, the sons' deaths as a consequence of one ritual fault was problematic. Even for God, the punishment was not an easy matter.

The opposite approach asserted that the two Priests somehow deserved to die. The Sages who taught this must have felt that the sin mentioned in the Torah — "alien fire" — was not sufficient in itself to explain the Priests' deaths. God must have had other reasons to slay them. Thus, besides the alien fire, the sons had to have committed other sins.

Various suggestions of their sins were then offered. Some of these imagined transgressions were also ritual in nature, such as approaching the Divine Presence by entering the Holy of Holies or bringing an extra, unwarranted sacrifice. Some were faults of character: the sons did not consult or cooperate with one another, they were dissolute, they acted arrogantly, they did not revere their teachers and elders, they coveted Aaron's and Moses's positions, they were too haughty, they neglected to help those in need of their expertise.

Many of these scenarios were in fact drawn from the Sages' personal experiences. In the Sages' time, for example, disciples were supposed to demonstrate humility and respect for their teacher. Such comportment was supposed to be a main characteristic of a Sage — but often was not. The Sages' criticism of Aaron's sons, then, was really aimed at teaching their own students what they, as Sages, should or should not do.

D'rash: Personal Reflection

CELEBRATING A WOMAN'S FREEDOM

Of all the reasons the Sages list for the deaths of Aaron's sons, the one that touches me the most is their sons' supposed failure to help women who are desperate to be freed from their marriages. This problem of the *agunot* (women who cannot obtain a divorce and consequently marry again because their husbands refuse to grant it) is prevalent in Jewish life today, especially though not only in Israel, and the problem is the same: the refusal of rabbinical authorities to do something about it. Since Jewish law gives husbands the right to grant or deny a divorce, many husbands have taken undue advantage, forcing their wives to agree to relinquish financial or other benefits in order to obtain that divorce. Some do this merely out of spite, to punish the woman who wants to divorce her husband for whatever reason.

In Israel all divorces go through the official courts of the Orthodox Chief Rabbinate, which has certain legal powers to attempt to force a recalcitrant husband to grant a divorce but unfortunately has all too often been reluctant to do so and has sided with husbands. As a result, hundreds of women, as *agunot*, have waited many years for the right to become free to marry again. Some never receive it.

There are various proactive solutions to this problem. In America in the 1950s the eminent talmudic authority Prof. Saul Lieberman created a clause, added to the *ketubah* (the wedding agreement), that grants the Rabbinical Court the right to insist that the husband grant his wife a Jewish divorce. The Conservative Rabbinical Assembly adopted this arrangement, and it has proved effective, since in effect the husband has agreed in advance to grant a divorce if the rabbinical court so decrees.

Another solution is a premarital agreement on the subject. Both parties agree in advance on the terms of a potential divorce agreement and sign a legal document to this effect in the presence of lawyers.

Years ago I was part of a special ceremony at my Jerusalem synagogue celebrating the new status of a woman who, after sixteen years of being an *agunah*, had finally managed to obtain a divorce. In attendance were her children, other family members, and dozens of women belonging to organizations devoted to this struggle who had helped her over the years. She recited a blessing praising God for her freedom, and everyone sang and danced in celebration. In addition, I offered a public prayer that the authorities who delay and do not help these women will realize the seriousness of their actions. They should remember what the Sages taught hundreds of years ago when they condemned Nadab and Abihu as arrogant men. These authorities are just as unworthy of their positions, and just as guilty.

Tazria^c

Dealing with Impurity

LEVITICUS 12:1–13:59

The Lord spoke to Moses saying: Speak to the Israelite people thus:
When a woman at childbirth bears a male, she shall be unclean
seven days; she shall be unclean as at the time of her menstrual
infirmity. On the eighth day the flesh of his foreskin shall be
circumcised. . . . If she bears a female, she shall be unclean two weeks
as during her menstruation. . . . On the completion of her period of
purification, for either son or daughter, she shall bring to the priest,
at the entrance to the Tent of Meeting, a lamb in its first year for
a burnt offering, and a pigeon or a turtledove for a sin offering.
—Numbers 12:1–3,5–6

P'shat: Explanation

This section and the subsequent one constitute a long and detailed discussion of the sources of impurity that will render people or objects ritually unclean. The text prescribes various ways to treat this condition so that purity will be regained.

The placement of this discussion in the book of Leviticus seems appropriate. After all, the priest is the one who is charged with determining impurity and purity and overseeing the related rituals. The text delineates the rules and regulations that the priest must know in order to fulfill these functions.

The cases of impurity described here begin with childbirth, which is compared to menstruation. There is no explanation for the fact that the period of impurity is doubled when the infant is female. A following discussion concerns skin infections, which are referred to as "leprosy" but (as the text makes clear) are not really the same thing as that dreaded disease, as well as "an affection" found in cloth or leather. The following Torah section (Metsoraᶜ) adds eruptive plagues in houses and male and female discharges to the list.

Here, the priest does not function as a healer but as the one who decides if the individual or the object is pure or impure and the one who offers the brought sacrifices once purity has been achieved. The Torah does not imply that these occurrences of impurity are punishments for misdeeds, although, as we shall see in the following section, a connection was sometimes — but not always — made between leprosy and punishment for speaking evil.

D'rash: Exposition of the Sages

"When a woman at childbirth bears a male, she shall be unclean seven days. . . ." Why is she unclean seven days when bearing a male but fourteen days when bearing a female? [Said Rabbi Shimon bar Yochai]: In the case of a male, when all rejoice in his birth, she becomes pure after seven days. In the case of a female, when all are sad because of her birth, she becomes pure after fourteen days.
—Midrash ha-Gadol to the verse

Rabbi Isaac in the name of Rabbi Ammi said: When a male comes into the world he brings peace. . . . When a male comes into the world he brings his provisions with him. . . . When a female comes into the world she brings nothing with her.
—Niddah 31b

"And the Lord had blessed Abraham in all things" (Genesis 24:1). Rabbi Judah says: "in all things" means that He granted him a daughter. Rabbi Nehemiah says: "in all things" means that he did not grant him any daughters at all!
—Genesis Rabbah 59:4

*A woman once came to Rabbi Akiba and said, "I have seen
a blood stain." He said to her, "Did you have a wound?"
"Yes," she replied, "but it has healed." "Is it possible," he
asked, "that it might have opened again and bled?" "Yes,"
she replied, whereupon he declared her clean. When
his disciples looked astonished, [Akiba] said to them,
"Why do you find this difficult? The Sages did not say
these things to be stringent, but rather to be lenient."*
—Niddah 8:3

Some scholars have suggested that this period of impurity was really
established for the mother's benefit, since at the time childbirth was
an extremely dangerous matter, and this ruling gave the mother
time to recover. No reasonable explanation has ever been offered
for the disparity in time taken for a woman to achieve ritual purity
after childbirth when giving birth to a daughter (fourteen days) as
opposed to a son (seven days). Why having a female child should warrant double the purity recuperation time is unclear, but the fact that
the male child undergoes circumcision on the eighth day may have
something to do with it.

Because the matter is so puzzling, Shimon bar Yochai, one of Rabbi
Akiba's close disciples, is said to have offered the above-mentioned
explanation in response to a student's request. In the full account
as presented in the Talmud, he said that while in the pain of travail,
women would vow not to have more children, and it would take that
long for them to be willing to nullify that vow—longer when they had
a daughter than a son, since they were happy to have a male child and
not happy when the child was female. Bar Yochai was often known for
having rather extreme positions, and one wonders if he meant this one
to be taken seriously. Other Sages did not agree with his statement.

It is likely that this expressed prejudice against daughters was not
unknown at that time (the second century CE). Rabbi Ammi (a third-
to-fourth-century CE Babylonian *amora*) commented that a draw-
back about having daughters was that they had no way of providing

for themselves financially. In other cultures, daughters were in fact so undesirable that steps were taken to see that they did not survive. Nothing that extreme happened in Jewish life, although the preference for sons may have been strong in the era.

An ambivalent attitude about daughters is also seen in the interpretations given by two second-century *tannaim*, Judah and Nehemiah, concerning God's blessing granted to Abraham. While Judah says that Abraham was blessed with a daughter, Nehemiah says that he was blessed in not having any daughters. No daughters of Abraham are mentioned in the Torah, but that does not prove the matter either way. Obviously, for Rabbi Judah, a daughter was seen as a blessing, while Rabbi Nehemiah took the opposite view. I would hope that Rabbi Judah's position is the accepted one today.

When it came to questions of ritual purity and when women were considered permitted to engage in marital relations, it is interesting to see that Rabbi Akiba, the most influential authority of his day, took the position that the general attitude of Rabbinic law was to be lenient and not overly stringent whenever possible. This accords with Akiba's opinion that love was the basis for a good marriage. Akiba even took the description of such love in the Song of Songs as the paradigm for the love between God and Israel.

D'rash: Personal Reflection

THE BLESSING OF DAUGHTERS

We were blessed with three daughters in a row, and we never felt downcast at their births. On the contrary, we rejoiced in each one of them. Like Rabbi Judah, we felt that having a daughter was a blessing. Having three was a triple treat.

When our fourth child was expected, we never imagined that it would be a son. We were so certain we would continue as before that we didn't have a boy's name picked out. When a big strapping boy emerged we were delighted, not because sons were better than daughters, but because having children of both sexes seemed to complete the family circle.

Years later, one of our daughters had the opposite experience: giving birth to five sons. Her sons then became fathers and also produced four male children, so that when the fifth child, a daughter, was born to one of them, it was a time of rejoicing for the entire family.

My own view has always been that although daughters and sons are different, they deserve to be treated as equals. In the early 1970s, leaders of the synagogue I was serving as rabbi asked me whether I believed women should be given *aliyot* to the Torah. I gave a lecture on the subject, namely, that although at that time this was not considered to be appropriate to the "honor of the congregation," from the perspective of Jewish law, women could in fact receive *aliyot*, and I favored instituting the practice. Then, the congregation voted— and turned down the idea. Today, that congregation has a woman as its rabbi!

Metsoraᶜ

LEVITICUS 14:1–15:33

The Lord spoke to Moses, saying: This is the ritual for the leper at the time he is to be cleansed. When it has been reported to the priest, the priest shall go outside the camp. If the priest sees that the leper has been healed of his scaly affection, the priest shall order two live clean birds, cedar wood, crimson stuff, and hyssop to be brought to him who is to be cleansed. . . . Thus the priest shall offer the burnt offering on the altar, and the priest shall make expiation for him. Then he shall be clean. . . . Such is the ritual for every eruptive affection—for scalls, for an eruption on a cloth or a house, for swellings, for rashes, or for discolorations—to determine when they are unclean and when they are clean.
—Leviticus 14:1–4,20,54–57

P'shat: Explanation

This Torah portion completes the discussion of leprosy-like infections begun in the previous parashah (weekly Torah reading). On most years the two portions are read together on one Shabbat.

The preceding portion had described the disease in detail and instructed the priest on the means of determining if a person truly was afflicted with this disease. If the answer was yes, then the individual was considered ritually unclean and required isolation. Now, in this portion, the Torah comes to the end of the process. After the individual has been cured, the text describes the rituals the priest is to perform that will render this person ritually pure once again — and thereby able to reenter the camp and resume normal living.

The chapter also adds a description of similar "eruptive plagues" that can afflict houses, how the priest can determine if the house is plague-ridden or not, what to do if it is, and under what conditions the house will have to be destroyed altogether.

In all of these instances the priest has two functions: to determine if the disease or the plague really exists and when it has disappeared, and only then to perform rituals that expiate the ritual impurity, rendering people and objects ritually pure once again. Notably, the priest never takes action to bring about the change, to heal the affliction. It either comes of itself, or it does not. Thus the priest does not possess any magical formulae or special powers.

D'rash: Exposition of the Sages

"This is the ritual for the leper." As it is written, "Who is the man who is eager for life, who desires years of good fortune? Guard your tongue from evil, your lips from deceitful speech" (Psalm 34:13–14). An incident concerning a peddler who would go around to the settlements near Tzipori and would proclaim, "Who wants to buy the balm of life?!" Rabbi Yannai heard him from his residence and said to his daughter, "Go and buy me some." He [the merchant] said, "Neither you nor your group need this." He took out a book of Psalms and showed him [Rabbi Yannai] this verse: "Who is the man who is eager for life, who desires years of good fortune?" What is written after that? "Guard your tongue from evil, your lips from deceitful speech. Shun evil and do good, seek peace and pursue it." Rabbi Yannai said, "All my life I read that verse and did not understand its simple meaning until this peddler came and explained it!" Rabbi Haggai added, "Solomon similarly said, 'He who guards his mouth and tongue guards himself from trouble — mi-tzarot' (Proverbs 2:23) — He guards himself

from leprosy—mi-tzarat. That is why Moses warns Israel,
'This is the ritual for the leper—ha-metzora'—the ritual
for one who brings forth evil [speech]—ha-motzi—ra."
—Leviticus Rabbah Metsora^c 16:2

This midrash begins by citing two verses, one from today's portion that speaks of leprosy and the other from Psalms that talks about deceitful speech after mentioning being "eager for life." It is not immediately clear what one has to do with the other.

That is clarified only in the tale told about Rabbi Yannai and the peddler. In order to understand this fully we need to understand the reason for the connection between the leper and "evil speech" that the Sages make in this midrash and many other places. As discussed in this midrash, the two Hebrew words are similar. The Hebrew word for leper is *ha-metzora*, and the Hebrew term for speaking evil about others is *ha-motzi—ra*, literally, "one who brings forth evil"—or, in its fuller form, *ha-motzi shem ra*, defaming someone's name.

The other connection appears in the biblical story of Miriam's punishment. After Miriam speaks evil about her brother Moses because he married a Kushite woman, God punishes her by making her leprous: "Miriam was stricken with snow-white scales—*m'tzora-at*" (Numbers 12:10). From this the Sages concluded that just as Miriam was struck with leprosy for slander, so all cases of leprosy are punishments for slander, which they termed "evil speech." (Under discussion is not the actual disease of leprosy but the appearance of many kinds of skin eruptions as described in the Torah.)

After the Temple's destruction in 70 CE, priests were no longer practicing the rituals of leprosy and subsequent rituals of purification. Nonetheless, the Sages were so opposed to the use of language to defame others that they proffered these interpretations to denounce slander whenever the topic of leprosy appeared in biblical passages. The comments on this week's portion are perfect examples of this.

Returning to our tale about Rabbi Yannai and the peddler: Rabbi Yannai, a third-century *amora* and pupil of Rabbi Judah the Prince, was a very wealthy man who ran an important academy and lived in the upper Galilee, then a flourishing place of Jewish settlement. Galilee towns such as Tzipori (Sepphoris) were major centers with lavish homes and public buildings, including synagogues (the archaeological remains can still be seen today). Peddlers have long been known for selling all kinds of potions touted to improve the body and heal illnesses, although most often those potions do not have any real healing powers (as an example see Donizetti's comic opera *L'elisir d'amore* about peddling fake love potions). The peddler in this midrash is also selling a potion—one that he says will guarantee a good and long life. But he is also smart enough to know that for the revered Rabbi Yannai, his family, and his circle of students, there is no need for what the peddler has to sell. The true elixir of life and "years of fortune" are not to be found in a bottle. All you have to do is follow the advice of the verse: watch your tongue, stop speaking evil, and do only good. As the peddler conveys it, a true Sage such as Rabbi Yannai obviously lives according to this rule and therefore will have a long life. Rabbi Yannai appreciates the peddler's clever use of the verse.

This story is told in order to explain the two verses cited at the beginning of the midrash. Disease comes from evil speech. Long life comes from avoiding it. Rabbi Haggai adds another verse, from Proverbs, that also makes this connection through a play on the words *tzarot* (troubles) and *tzarat* (leprosy). If you watch your tongue, you guard yourself not merely from troubles but from disease.

D'rash: Personal Reflection

A PLAGUE ON THE HOUSE

I certainly do not believe that leprosy or any other disease is a punishment for slander or any other transgression. This Torah portion does not say that. Nor am I positive that the Sages really believed that—certainly not in all instances. What they did believe, and so do I, is that speaking evil is itself a terrible act that must be eliminated. When the disease of slander appears in any one of us, we must take steps to eliminate it and to purify ourselves of it. Obviously, both the Torah and the Sages took Miriam's actions seriously and condemned them. If a person of her character could fall prey to the ease with which words become harmful, all of us have to be on our guard.

On another level, whenever I read this portion I remember my personal encounter with 'leprosy' of a house. Our week's portion describes this in most unpleasant detail. The idea of a house having a plague always struck me as strange, and for a long time I could not imagine it.

When my family and I came on *aliyah* to Israel, before we moved into our as yet unfinished apartment, we lived in a *merkaz k'litah*, an absorption center in the Judean hills outside of Jerusalem. The houses within the center complex were basically unheated except for small oil stoves. In the winter, which in Israel is the rainy season, our house was cold and damp. We huddled around the stove to keep warm, with little success. As time went on we noticed patches of a kind of greenish mold appearing on the walls. These continued to spread until large sections of the walls and ceiling were covered with this noxious growth. We tried various cleaning methods, but they did not help very much.

As I pondered the situation, I thought of this portion, Metsora᷄, and wondered if this was exactly the kind of "leprosy" it described. I then realized that the Torah's harsh description was not imaginary; the "leprosy" must have been quite common at the time. If we were living in biblical days, I mused, I could have called in a priest and heard what he had to say. I suspected he might have told us to tear the place down.

But since these were not biblical days, we simply had to put up with it until we were able to move out a year later.

'Aharei Mot

Attaining Atonement

LEVITICUS 16:1–18:30

> *And this shall be to you a law for all time: In the seventh*
> *month, on the tenth day of the month, you shall practice self-*
> *denial; and you shall do no manner of work. . . . For on this*
> *day atonement shall be made for you to cleanse you of all your*
> *sins; you shall be clean before the Lord. It shall be a Sabbath of*
> *complete rest for you, and you shall practice self-denial; it is a*
> *law for all time. The priest who has been anointed and ordained*
> *to serve as priest in place of his father shall make expiation. . . .*
> *He shall purge the innermost Shrine; he shall purge the*
> *Tent of Meeting and the altar; and he shall make expiation*
> *for the priests and for all the people of the congregation.*
> —Leviticus 16:29–32

P'shat: Explanation

This section of the Torah reading instructs the common people about what they must do on Yom Kippur so they "shall be clean before the Lord." The previous verses describe what the High Priest does on that day in order to purify the sanctuary and insure that all Israel will be free of iniquity. That description includes the ritual of the scapegoat and the sprinkling of blood in the Holy of Holies—rites of expiation, that is, ridding the place and the people of impurity.

The burden and the responsibility fall on the priest. Without the priest's actions, there is no atonement.

It is quite clear that these rites are performed on this particular day because it comes five days before the great pilgrimage holiday of Sukkot. It would be impossible to hold the rituals of the holiday if the sanctuary and the people were impure.

Notably, the text places greater emphasis upon the ritual purity of the sanctuary than upon that of individuals. In First Temple times only the priests—not the people—would go to the central shrine on Yom Kippur. The people stayed at home, avoided work, and fasted.

This changed drastically in Second Temple times, when the Temple rituals were greatly expanded and crowds of people came to see and participate in them.

D'rash: Exposition of the Sages

For transgressions between humans and God Yom Kippur atones. For transgressions between one person and another Yom Kippur does not atone until the other party has been appeased.
—Yoma 8:9

They asked Wisdom, "What is the punishment of the sinner?" Wisdom replied, "Misfortune pursues the sinner" (Proverbs 13:21). They asked Prophecy, "What is the punishment of the sinner?" Prophecy replied, "The person who sinned shall die" (Ezekiel 18:4). They asked Torah, "What is the punishment of the sinner?" The Torah replied, "Let him bring his guilt offering, and it will be forgiven him, as it is said, 'that it may be acceptable on his behalf, in expiation for him'" (Leviticus 1:4). They asked the Holy One, "What is the punishment of the sinner?" The Holy One replied, "Let him repent and it will be atoned, as it is said, 'Good and upright is the Lord; therefore He shows sinners the way'" (Psalm 25:6).
—Y. Makkot 31d

During the Second Temple period, the ritual emphasis on Yom Kippur changed: the sins of the people became more important than the purity of the Temple, and the masses became an integral part of the service. After the Temple was destroyed, the Sages went out of their way to develop this emphasis on human sin even more. They greatly emphasized personal confession. They also made it very clear that one could not atone, cleansing oneself from sin, simply by observing the rituals of the day. An individual had to have truly repented and made amends to any injured party. For offenses against God, repentance, prayer, and fasting would be sufficient. God could and would forgive offenses against God but not those against other people. That is the meaning of the verse "you shall be clean *before the Lord*"—you shall be clean of your sins against God but not yet of those that have affected other human beings.

All human beings go astray. That is human nature. Even the most pious will err in one thing or another. The Torah says explicitly that the priest "shall make expiation . . . for all the people of the congregation." The expiation of sin—turning sins from scarlet into white—was considered the most important function of the Temple and its priesthood.

Nevertheless, for the Sages, writing when the Temple no longer existed, it was important to emphasize that one could expiate sin and be forgiven without the Temple and the priesthood, indeed without any rituals at all. Although the Torah said that bringing a sacrifice was required, the final answer to the question "What is the punishment of the sinner?" is "Let him repent and it will be atoned." Repentance, truly being sorry, making up with whomever you have sinned against, and changing your actions will be sufficient for God's forgiveness.

D'rash: Personal Reflection

THE DEPTH OF GUILT

Was eliminating sin the most important thing about the Temple? After all, people brought sacrifices there for many other reasons, such as thanksgiving, and they rejoiced during times of festivity. Still, certainly one of the Temple's main functions was ridding the people of guilt.

Throughout the ages, people have frequently been guilt-ridden, sometimes with cause, other times for no good reason. The Torah thus speaks to the cleansing, the elimination of the burden of guilt, that Yom Kippur brings. While for us in the twenty-first century, ritual purity is hardly a major concern, our feelings of regret for things we've done wrong or not done, our feelings of guilt for what religion calls "sin," can really ruin our lives.

As with so many other human feelings and frailties, Shakespeare expressed this one very well. In *Hamlet* the guilty King Claudius find himself unable to pray because of his guilt: "Pray can I not. Though inclination be as sharp as will, my stronger guilt defeats my strong intent. . . . Try what repentance can. What can it not? Yet what can it, when one cannot repent? . . . My words fly up, my thoughts remain below. Words without thoughts never to heaven go" (iii:3).

I was quite startled once to receive a letter out of the blue from a member of a congregation I had served some twenty years earlier. We had not been particularly close, and I had never heard from him in all those years. He explained that he was writing to apologize. At one time he had been angry or annoyed with me for some reason, and because of that he had not invited me to an important event he had held in his home. He was certain that it must have hurt me to have been treated in that way, and for many years he had felt guilty about it. He regretted his action, which, he said, was really unwarranted. However, he had always been reluctant to write and ask my forgiveness, but he was finally doing so now. Would I be willing to forgive him?

The truth was that I had no idea what he was writing about. I had not been aware that he was angry, and I never knew about the event or that I had been slighted. Yet for so many years this had weighed on his conscience. I wrote back, simply assuring him that he had nothing to feel bad about and that I held nothing against him.

His letter gave me a new understanding of how pernicious guilt can be and why Yom Kippur is so therapeutic and so important. Properly observed, it can truly cleanse us and give us the chance to start afresh. We do not need the Temple for this. The prayers and rituals of Yom Kippur play this important role.

Kedoshim

The Essence of Torah

LEVITICUS 19:1–20:27

You shall not take vengeance or bear a grudge against your countrymen. Love your fellow as yourself: I am the Lord.
—Leviticus 19:18

P'shat: Explanation

This Torah portion is so full of inspiring verses that one is tempted to say that if nothing remained of the Torah but these chapters, we would still have the basic ideals and principles upon which Judaism is founded.

In addition to the verse quoted above, this portion also teaches us to love the stranger as yourself (19:34) and to use only honest weights and measures (19:35–36). It also recapitulates many of the Ten Commandments, such as do not steal, do not take false oaths, do not worship false idols, honor parents, observe the Sabbath, and revere God. Rabbi Hiyya once proclaimed about this portion that "most of the essential laws of the Torah can be derived from it" (Leviticus Rabbah 24). What more could one want?

Another amazing thing about this is that all of these directives are found in Leviticus, the book of the instructions and teachings of the priests. The priests are usually thought of as placing ritual at the center of religion; the prophets, by contrast, are seen as the teachers of morality. In his famous essay "Priest and Prophet," the great Zionist thinker Ahad Ha-Am contrasted the two: the prophet's unwavering dedication to great ideals such as justice and mercy and the priest's tendency to take many factors into account and compromise ideals. As one example, the Priest Aaron permits the building of the Golden Calf, for which he is castigated by the prophet Moses.

That criticism is not totally without justification. Priests were often part of the establishment, defending the kings and the government, while prophets spoke truth to power. The prophet Amos (eighth century BCE), for example, famously denounced the injustice of the northern kingdom of Israel and predicted the destruction of its shrine at Bethel. Amaziah, the priest of Bethel, declared Amos's teachings as traitorous and called on King Jeroboam to exile him and forbid him to prophesize. Later, in Second Temple days, the priesthood seems to have represented an aristocracy concerned more with wealth, prestige, and power than with moral and ethical teachings.

And yet in this portion we see very clearly that the basic priestly teachings embodied the very essence of morality. When priests, be they Amaziah or others later on, deviated from these concepts found in the book of Leviticus, they represented the corruption—not the fulfillment—of the true priestly ideals. The teachings of the priests themselves as found in this Torah portion, commonly known as "the holiness code," came to represent the fundamental concepts of justice and morality upon which the entire Torah is built.

D'rash: Exposition of the Sages

Said Rabbi Akiva, "Love your fellow as yourself" (Lev. 19:18)—
this is a fundamental principle of the Torah. Ben Azzai said,
"'This is the record of Adam's line—When God created man,
He made him in the likeness of God' (Genesis 5:1)—this
is an even greater fundamental principle in the Torah!"
—Sifra 89b

A pagan once came to Shammai and said, "Convert me—on
condition that you teach me the entire Torah while standing
on one foot." Shammai drove him away with the builder's

ruler that he had in his hand. He then came to Hillel and
said, "What is hateful to you, do not do to your fellow. That is
the entire Torah. The rest is commentary. Now go—learn."
—Shabbat 31a

When Rabbi Akiva, perhaps the greatest of all the Sages, had to choose one verse that represented the very essence of the Torah, the ideal on which all else rests, he chose "Love your fellow as yourself."

Ben Azzai, a younger contemporary of Akiva who disagreed with him, was not of the same stature. It is not clear that the two really had a face-to-face dispute as to which was the more important verse of Torah or if each one at some point had simply said whichever verse he felt to be the underlying principle of the Torah, and the sources contrasted the two. One thing is certain: Rabbi Akiva's verse became the dominant choice.

Akiva also believed that all human beings were made in the divine image. He stated this forcefully: "Beloved is the human being, for he was created in the image of God. Greater still was that love in that it was made known to him that he was created in the image of God, as it says, 'For in His image did God make man' [Genesis 9:6]" (Pirkei Avot 3:15). Still, Akiva insisted on the primacy of the verse that called upon us to love (and not merely honor) others.

In another source Rabbi Akiva explained his choice: "So that one should not say, 'Since I am disdained, let others be disdained as well'" (Genesis Rabbah 24:7). In other words, by choosing a verse that specifies that one must love others, Akiva makes clear that in all cases love is the requirement. It is not enough to insist that we treat others as we want to be treated, since some people disdain themselves. It is not sufficient to say that all people are created equal. Love is the basic requirement.

In making this assertion Akiva was building upon the earlier teaching of Hillel the Elder (first century BCE), who also contended (by citing an Aramaic interpretation of it) that this verse is the essence of Torah. Both Akiva's and Hillel's concepts of Judaism were built upon love.

Time and again Akiva taught that our human relationship to God had to be one of love. Of all the books of Scripture, Akiva considered Song of Songs to be the "holy of holies" for a similar reason: its description of love could be applied to both divine and human love (Yadayim 3:6).

Akiva also stressed that Deuteronomy 6:5 required us to love God with all our faculties—even unto death. When he himself was confronted with such a quandary—either acquiescing to Roman decrees or possibly losing his life—he commented that all his life he had wondered if he would be able to fulfill this command. Now that he was faced with this dilemma, he would do so with a smile on his lips! (Y. *Berachot* 9:7).

D'rash: Personal Reflection

THE RELIGION OF LOVE

I was once the rabbi of a synagogue in a city where once a year all houses of worship were asked to support the united community charity drive by holding Shabbat or Sunday services dedicated to that drive. A special bulletin in pamphlet form, printed by the United Fund, was to be disseminated in all houses of worship that weekend.

Somehow I discovered that the pamphlet for synagogues was different from the one for churches. The church pamphlet featured the quote "Love your neighbor as yourself." The synagogue pamphlet had "Justice, justice you shall pursue." When I called to ask why synagogues had received a different one I was told, "We did not think you would want to use a quote from the New Testament." When I told them that when that verse "Love your fellow . . ." appeared in Christian Scripture it was as a quote from Leviticus, they were taken aback. Here was the ancient prejudice that "love" is appropriate for Christianity but not for Judaism.

Unfortunately, Judaism is often presented as a religion of sternness, of strictness, rather than of love and mercy. This concept, promulgated by early Christianity in its anti-Jewish polemic, has stuck to

Judaism not only in religious writings but in Shakespeare and Dickens as well, becoming a primary source of antisemitism through the ages, often with disastrous consequences for Jewish life.

The Sages of Israel would have been astonished at this thought. They knew very well that love and mercy epitomize the essence of Judaism, just as the ancient Priests had taught by enshrining such ideals in their holiness code.

'Emor

Am I a Barbarian?

LEVITICUS 21:1–24:23

*And when you reap the harvest of your land, you shall
not reap all the way to the edges of your field, or gather
the gleanings of your harvest; you shall leave them for
the poor and the stranger: I am the Lord your God.*
—Leviticus 23:22

P'shat: Explanation

This portion is concerned with outlining the festivals and sacred days
of the year. The Sabbath, occurring each and every week, is the first of
them. The others are the three *pilgrimage* festivals, Pesach, Shavuot,
and Sukkot; the first day of the seventh month, later to be known as
Rosh Hashanah; and the tenth of that month, the Day of Atonement.

In the midst of this discussion, when the harvest festival of Shavuot
is described, the Torah pauses to caution us that when reaping the
harvest we must leave a part of it for those in need. The corners of
the field and the parts of the harvest that fall by the wayside are not
to be taken by the owner but left for the poor and the stranger. The
stranger is the non-Israelite who lives permanently within the land.

This is one of several laws that were to serve as a foundation for
the new society that would be established by the Israelites once they
reached their own land.

Many specific laws concerning the treatment of the stranger—the
non-Israelite dwelling among the people—are scattered throughout
the Torah. These laws are repeated over and over again both to stress
their great importance and to make certain that the people never

applied a double standard, treating fellow Jews one way and everyone else differently. Having experienced discrimination and even slavery in Egypt, Israel was never to cause others to suffer what we had endured. We were not to mistreat the stranger, we were not to wrong the stranger, we were not to cheat the stranger. Indeed, as Leviticus 19:34 stipulates, we were even commanded to love the stranger.

D'rash: Exposition of the Sages

It once happened that Shimon ben Shetah was occupied with winnowing flax. His disciples said to him, "Our Master, let us go and make things easier for you. We will go and purchase an ass for you." They went and bought an ass from an Ishmaelite and discovered a precious stone hanging around its neck. They said to him, "'The blessing of the Lord enriches . . .' (Prov. 10:22). You will not have to work anymore!" Shimon ben Shetah asked, "Why not?" They said to him, "We purchased this ass from an Ishmaelite and found a precious stone tied around its neck." He asked them, "Did the owner know of it?" "No," they replied. He said to them, "I will return it." They said, "But even those who say that it is forbidden to steal from a gentile admit that one need not return something a gentile has lost!" He said to them, "Do you think Shimon ben Shetah is a barbarian?! I purchased an ass. I did not purchase a precious stone. I would rather hear him say, 'Blessed is the Lord, the God of the Jews!' than have all the treasures of the world." They returned it to the Arab, who proclaimed, "Blessed is the Lord, the God of Shimon ben Shetah!"
—Jerusalem Talmud Bava Metzia 2:5;
Deuteronomy Rabbah Ekev 3:3

Rabbi Shimon the Pious said: It is forbidden to steal from a non-Jew but it is permissible to retain an article he has lost. . . . Rabbi Pinhas ben Yair said that where there is a danger of

causing Hillul haShem (the public desecration of the Name
of God), retaining an article lost by a non-Jew is forbidden.
—*Bava Kamma* 113b

Shimon ben Shetah, the hero of this morality tale, carried great authority. He was both a scholar and a Pharisaic leader of the Sanhedrin in Second Temple times, during the reign of Alexander Yannai (first century CE). His actions served to exemplify proper conduct in the relations between Jews and non-Jews.

That the Sages of Israel were serious about the injunction to treat the stranger well and honestly can be seen in the story told about this great Sage. The tale emphasizes the imperative of honesty; Shimon goes beyond what the strict letter of the law requires to uphold it.

Such an action came to be called *middat ha-hasidut*—the quality of loving-kindness—in which one acts not only legally but also in a civilized and highly ethical manner, even if the cost is great loss.

Shimon's disciples rejoice that this precious jewel will enable their master to live comfortably throughout his life. His concerns, however, are the ethical—not the legal—propriety of taking something the owner had not intended to forsake and the possible consequences of feeling justified in doing so just because the owner happens to be a Gentile and not a Jew.

Many of the Sages' teachings stress the importance of acting ethically in our relations with non-Jews. In certain instances, the Rabbis note, it is even more serious to cheat a non-Jew than a Jew, because such cheating, in addition to being a transgression itself, also induces *hillul ha-Shem* (public desecration of the name of God), thus bringing shame to both God and Judaism.

That is the case in this story, which advocates that we act to uphold the very opposite: the major Rabbinic value of *kiddush ha-Shem*, the sanctification of the name of God. Although Judaism teaches that the ultimate act of *kiddush ha-Shem* is martyrdom, the willingness to sacrifice one's very life rather than defame God, *kiddush ha-Shem* also applies to any act that bestows glory and honor onto God and the Torah. In this case, it caused the Ishmaelite to proclaim God's greatness.

Thus, Rabbi Pinhas ben Yair teaches that if *hillul ha-Shem* is involved, even keeping a lost item is not permitted. All the riches of the world are not worth bringing shame upon God and God's teachings.

D'rash: Personal Reflection

CARING FOR THE STRANGER

One of the things that impresses me deeply about this story is the way in which Shimon ben Shetah rebukes his disciples for even suggesting that Shimon should cheat the Ishmaelite. He says rather sharply, "Do you think Shimon ben Shetah is a barbarian?" Barbarian is a very strong epithet. For Shimon, taking advantage of any person, be it within or outside the law, makes one uncivilized.

To my mind, Shimon is setting a very high standard for appropriate Jewish conduct. One is forbidden to play games and find ways of getting around the laws and the commandments. Nor should one ask "what is permitted?" but rather "what is right and honorable?" Anything else is barbaric. This and only this is appropriate conduct for a Jew.

The year 2010 saw the publication in Israel of the book *Torat HaMelech* (The king's Torah), which claimed that according to Jewish law, non-Jews living in Israel could be discriminated against in many different ways—and it was even permissible to harm them physically. Furthermore, it justified select actions taken against non-Jews and rulings by certain official rabbis who countenanced such discrimination. Although this work was the product of a small, radical sect and certainly did not represent the teachings of most Orthodox rabbis, it influenced those seeking legitimacy for their racist opinions and actions.

I decided then that it was necessary to write a rabbinical responsum showing that this was not the true teaching of Jewish law. After centuries of us Jews being the objects of discrimination by non-Jews when we lived in other lands, for us to now treat others in our land as we had been mistreated seemed to be the ultimate irony.

In a sense, the responsum I wrote answered Shimon ben Shetah's rhetorical question, "Do you think Shimon ben Shetah is a barbarian?" In essence, it said that we are not barbarians when we follow the Torah's many commands to care for the stranger in our land.

The Rabbinical Assembly's Committee on Jewish Law and Standards unanimously accepted the responsum, and it was subsequently disseminated in both English and Hebrew. I am pleased to see that as a consequence, the responsum has helped to promote changes in the way in which this subject is taught in schools. I hope it will continue to aid in reducing, if not eliminating, the all-too-frequent misrepresentations of Judaism's true teachings regarding the treatment of non-Jews.

Be-har

Do No Wrong

LEVITICUS 25:1–26:2

In this year of jubilee, each of you shall return to his holding.
When you sell property to your neighbor, or buy any from your
neighbor, you shall not wrong your brother. In buying from
your neighbor, you shall deduct only for the number of years
since the jubilee; and in selling to you, he shall charge you only
for the remaining crop years: the more such years, the higher
the price you pay; the fewer such years, the lower the price; for
what he is selling you is a number of harvests. Do not wrong
one another, but fear your God; for I the Lord am your God.
—Leviticus 25:13–17

P'shat: Explanation

The law of the jubilee, the fiftieth year following a succession of seven
periods of seven sabbatical years, is a unique institution that was
intended to promote social justice among the people of Israel. Debts
were canceled, slaves were freed, and land was returned to its owners.
When the Israelite tribes entered the land, it was divided among the
tribes, and then equal portions were given to each family. If someone
had to sell his land, the sale was valid only until the next jubilee year,
so that if this was the twentieth year of the jubilee period, the land
was being "sold"—really leased—for only thirty years.

The Torah is very concerned that there be no deception about this
and that people do not try to take advantage of someone else's problematic situation by demanding an unfair price for the land. Therefore, it commands that we "not wrong one another" in this matter.

D'rash: Exposition of the Sages

*"Do not wrong one another. . . ." This refers to verbal wrong.
Perhaps it means financial wrong? ". . . you shall not wrong
your brother . . ." refers to financial wrong, therefore how
shall I interpret "Do not wrong one another"? It refers
to verbal wrong. How is that? For example, if one was a
repentant sinner, one should not say to him, "Remember
your former misdeeds!" If one was a descendant of converts,
one should not say to him, "Remember your ancestors'
actions!" . . . If someone was looking to buy produce, do not
say to him, "You should go to Mister X" when he [Mister
X] never sold such produce. Rabbi Judah says: Similarly
one should not look at something and ask, "How much does
this cost?" when one has no intention of buying it. . . . All
of this is a matter of conscience, and whenever there is a
matter of conscience [the Torah] says, "fear your God."*
—Sifra Be-har 4:1

*"You shall not wrong your brother." "Death and life are
in the power of the tongue . . ." (Proverbs 18:21). Rabban
Gamliel said to his slave Tabi, "Go and buy me something
good from the market." He went and brought back tongue.
He said to him, "Go and buy me something bad from the
market." He went and brought back tongue. He said to him,
"What is this? When I told you to go and buy me something
good, you brought back tongue and when I told you to go
and buy me something bad, you brought back tongue!" He
replied, "Good comes from it and bad comes from it. When
it is good, there is nothing better and when it is bad, there
is nothing worse!" . . . That is why Moses warned Israel,
"When you sell property to your neighbor, or buy any
from your neighbor, you shall not wrong your brother."*
—Leviticus Rabbah 33:1

The warning "do not wrong" is unusual in that it appears twice in this biblical passage. Therefore, the Sages attempted to find a reason for the ostensible duplication. *Sifra*, the early tannaitic midrash to the book of Leviticus, interprets each verse containing "do not wrong" as referring to a different way of causing harm to others. The first time it appears it connotes causing someone financial harm, which could easily happen during the property transfer before a jubilee year, since land values would change over each year of the jubilee period. The Sages conclude that the second iteration of "do no wrong" must then refer to hurting another person through verbal abuse. All of the cited examples of verbal abuse harm the victim by somehow embarrassing that person or, in the case of a merchant, stealing his time and deceiving him. No financial loss accrues in any of this, but the practice is nevertheless forbidden.

This midrash demonstrates great sensitivity to people's feelings. When the text was written, all converts had formerly been pagans, and in Jewish eyes paganism was shameful. It is noteworthy that even beyond reminding people of their previous misdeeds, the Sages deemed that reminding a convert or the convert's children that they once were adherents of what was considered to be a false religion would cause them harm.

Since verbal abuse, unlike financial abuse, was not a matter for the courts (and was ultimately a question of intent, which cannot easily be determined), these matters were left to one's conscience. For this reason, in such instances the Torah always invokes fear (or reverence) of God as the only way of preventing abuse. Our awareness that a powerful God understands what we are saying and why is meant to make us think twice before opening our mouths.

A later midrash, Leviticus Rabbah, assumes that the warning against wronging our fellow regarding the selling of property is designed to emphasize the severity of the sin of manipulating others through verbal trickery. From this springboard comes a larger discussion about the power and damages inherent in speech. As Proverbs 18:21 says, "Death and life are in the power of the tongue." The story of purchasing tongue is a popular way of illustrating this. Gamliel's slave Tabi is mentioned in many places as being an unusually learned and ethical person from whom even an important Sage such as Gamliel (second century CE) could learn. (Tabi is also said to have observed many of the commandments, including wearing tefillin, and when he died Rabban Gamliel observed mourning customs in his honor.)

The jubilee year was not observed during the Second Temple period and thereafter. The reason is not entirely clear, but it seems that conditions were no longer the same. Tribes and tribal land were no longer in existence. Nevertheless, the Sages continued to interpret the jubilee texts in the Torah as a way of teaching these important ethical principles.

D'rash: Personal Reflection

SENSITIVITY TO OTHERS

One of the most blatant instances of verbal wrongdoing I have ever witnessed occurred at a festive gathering held in an important cultural institution that was investing a new director. The former director, who had served there with distinction for the better part of a lifetime, had recently retired and was present at the event. The speaker, who was head of the entire institution that oversaw this particular program (among others), spoke enthusiastically about the new director and the plans to further the activities of this institution.

That was fine, but the speaker then did two things that spoiled the event. First, he neglected to say anything at all about the previous director. Second, he spoke in a negative fashion about how the institution had been run up to now and contrasted this to how the new person was going to conduct it.

I was seated near the retiring director and saw how his face turned pale. Indeed, the power of life and death was in the tongue that was speaking. Insensitivity had produced an act of verbal wrongdoing that the Sages warned against.

The age of social networking has also drastically increased the dangers of perpetrating verbal abuse. Words written on various social networks or photos distributed on them have induced terrible distress, including many instances of suicide. The phenomenon of school-children who become victims of orchestrated defamation campaigns to the point where they can no longer continue in their school class has become an epidemic that no one seems to know how to control. When postings can be published anonymously, no one can be held accountable and made to stop.

I belong to several professional networks on which colleagues share their perspectives concerning issues of the day. Sometimes the conversations get heated. Every once in a while, one member will speak in a disrespectful manner about another colleague. This is usually followed by an apology, but by then it is too late. The harm has been done—not only to the person maligned but to the reputation of the person who sent out the message.

That is exactly what is meant by the Rabbinic statement: "All of this is a matter of conscience, and whenever there is a matter of conscience [the Torah] says, 'fear your God.'" To me it seems more important than ever that we inculcate moral values and sensitivity to others in those we can influence. I myself try very hard to think twice before sending out messages over the web. Once you press that button it is too late.

Be-ḥukkotai

The Hope

LEVITICUS 26:3–27:34

When I, in turn, have been hostile to them and have removed them into the land of their enemies, then at last shall their obdurate heart humble itself, and they shall atone for their iniquities. Then will I remember My covenant with Jacob; I will also remember My covenant with Isaac, and also My covenant with Abraham; and I will remember the land. . . . Yet even then, when they are in the land of their enemies, I will not reject them or spurn them so as to destroy them, annulling My covenant with them: for I the Lord am their God. I will remember in their favor the covenant with the ancients, whom I freed from the land of Egypt in the sight of the nations to be their God: I the Lord.
—Leviticus 26:41–42,44–45

P'shat: Explanation

The concluding portion of the book of Leviticus, Be-ḥukkotai, is one of two places in the Torah that contain both curses and blessings. (The other is Ki Tavo' in Deuteronomy.) When the curses—descriptions of punishments—are read as part of the Torah reading, they are usually recited very quietly, as if to say, We never want to hear this, much less experience it.

These blessings and curses are intended to impress upon the Israelites the serious consequences of disregarding the covenant they have just made to be God's treasured people and observe God's laws. God instructs Moses to so warn the people while they are still at Sinai, before they begin their journey to the Promised Land. Moses does so again forty years later. The blessings will come if the Israelites observe the commandments. The curses will follow their disobedience. It is up to them to choose.

For this reason Jewish tradition later taught that the destruction of Jerusalem, twice—first in 586 BCE by the Babylonians and then in 70 CE by the Romans—was punishment for Israel's sin.

What is unusual and important about this passage is that even though the Israelites are warned of terrible destruction and exile, they are simultaneously told that at a future time they will atone for their misdeeds, at which point God will forgive them and bring them back to their own land. In other words, the people will never be totally abandoned. The covenant made with their ancestors, Abraham, Isaac, and Jacob, will always remain in force.

Thus, even God's most dire warnings contain a ray of hope. The return to the land, the end of suffering, will come.

This very promise enabled the Jewish people to endure through eons of exile. Even though adherents of other religions disparaged God as having rejected the Israelites, the people as a whole maintained their faith in God.

Prophets such as Jeremiah also offered comfort, assuring the people that in time they would return to their land, even as they warned that destruction was imminent. As Jeremiah put it, "See, I will gather them from all the lands to which I have banished them in My anger and wrath and in great rage; and I will bring them back to this place and let them dwell secure. They shall be My people and I will be their God" (Jeremiah 32:37–38).

D'rash: Exposition of the Sages

Once Rabban Gamliel, Rabbi Joshua, Rabbi Eleazar ben Azariah, and Rabbi Akiva were going up to Jerusalem. When they reached Mount Scopus they tore their garments [as a sign of mourning]. When they descended to the Temple Mount they

*saw a fox running out of the Holy of Holies and they began to
weep while Rabbi Akiva laughed. They said to him, "Akiva,
you always astonish us — we weep and you laugh!" He replied,
"Why are you weeping?" They said to him, "Should we not
weep when a fox emerges from the place no common person
was allowed to enter? We have seen the fulfillment of the verse,
'Because of Mount Zion, which lies desolate; jackals prowl over
it'" (Lamentations 5:18). He said to them, "That is exactly why
I laughed! One prophet said, 'Zion shall be plowed as a field,
and Jerusalem shall become heaps of ruins, and the Temple
Mount a shrine in the woods' (Jeremiah 26:18). But there is
another prophecy, that of Zachariah, 'There shall yet be old
men and women in the squares of Jerusalem, each with staff
in hand, because of their great age. And the squares of the city
shall be crowded with boys and girls playing in the squares'
(Zachariah 8:4–5). Since the words of the first prophet have
now been fulfilled, so will the words of Zachariah be fulfilled.
I therefore rejoiced seeing the fulfillment of the first prophecy
because this means that the words of Zachariah will also be
fulfilled!" They said to him, "Akiva, you have comforted us."*
— Sifre Deuteronomy 43

This incident occurred some forty or fifty years after the destruction
of the Temple and Jerusalem. At that time, ruins of the Temple still
stood on the Temple Mount. The western wall of the Temple that had
been part of the Holy of Holies still stood. (This is not to be confused
with what today is called the Western Wall, which is only a part of
the retaining wall that Herod had constructed around the Temple
Mount.) The Romans had left these ruins deliberately to remind
everyone of the magnificence of what they had been able to destroy
and thus demonstrate the extent of their victory.

This story illustrates the enduring power of the promise of return.
The greatest Sages of the age visit these ruins and mourn the destruction of Jerusalem. Seeing a wild animal roaming about the most

sacred place of all—which, when the Temple existed, only the High Priest could visit, and only then on Yom Kippur—the Sages weep in despair. Akiva, however, has never given up hope of seeing the restoration of Jerusalem and its Temple. After all, not too long after the First Temple was destroyed and the people were sent into Babylonian exile, Cyrus let them return and rebuild the city and the Temple. When these Sages make their visit to the ruins, a similar period of time has elapsed since the second destruction of Jerusalem. Perhaps the rebuilding will happen yet again.

Akiva, always the optimist and the comforter, therefore views what the other Sages see not as a reason for despair but as a sign of the fulfillment of God's promise. Since one ancient prophecy of destruction has come to pass, he declares that another prophecy, one of restoration and rebuilding, is about to be fulfilled. Once again the streets of Jerusalem will be filled with contented people, old and young.

Unfortunately, this was not to be in Akiva's time, but the return did happen: in the twentieth century, nearly two thousand years later.

D'rash: Personal Reflection

FULFILLING THE DREAM

When I was growing up in 1940s America, the question of the Jews' return to the Land of Israel and the creation of a Jewish state in what was then Mandatory Palestine was a very live issue. Would it happen? One could not be certain, but one could hope.

One of my first so-called journalistic endeavors as a young teenager was to write letters to the local newspaper refuting the letters written by an anonymous person who argued that the Jewish people had no rights whatsoever to the land of Palestine. Our lively interchange on the subject continued for some period of time, until he stopped writing letters. I do not know if I won the argument, but at least the local readers were not left with only his side.

I have a very vivid memory of how the Jewish community of Syracuse, New York, where I was born, celebrated the State of Israel's creation in 1948. The community came together in the largest synagogue in town, the Conservative Temple Adath Yeshurun, which was filled to overflowing. All the rabbis of the city participated in leading prayers, sharing biblical readings, and singing Hebrew songs. The most emotional speech was given by a revered Orthodox rabbi, the aged scholar Rabbi Yallow. I do not remember what he said, only that it was accompanied by tears — both his and those of the entire group assembled, myself included. The evening concluded with the sounding of the shofar and the singing of "Hatikvah," the anthem of hope.

I am not certain if those younger than myself who grew up after Israel came into being and take it for granted can appreciate what it meant to those of us who experienced that great event. Coming as it did immediately after the Shoah, it had all the makings of a miracle. No one could take for granted that it would occur. On the contrary, although our tradition always assured us that there would be a return, there was no assurance of when that would happen, and this seemed the most unlikely time of all. Yet it did happen.

I have always wished that it was possible to tell Rabbi Akiva that although his timing was off, he and his words of comfort and hope were ultimately vindicated.

IV

Numbers (Be-midbar)

Be-midbar

Surviving the Wilderness

NUMBERS 1:1–4:20

> *On the first day of the second month, in the second year*
> *following the exodus from the land of Egypt, the Lord*
> *spoke to Moses in the wilderness of Sinai, in the Tent*
> *of Meeting, saying: Take a census of the whole Israelite*
> *community by the clans of its ancestral houses, listing*
> *the names, every male, head by head. You and Aaron*
> *shall record them by their groups, from the age of twenty*
> *up, all those in Israel who are able to bear arms.*
> —Numbers 1:1–3

P'shat: Explanation

The Israelites have not yet left their camp at Sinai to undertake the journey to the land of Canaan, but this portion clearly indicates that they are about to do so. Everything in it is aimed at preparing them for the march and for what they will encounter in the wilderness. It begins with a census of those who can enter into battle, to be ready for the enemies they may meet on the way, as well as those they will have to fight when conquering Canaan.

The census gives this entire book its name. "Numbers" is derived from the ancient Hebrew title *Sefer ha-P'kudim*, "The Census Scroll." The current Hebrew name, Be-midbar, "In the wilderness," is taken from the first important word in the book's opening verse; the same is true for the names of all the other books of the Torah, as well as the individual portions.

Following the census comes the ordering of the tribes around the central sanctuary, each with its own standard. Then there is an accounting of the tasks of the tribe of Levi: first the family of Aaron, the Priests, and then counting the rest of the Levites, who are charged with caring for the sanctuary. The Levites are to substitute for the first-born, who until then had been dedicated to the service of the Lord.

If the journey is to be successful in its goal of getting the Israelites to Canaan safely and quickly, everything must be in order. If they are to endure in the wilderness, they cannot be a rabble but a properly structured society that can travel, breaking camp easily and setting it up again, and that is prepared to defend itself against its enemies along the way. With hindsight we know what will happen to the Israelites on their travels, and it is not a happy story, but since they could not predict this, they probably felt eager and ready—properly organized—to go forward.

D'rash: Exposition of the Sages

Rabbi Judah began [his exposition]: "O generation, behold the word of the Lord! Have I been like a wilderness to Israel, or a land of deep gloom?" (Jeremiah 2:31). . . . He [Jeremiah] took that jar of manna and showed it to [the people of Jeremiah's generation] and said, "Behold what delicacies your ancestors had in the wilderness when they followed God's will. 'Have I been like a wilderness to Israel?' [This means] has the Holy One been like a wilderness to you? When a human monarch wishes to send his legions out to battle, he supplies all their needs while still in their base, but when they go forth he only gives them enough to keep them from starvation because he does not have the supplies in the wilderness that he has at the base. The Holy One, however, did not treat your ancestors like that. Rather, he supplied all their needs for forty years in the wilderness, as it says, '. . . and in the wilderness, where you saw how the Lord your God carried you, as a man carries his

son . . .' (Deuteronomy 1:31). Did they lack anything? 'Have I
been like a wilderness to Israel . . . ?' [Jeremiah] said to them,
'Did He make them march in the dark at night or smite them
with heat during the day as happens with caravans traversing
the wilderness? Rather a pillar of fire illuminated them at
night and consumed any thorns or serpents or scorpions,
and a pillar of cloud guarded them from the sun and the
extreme heat during the day!' Then why do My people say,
'We have broken loose, we will not come to you any more?'
(Jeremiah 2:2). The wilderness testifies against you, for it
was there that the Holy One performed miracles and helped
you under Moses." What verse teaches this? As we read here,
". . . the Lord spoke to Moses in the wilderness of Sinai."
—Midrash ha-Gadol Be-Midbar 1:1

This midrash is found in a medieval Yemenite collection entitled
Midrash ha-Gadol, which incorporates sections from ancient Rabbinic teachings. In the format, known as a *petichah* (opening), a homily serves as an introductory statement leading up to the verse that
begins a section.

The *petichah* builds the text around the word *be-midbar* (in the
wilderness), found in that verse, and connects it to another verse
in the book of Jeremiah in which the same word appears. It begins
with the question, Why does the Lord ask there, "Have I been like a
wilderness to Israel?" It interprets this question as being God's way
of saying that when the Israelites were in the wilderness for forty
years, God did not allow them to suffer the usual deprivations one
encounters in the wilderness—shortage of food and supplies, darkness, dangers, unbearable heat. On the contrary: in the wilderness
God supplied all their needs, as the manna testifies, and took extraordinary care of the people. So too has God cared for them ever since.
Therefore, contends Jeremiah, the people have no right to abandon
God and rebel against the Lord. This homily thus explains why it was
important to mention there that all this took place in the wilder-

ness: because it was the place in which they did *not* suffer because of God's concern and care.

D'rash: Personal Reflection

IN THE WILDERNESS OF ISRAEL

After the peace treaty with Israel was signed, my wife and I drove through the area on the other side of the Jordan where the Israelites had marched thousands of years ago. The landscape was more difficult and dangerous than I had ever imagined. Even in a vehicle we experienced steep ups and downs. I thought how hard it must have been for my ancestors to walk through it. The wilderness was not a pleasant stroll. It must have been exhausting.

The wilderness experience plays a major part in biblical literature. Sometimes it was seen as a glorious honeymoon: "I accounted to your favor the devotion of your youth, your love as a bride—how you followed Me in the wilderness, in a land not sown" (Jeremiah 2:2). At other times it was described as a time of disastrous conflict: "Forty years was I provoked by that generation; I thought, 'They are a senseless people; they would not know My ways.' Concerning them I swore in anger, 'They shall never come to My resting-place!'" (Psalm 95:10–11). Which was it? Perhaps both.

I suppose that the modern equivalent of the wilderness would be the experience of preparing for and making *aliyah*, journeying to the Land of Israel. For some, especially now, it is a honeymoon, while for others, it has been a difficult trial—or a combination of both.

The early pioneers certainly did not have an easy time of it. My contemporaries who survived the Shoah and struggled thereafter to get to Palestine, defying the British blockade, surmounted terrible obstacles on their journey. Soviet Jews whom I met in the early seventies had been waiting for years with packed bags to get out. They had lost their positions and still persisted in trying to leave. Some languished in prison or in Siberian exile because of it. That was a wilderness I cannot even begin to fathom. Compared to them, my own experience was much closer to the "honeymoon" than to the treacherous journey—hardly a wilderness at all.

After many years of contemplating the possibility of *aliyah*, in 1971 my wife and I decided to take the plunge. We prepared for it as carefully as we could. That included finding a way to earn a living in our new country, which would not be easy, since in Israel the pulpit rabbinate was hardly a bankable profession. Nevertheless, after an exploratory visit I managed to put together a few positions so we would not starve. We also needed a place to live. Here the Jewish Agency helped us to find an apartment being constructed in a new area of Jerusalem where places had been allotted at reasonable prices for new *olim* (immigrants to Israel). We bought an apartment, sight unseen, on paper. It turned out to be on the fourth floor with no elevator, and the entire living space was probably no bigger than the basement recreation room we'd had in our expansive house in suburban Chicago. Still, it had a lovely terrace and a view . . . and it was to be ready two months after our arrival in Israel. What would we do in the interim? Well, we would have to go into the absorption center at Mevaseret Tzion outside of Jerusalem.

After selling or giving away our excess furniture, many of our books, and our two cars, we departed the United States and arrived at the absorption center in August 1973. With the exception of our suitcases, all of our possessions were in a container coming to Haifa by boat and would stay there until we moved into our apartment. The accommodations were hardly the Ritz, but they would do for a short period. We made friends with other *olim* from America, England, France, and Eastern Europe, many of whom would become as close as family or closer.

Of course, the Yom Kippur War changed everything. When it broke out we were shocked and dazed. At first we worried that Israel might not survive, but then it became only a question of enduring a difficult situation. Because of the war, our apartment was not completed as scheduled, so we remained in the center for fourteen months without possessions. Moreover, our now longer-term accommodations were damp, moldy, and improperly heated. Fortunately, our Israeli relatives and friends helped out with the warm clothes we absolutely needed for the winter. All in all, though, for us the war was not nearly as bad as it was for Israelis whose husbands, fathers, and sons were sent into battle, often with disastrous consequences.

Eventually, we moved into our apartment, received our possessions, and settled into life in our new home in the Jewish state. From here on, our experience was much more like what Jeremiah described when he told his generation that God had taken all the difficulties out of the wilderness journey. The wilderness was not a time of suffering at all.

Naso'

Great Is Peace

NUMBERS 4:21–7:89

Speak to Aaron and his sons: Thus shall you
bless the people of Israel. Say to them:
The Lord bless you and protect you!
The Lord make His face to shine upon you
and be gracious to you!
The Lord lift up His countenance to you and
grant you peace!
Thus they shall link My name with the people
of Israel, and I will bless them.
—Numbers 6:23–27

P'shat: Explanation

The Priestly Blessing, as these verses are called, is the most ancient liturgical formulation in Judaism. Since its inception thousands of years ago, the *Kohanim*—the religious leaders of Israel—have recited it whenever the people gathered for worship. Psalm 24 (which the pilgrims recited as they prepared to ascend the Temple Mount) recounts that only those who are worthy will be able to "ascend the mountain of the Lord" where the Temple stood and that from there they will "carry away a blessing from the Lord," meaning the Priestly Blessing recited at worship services at the Temple.

In the Hebrew original, the blessing is carefully constructed in three levels. The first has three words, the second has five, and the third has seven, the number that stands for holiness in Israelite thought. The text carefully makes it clear that although the Priests recite the blessing, the blessing does not come from them but from God alone: "And *I* will bless them." Only God has the power to confer blessings. The Priests are solely the megaphone through which God's blessing is conveyed.

D'rash: Exposition of the Sages

"Thus shall you bless the people (literally 'the sons') of Israel."
This would indicate that only the male Israelites (receive the blessing)! What about converts, women and emancipated slaves? The verse says: "Say to them"—meaning all of them. "To them" also teaches that this is done face to face, not with their backs to them. "To them" also means "to the Kohanim"—the words are also said to them, prompting them (so that they will say each word exactly correctly).
—Numbers Rabbah 11:4

Great is peace, for all blessings conclude with shalom—peace. Rabbi Eliezer the son of Rabbi Eliezer Ha-Kappar says: Great is peace but controversy is despised. Great is peace for peace is needed even at a time of war. Great is peace for even the dead require peace. Great is peace for it is granted to those who return in penitence. Great is peace for it is bestowed upon the righteous. Great is peace for it is not bestowed upon the wicked. Great is peace for it is bestowed upon those who love the Torah. Great is peace for it is bestowed upon those who study Torah. Great is peace for it is bestowed upon the lowly. Great is peace for the name of the Holy One is designated "Peace." Great is peace for it is as important as the entire work of creation. Great is peace for even those who dwell on high need peace.
—Sifre Numbers 42

The Sages determined exactly how this blessing was to be recited by carefully interpreting the introductory verse, "Thus shall you bless the people (literally 'the sons') of Israel."

In accordance with these instructions, when the *Amidah*, the central prayer of each service, is repeated aloud, the *Kohanim* stand at the front of the synagogue and recite a blessing thanking God for commanding them to "bless His people with love." As they then turn to face the congregation, they cover their faces with the tallit, extend their arms, and arrange their fingers to form the letter *shin*, which stands for *Shadai*, one of the names of God. The service leader recites each word quietly, and the *Kohanim* repeat it, chanting a beautiful melody. The congregation faces them and responds to each of the three stanzas with "Amen." In Israel and in many Sefardi synagogues, this ritual is performed daily, at morning services. Elsewhere, the custom is to do it only on holidays. At other times, the blessing is recited by the service leader.

The Sages noted that the climax of the blessing, its very last word, is *shalom*, "peace." They found this to be very significant. They learned from the blessing how important peace truly is and that peace can prevail on many different levels, starting with the individual and extending even to the entire universe. The existence of so many different elements in the heavens is in itself a sign of peace, taught Rabbi Eliezer, the son of the late second-century Sage Rabbi Eliezer Ha-Kappar.

The power of this Rabbinic teaching is to be found in its multiple repetitions of the phrase "great is peace." Indeed, it is true that "all blessings conclude with *shalom*—peace," since the main prayers of Jewish liturgy all end with a prayer for peace. The Priestly Blessing set the pattern, and later prayers followed it. The main prayer of each service, the *Amidah*, concludes with a blessing that repeats the word "peace" four times. It is simply an expansion of the Priestly Blessing: "Grant peace, grace, love, and mercy to us and all Israel Your people. Bless us all with the light of Your countenance, for in that light You have given us the guidance of life and the love of kindness, righteousness, blessing, mercy, life, and peace. May it be good in Your sight to bless Your people Israel at all times with Your peace. Blessed are You, O Lord, who blessed His people Israel with peace.

So, too, the *Kaddish*, a prayer sanctifying God that is repeated over and over in each service, concludes with "May the One who brings peace on high bring peace for us and all Israel."

"The ways of peace" is also a central concept of Rabbinic Judaism. It is based on the understanding that the purpose of the Torah is to instruct us in peaceful behavior. As Proverbs 3:17 explains about the Torah, "Its ways are ways of pleasantness and all its paths are peace." The Sages often invoked this precept when addressing the question of how a Jew should relate to non-Jews. It mattered not what the law required. More important was the general principle that there must be peace in society, along with the recognition that peace only comes when we treat others decently and fairly. It was therefore ruled, for example, that Jews should support the non-Jewish poor along with the poor of Israel, visit the non-Jewish sick along with the sick of Israel, and bury the non-Jewish dead as well as the dead of Israel because of the ways of peace (*Gittin* 61a).

D'rash: Personal Reflection

ECHOES OF THE PRIESTLY BLESSING

My maternal grandfather was a *Kohen*, and one of my most vivid and moving childhood memories is of hearing his melodious voice chant the Priestly Blessing on Yom Kippur. I would watch in awe as he stood in front of the congregation together with other *Kohanim*, his face covered by his tallit, his arms extended as if reaching out to me. His voice was stronger than the others, and I could almost feel the vibrations of sound entering my body. To this day, whenever I hear the priestly blessing, my grandfather's rendition still echoes in my mind.

That may be one of the reasons I have always advocated having the *Kohanim* recite the blessing in synagogues. At one time this ancient practice fell out of favor. When the question came up in Israeli Masorti congregations as to whether the practice was still valid in our day, I wrote the responsum that declared it valid for modern times as well. As I explained, this practice connects us with thousands of years of Jewish worship and emphasizes that the blessing itself comes directly from the Divine Presence.

One year when Naso' was being chanted, my friend and fellow worshipper, the noted archaeologist Prof. Gavriel Barkai, came over to me and asked me several questions about the Priestly Blessing. He then revealed to me that in one of his digs in Jerusalem he had discovered a small silver amulet dating from the First Temple period (i.e., no later than 586 BCE) inscribed with the text of the Priestly Blessing. It was slightly abbreviated but almost exactly as we have it in the Torah. To date, this is the oldest text of the Torah ever to be found. This treasured blessing was probably worn around the neck and buried with the wearer. Today it is on display in the Israel Museum in Jerusalem.

Every year when I hear this blessing recounted in this Torah portion I think of that ancient amulet discovered by my friend in Jerusalem thousands of years after it was created. It has survived all this time as a direct connection between this generation and our ancestors who also lived in Jerusalem as we do today. The blessing of the Priests somehow comes to life when you realize that it was considered so important by our ancient ancestors that they would have it cast in silver, wear it around their necks daily, and want to be buried with it on their body. These are not mere words written in a sacred text but the deeply felt hopes and prayers for the greatest blessing that God can convey: peace.

Be-haʿalotekha

The Evil Tongue

NUMBERS 8:1–12:16

When they were in Hazeroth, Miriam and Aaron spoke against
Moses because of the Cushite woman he had married: "He
married a Cushite woman!" They said, "Has the Lord spoken
only through Moses? Has he not spoken through us as well?"
The Lord heard it. . . . The Lord came down in a pillar of cloud,
stopped at the entrance of the Tent, and called out, "Aaron and
Miriam!" The two of them came forward and He said ". . . My
servant Moses is trusted throughout My household. With him
I speak mouth to mouth, plainly and not in riddles, and he
beholds the likeness of the Lord. How then did you not shrink
from speaking against My servant Moses!" Still incensed with
them, the Lord departed. . . . As the cloud withdrew from the
Tent, there was Miriam stricken with snow-white scales.
—Numbers 12:1–2,5,7–10

P'shat: Explanation

This Torah portion finds Moses embroiled in conflict. The people have been constantly complaining; Moses now says he cannot bear their burden alone. And soon after this comes the story of bickering among the troika: Moses, Aaron, and Miriam. Up until now they have worked together harmoniously; this is the first indication of jealousy among them.

Nothing that has happened beforehand prepares us for this story of Miriam and Aaron speaking against Moses. They make two statements that appear unrelated. First, they grouse about the ethnic origins of his wife; then, they protest that Moses acts as if he alone is the recipient of God's word. As for the first assertion, are they referring to Tziporah, or did Moses take a second wife? It seems a little late to be gossiping about Tziporah, since the two were married long before Moses came back to Egypt. Furthermore, she was not previously identified as a Cushite. Yet we have heard nothing of a second wife. If there was one, where did she come from? It has been suggested that since Tziporah only joined them at Sinai and not in Egypt, she was still a relative newcomer. Or perhaps Cushite is another name for Midianite.

It is also puzzling that while both Aaron and Miriam are implicated in their protest of Moses, only Miriam receives a physical punishment. Perhaps the Torah's use of the Hebrew feminine singular verb for "speaking" is intended to indicate that it was Miriam who actually spoke out, while Aaron simply followed her lead. Regardless, it is important to note that when God rebukes them, God speaks only about their claim to be on the same level of prophecy as Moses; God says nothing about his wife. In the Torah, then, God's concern is mainly with the challenge to Moses's standing as the supreme prophet and not with talebearing. The Sages, however, take a very different view.

D'rash: Exposition of the Sages

Rabbi Shimon says, "Plagues come upon those who speak
disparagingly, for thus we find that Aaron and Miriam
spoke disparagingly concerning Moses and were punished
for it, as it says, 'Miriam and Aaron spoke against Moses.'"
Why is Miriam mentioned before Aaron? Tziporah went and
told Miriam. Miriam went and told Aaron and both of them
spoke against that righteous man and were punished for it, as
it says, "Still incensed with them, the Lord departed." Miriam,
however, who was the tale bearer, was punished more severely.
—Avot de-Rabbi Natan A 9

*If Miriam, who spoke in such a way that only God heard it,
was punished thus, how much more so will this happen to
one who speaks disparagingly about another in public!*
—Sifre Deuteronomy 1

The Sages remark about this incident in several places. Their general consensus is that the wife referred to is indeed Tziporah. But they do not believe that Miriam is speaking negatively about her; quite the contrary, they sympathize with Tziporah. The complaint is totally about Moses. According to Rabbinic legend, when Moses returns from his forty days on Mount Sinai, he feels he has achieved such a high degree of holiness that he is required to avoid marital relations with his wife. Tziporah informs Miriam of this. Miriam then tells Aaron, and the two agree that while they too have spoken to God, they have not then turned themselves into celibates as a result. In this way, the Sages were able to establish a connection between two seemingly different matters. Miriam and Aaron mention Moses's wife because Moses is justifying his neglect of her by claiming superior holiness after receiving revelations from God, but hasn't God also revealed Himself to them?

Whereas the Torah specifies that God is angry because Miriam and Aaron challenge Moses's superiority as a prophet, the Sages dwelt on the general sin of speaking negatively about someone rather than on the content of the comment. When preaching about and interpreting the Torah, the Sages were concerned about finding meanings and messages that would inspire the constituents of their day. For them, the important lesson to be learned here was to never speak evil about anyone. They connected this with the fact that Miriam was punished by turning leprous. As they pointed out, the Hebrew for "leper" is *metzorah*, which easily becomes the phrase *motzi shem ra*, "speaking evil." Therefore, Miriam's leprosy was a punishment for speaking evil, almost as if the physical corruption was an outward manifestation of the inner moral corruption of speaking evil, a kind of "picture of Dorian Gray."

This story of Miriam became the main source of the prohibition against speaking evil of anyone. The Sages called this practice *lashon ha-ra*, "the evil tongue." The term itself derives from the verse "Guard your tongue from evil, your lips from deceitful speech. Shun evil and do good, seek peace and pursue it" (Psalm 34:14–15). "Guard your tongue from evil"—*l'shonkha mei-ra*—became *lashon ha-ra*, literally, "the evil tongue." It is not exactly slander, since slander usually refers to an untrue statement. *Lashon ha-ra* may be either true or false. It simply means spreading negative things about a third party, true or not. The closest English equivalent would be "gossip," but that sounds trivial, whereas "the evil tongue" is anything but.

The Sages railed against it. They said it was as bad as the most serious sins of shedding blood and idolatry.

D'rash: Personal Reflection

A DIFFICULT MITZVAH TO FULFILL

The nominations committee of an organization in which I was very active once asked me if I would like to be nominated for president. I agreed. The nominated slate was announced, and no one else came forward to run for the position. Surprisingly, a very short time before the election, someone else offered his candidacy. I did nothing in particular in response, assuming that I would probably be elected, and if not, so be it. The election was very close, but I lost. I admit that I was somewhat taken aback, but it was no great tragedy.

I was hurt, however, when I discovered why I had lost. My rival's campaign had been well organized by a friend of his who had spread rumors about me and my plans for the organization if I were elected, none of which happened to be true. I had not refuted the accusations, because I never knew of them. To be the victim of *lashon ha-ra* is never pleasant. In my case it was not tragic, but often the outcome is much more serious.

The modern age could easily be called the age of *lashon ha-ra*. This is a time in which we all talk too much and too quickly. Whereas previously, leaders and prominent people carefully measured their words, now they simply send out messages at all hours with no hesitation. We all have thoughts that we might be ashamed to reveal, but we also have the power to keep them to ourselves. That power seems to have diminished or been lost altogether in our times, and the damage is severe. Would that everyone would heed the wise words of the ancient Sage Avtalyon, "Sages, watch your words carefully . . . lest you be responsible for desecrating the name of God!" (Pirkei Avot 1:11). Thoughtless statements made public have caused thousands of people embarrassment, pain, and suffering. The only way we can help temper this state of affairs is to make certain that we ourselves do not initiate or spread defamation.

This negative mitzvah—avoiding *lashon ha-ra*—may well be one of the most difficult to fulfill. How often when simply engaging in conversation do we talk about someone else and suddenly find that conversation veering into negative remarks. It requires great self-control to measure one's words and to employ self-censorship. No wonder one Sage said that he found that there was "nothing better than silence" (Pirkei Avot 1:17).

Shelah-Lekha

Fringe Benefits

NUMBERS 13:1–15:41

The Lord said to Moses as follows: speak to the Israelite people and instruct them to make for themselves fringes on the corners of their garments throughout the ages; let them attach a cord of blue to the fringe at each corner. That shall be your fringe; look at it and recall all the commandments of the Lord and observe them, so that you do not follow your heart and your eyes in your lustful urge. Thus you shall be reminded to observe all My commandments and to be holy to your God. I the Lord am your God, who brought you out of the land of Egypt to be your God: I, the Lord your God.

—Numbers 15:37–41

P'shat: Explanation

This Torah portion is a mixture of law and lore. It begins with the sending of spies "to scout the land of Canaan." The spies' negative, discouraging report incites the people to revolt. They refuse to go on. They wish to die in the wilderness or return to Egypt.

Only Moses's intervention prevents God from annihilating the Israelites completely and creating a new people from the family of Moses. God instead metes out a different punishment for the people: wandering for forty years in the wilderness. The entire generation that left Egypt will die there, never reaching the land they had been promised. Their wish to die in the wilderness becomes their fate.

This is undoubtedly the most crucial event in the people's journey. Had it not occurred, the Israelites would have been in their own land in a matter of weeks, and all the events recorded from here until the end of the Torah would never have taken place.

Yet immediately after relating this tragic event, the portion continues blandly as if nothing has changed. God gives instructions regarding how to bring the offerings once the people enter the land—even though only their children will be able to do that. It is an ironic touch that underlines the enormity of the Israelites' misdeed.

At the very end of the portion comes the command to make and wear fringes—*tzitzit*—on the people's garments. Why is this commandment inserted here, of all places? There seems to be no logic to it. Since the clearly stated purpose of the fringes is so that "you shall be reminded to observe all My commandments and to be holy to your God," wouldn't the command belong in Leviticus 19, as part of the holiness code, Kedoshim? You are to be holy, and the fringes are to be worn to remind you of this.

A close reading of the text, however, reveals a linguistic connection to the spies story. The spies are sent *v'yaturu*—"to scout the land" (13:1). This Hebrew verb is repeated in 13:16 ("the men whom Moses sent to scout the land [*latur*]") and in 13:17, 25 and 14:6, 7, 34, 36, 38 as well. And this very same verb appears in the command to wear fringes "so that you do not follow [*taturu*] your heart and your eyes in your lustful urge" (15:39). Considering that this verb is not very common in the Torah, it cannot be mere coincidence that it is used here. The fringes are needed, that verb tells us, in order to prevent us from doing what the spies did, namely, they followed their own inclinations to their own detriment rather than hearkening to God's commands. It is as if the Torah has determined that in light of the Israelites' rebellious nature, as seen in the story of the spies, something very concrete and tangible is needed to keep them on the straight path—something they can see that will remind them constantly of their task to be "a kingdom of priests and a holy nation" (Exodus 19:6). Fringes are to serve that purpose.

Drash: Exposition of the Sages

Our Rabbis taught: The law of fringes applies to everyone:
Priests, Levites and Israelites, proselytes, women and
slaves. Rabbi Shimon exempts women because it is a
positive commandment dependent upon a fixed time.
— *Menachot 43a*

Once a man who was diligent in observing the commandment
of fringes . . . heard tell of a prostitute in a great city whose
fee was four hundred gold pieces. He sent her four hundred
gold pieces. . . . When he entered her house she offered him
seven beds, six of silver and one of gold and she sat on the
highest one. Between the beds there were stools of silver and
the highest one was of gold. When he was approaching her
his four fringes suddenly struck him upon the face like four
witnesses. He immediately ceased. . . . "By the power of Rome,"
she said, "I will not let you go until you tell me what flaw you
saw in me!" He replied, "By the Temple Service — I saw no
flaw at all since there is none as beautiful as you in all the
world. But there is one simple commandment that the Lord
our God has commanded us concerning which 'I the Lord am
your God' is written twice, indicating that 'I, the Lord, will
reward you and I, the Lord, will punish you.' These four fringes
appeared as witnesses against me." She then said to him, "By
the Temple service I will not let you go until you write down
your name, your city and where you study Torah." He did
so . . . and she went there [and converted, so that] what she
had offered him illicitly she could now offer him lawfully.
— *Menachot 44a*

These two selections are samples of the way in which the Sages interpreted this section in Jewish law and in Jewish lore. Originally, the

four fringes decorated the four bottom corners of a unique robe worn by all Israelites to indicate their status as members of this sacred, priestly people. At a later period, the fringes were attached to an outer cloak worn over regular clothes and in time became the ritual tallit Jews wear.

According to the Talmudic passage above, the command to wear fringes applied equally to men and women. Only one authority, Rabbi Shimon, ruled that women were exempt. Nevertheless, the common custom, with a few notable exceptions, became that only men wore them. This has begun to change among various circles in recent times.

The delightful story of the observant man whose fringes kept him from transgressing and who is greatly rewarded for his abstinence is in essence a morality tale based on the words "so that you do not follow your heart and your eyes in your lustful urge." In the story these words are taken literally. This man followed his lustful urge at great expense and trouble but was thwarted from continuing by the fringes. Thus they fulfilled the exact purpose assigned to them by the Torah.

D'rash: Personal Reflection

JEWISH GARMENTS

Typically, after flying from Israel to New York, I would wait with all the other passengers in a long line at JFK Airport for my bags to be inspected. One time, the customs officer, who was not Jewish, noticed on some documents that I was a rabbi. "Rabbi," he said, "I apologize for having to search your bags, but if I didn't, the other people watching would wonder why you weren't searched like everyone else." I told him that was perfectly all right; I didn't need special treatment. Then he added, "But if you were wearing your uniform, I wouldn't have to do it, because everyone would know." I was puzzled. What uniform did he mean? The one I had worn as an air force chaplain? "You know," he said, "the round fur hat and the long black coat."

I had a good laugh when I realized that he thought the *shtreimel* and kaftan worn by Hasidic Jews indicated that one was a rabbi. I did not bother to correct him.

There is no special garment for rabbis. The so-called canonicals or robes once worn by many rabbis of all denominations were only imitations of clerical garb worn by Christian clergy. Nor is there even a truly Jewish garment other than the *tzitzit*. The Hasidic garb and that worn by many ultra-Orthodox Jews today is merely a leftover from the fancy dress of Polish nobles. There is nothing Jewish about it, and certainly nothing rabbinical. Furthermore, any artwork we have from Jewish illuminated manuscripts indicates that no matter where they have lived, Jews have always dressed like everyone else, unless, as sometimes happened in the Middle Ages, the authorities required Jews to wear special hats and garments to differentiate them from others.

The Torah does require special garments to be worn by the priests, but that is only when they are officiating in the Temple, something that has not happened since the year 70 CE. The only long-standing clothing requirement is the *tzitzit*, which all Israelites were required to wear to show that they too were part of a priestly people and to remind them to observe the commandments. This particular commandment was intended to strengthen observance of all the commandments.

It is clear from the Talmud passage that the majority of Sages considered the wearing of *tzitzit* to be a biblical command for both women and men. Only one authority is mentioned as taking the opposite position. Yet custom is often more powerful than the law. When some women began to wear tallit with *tzitzit* in synagogues in the last part of the twentieth century, the more conservative members of congregations were often outraged. Quoting the talmudic law to these individuals was not effective in overcoming their opposition. I know of at least one congregation that actually split in two as a result.

It is difficult to understand why it should be so offensive to see women wearing this garment, especially when Jewish law in ancient days permitted it, and some great Rabbinic authorities—among them

Rav Yehudah—even required it of all female members of their household. Obviously, opposition to women wearing *tzitzit* does not come from halakhic reasoning based on Jewish law but, at its best, from emotional objection to change of custom and, at its worst, from misogyny, the desire to preserve male dominance in the realm of Jewish ritual. The Torah's injunction to look at *tzitzit* and "recall all the commandments of the Lord and observe them" should take precedence over any such objections.

Korah.

Controversies Proper and Improper

NUMBERS 16:1–18:32

Now Korah, son of Izhar son of Kohath son of Levi, betook
himself along with Dathan and Abiram sons of Eliab,
and On son of Peleth — descendants of Reuven — to rise
up against Moses, together with two hundred and fifty
Israelites, chieftains of the community, chosen in the
assembly, men of repute. They combined against Moses and
Aaron and said to them, "You have gone too far! For all the
community are holy, all of them, and the Lord is in their
midst. Why then do you raise yourselves above the Lord's
congregation?" When Moses heard this he fell on his face.
—Numbers 16:1–4

P'shat: Explanation

Tragedy follows tragedy. Rebellion follows rebellion. Immediately
after the episode of the spies and the punishment of that entire generation, two groups rise against the leadership of Moses and Aaron.
Korah, a Levite of Moses's own tribe, leads a group opposed to the
Priesthood given to Aaron and his family. Datan and Abiram, of the
tribe of Reuben, descendants of the first-born son, protest against
Moses's leadership and his claim of prophetic powers. The Israelites
have been led by a prophet and a Priest. The resentment against both
now rises to the surface. Why should either of them be considered
superior to others when the entire people is holy?

Once again God threatens to destroy the entire community because
of its rebelliousness, but upon Moses's and Aaron's pleadings, the pun-

ishment is mitigated and limited to "Korah and his band" and those from the community who followed their ways. The conclusion of the portion, the miraculous flowering of Aaron's rod and God's charge to Aaron, reiterates in the strongest possible language that he and his family alone are the anointed Priests, while the rest of the Levites are to minister to them. This is a clear justification of the rights and privileges of the Priesthood and a clarification of the proper status of the Levites. The status of the leadership of Moses and Aaron is reaffirmed so that it should not be questioned for the remainder of the long journey ahead.

D'rash: Exposition of the Sages

*A controversy for the sake of Heaven will endure. A
controversy not for the sake of Heaven will not endure. What
is a controversy for the sake of Heaven? The controversy
of Hillel and Shammai. What is a controversy not for the
sake of Heaven? The controversy of Korah and his band.*
—Pirkei Avot 5:19

*What is written just before this incident? ". . . make for
themselves fringes . . . and let them attach a cord of blue to
the fringe at each corner" (Numbers 15:38). Korah burst
out and said to Moses, "A tallit that is completely blue —
does it require fringes?" He replied, "It requires fringes."
Korah said to him, "A tallit that is completely blue does not
fulfil the requirement, but four blue threads do?! If a house
is filled with Torah scrolls, does it require a mezuzah?"
[Moses] said to him, "It requires a mezuzah." [Korah] said to
him, "An entire Torah, two hundred seventy-five portions —
does not exempt a house from needing a mezuzah but one
portion does?! These matters," [Korah] continued, "were not
commanded to you. You made them up in your own mind!"*

Rabbi Levi said: At that time Korah gathered his band
together and said to [Moses and Aaron], "You have placed
more burdens upon us than did the Egyptians when we
were enslaved in Egypt! The priests receive Terumah,
tithes and twenty-four different offerings! It was better
for us when we were ruled by Egypt than under your
rule!" Therefore, "When Moses heard this he fell on his
face." Moses said to them, "I never sought sovereignty
nor did Aaron my brother seek the High Priesthood."
This controversy of Korah terrified Moses since this was the
fourth time that Israel had rebelled and complained, and he
said, "How many times can I beseech the Lord on their behalf?"
Therefore "When Moses heard this he fell on his face."
—Numbers Rabbah 18:3,4,6

For the Sages the story of Korah's rebellion became the symbol of needless controversy that brought only disaster. They interpreted this story as if it applied to their own times, when there were numerous controversies within the academies and also between the Sages and others.

The most extreme example was the ongoing difference of opinion between the two great Sages of the first century BCE, Shammai and Hillel. They varied radically in their outlook and in their decisions concerning what was permissible and forbidden in Jewish law, yet they did so with respect for one another. Although disagreeing about laws of marriage and divorce, for example, nevertheless "the school of Shammai did not abstain from marrying women from the school of Hillel" and vice versa (*Yevamot* 14b).

The well-known saying concerning these controversies was "Both these and those are the words of the living God" (*Eruvin* 13b). The differences between the schools could be tolerated and even encouraged as long as both groups were arguing from positions of sincerity, seeking to interpret God's will correctly, with no ulterior motives.

Korah, on the other hand, became an example of someone who was concerned only for his personal gain. The midrash depicts him as mocking laws taught by Moses not because he has an honest disagreement with them but because he seeks power for himself.

The controversies in the midrash are anachronistic. They could not have occurred in Korah's time but were possible at the time of the Sages. Perhaps they reflected heated discussions in the academies or mocking questions from individual Jews or Gentiles or heretical groups concerning the Sages' interpretations of Torah laws.

Rabbi Levi enunciates another example of what Korah might have said. In this account Korah is not interpreting the Torah's laws but questioning their validity in and of themselves. Korah complains about the burden of fulfilling the many required tithes and similar offerings. He then makes the claim that none of these rules really came from God. Moses made them all up. Certainly at the time of the Sages, both individuals and groups made similar claims, denying the Torah's divine origin and protesting that the commandments were overly burdensome.

For the Sages, controversy for its own sake or for personal gain was improper and could be destructive. Yet respectful controversy to determine truth was a positive matter of great value.

D'rash: Personal Reflection

A CONTROVERSY NOT FOR THE SAKE OF HEAVEN

In 1997 Prime Minister Benjamin Netanyahu appointed me to the Neeman Commission, named for justice and finance minister Yaakov Neeman. Our commission was charged with recommending a solution to the controversy over conversions conducted by Conservative and Reform groups in Israel that was threatening to bring down the government and cause a major rift between Israel and Jews in the Diaspora. I was representing the Conservative/Masorti movement on the panel, which also had representatives from the Reform and

Orthodox movements, as well as secular Jews. There were no official representatives from the Chief Rabbinate of Israel.

Meeting intensively for the better part of a year, the commission heard testimony and suggestions from divergent groups of Jewish leaders throughout the world. The meetings could be heated but nevertheless were always to the point: seeking acceptable compromise. This was not easy, since the differences were great, and it was not simple to find bridges to connect them.

Finally, a tentative proposal emerged. A new institute, to be run jointly by all groups, would prepare conversion candidates, while the actual conversion would be performed by special Orthodox courts consisting of rabbis selected for their willingness to be moderate and understanding in their requirements. This formulation would limit Conservative and Reform participation to teaching and preparation alone, a major concession, while the Orthodox would have to permit such participation and generally be much more liberal in their approach to conversions, major concessions on their part. This would have enabled us to work together to solve the problem of the hundreds of thousands of *olim* from the former Soviet Union who are not Jewish according to Jewish law and require conversion.

Our group agreed to try this on an experimental basis for one year, provided that the Chief Rabbinate agreed to this formulation, which we were led to believe they were prepared to do. To my mind this was a "controversy for the sake of Heaven."

When this was presented to the Chief Rabbinate, the reaction took us all by surprise. We received, in writing, a refusal to have anything to do with any proposal that included non-Orthodox groups. Furthermore, the response contained vitriolic denunciations of these groups. The controversy was now "not for the sake of Heaven" but intended to maintain the exclusive power of one group.

Under those conditions we had no choice but to withdraw our concurrence, and the Neeman Commission never issued an official report. To this day no agreed-upon solution has been found. The result has been continual controversy over the recognition of conversions performed by Conservative and Reform rabbis and even those by Orthodox rabbis who are not part of the official Chief Rabbinate. Time and time again it is necessary to appeal to the courts and to combat attempts to enact new legislation that would further curb the rights of all Jewish religious denominations, all of which is worsening relationships between Israel and the Diaspora.

For me, the experience of participating in this commission became a matter of bitter disappointment. I had wanted to advance agreed-upon ways of converting the thousands of *olim* from the former Soviet Union and to encourage cooperation among the diverse streams of Judaism. Instead, there was only more controversy. What a shame that the example of Hillel and Shammai could not be duplicated in our time.

Ḥukkat

A Perplexing Law

NUMBERS 19:1–22:1

> *This is the ritual law that the Lord has commanded: Instruct the Israelite people to bring you a red cow without blemish, in which there is no blemish and on which no yoke has been laid. You shall give it to Eleazar the priest. It shall be taken outside the camp and slaughtered in his presence. Eleazar the priest shall take some of its blood with his finger and sprinkle it seven times toward the front of the Tent of Meeting. The cow shall be burned in his sight—its hide, flesh, and blood shall be burnt. . . . He who performed the burning shall also wash his garments in water, bathe his body in water, and be unclean until evening. A man who is clean shall gather up the ashes . . . to be kept for lustration for the Israelite community. It is for cleansing.*
> —Numbers 19:2–5,8–10

P'shat: Explanation

The purpose of most commandments is fairly clear. We can usually discern what they were intended to accomplish and how they were to be performed. In the Middle Ages, Maimonides easily divided them into various categories on the basis of what they were intended to accomplish.

However, this particular law, the ritual of the *parah adumah*, the red cow (sometimes called the red heifer), has long raised questions from both ancient and modern commentators. It is one of four commandments that Rabbi Levi said seemed to contradict other verses

205

in the Torah, thus causing people to question their validity (*Pesikta de-Rav Kahana* 4:6).

The ultimate purpose of the red cow is clearly stated: "for lustration of the Israelite community," meaning that the ashes were to be used to purify individuals who were in a state of ritual impurity. Only those who were ritually pure were permitted to enter the Temple sanctuary.

Yet several things are puzzling about this commandment. The cow is not slaughtered in the sanctuary, as sacrifices were. It is the only instance in which the entire animal, including its blood, is burned and turned into ashes. It is the only time the color of any sacrificial animal is ever specified. It is strange that everyone involved in this procedure is rendered unclean by it when its entire purpose is to ritually cleanse people. Above all is the question, Why does this ritual eliminate ritual impurity?

D'rash: Exposition of the Sages

> A pagan asked Rabban Yohanan ben Zakkai, "Some of the things you Jews do appear to be sorcery. You bring a cow, burn it, make it into ashes and gather them up. Then when someone becomes defiled by coming in contact with a dead body, you mix some of it with water, sprinkle it on him and declare, 'You are purified!'" Rabban Yohanan asked the pagan, "Have you ever been possessed by the spirit of madness?" He replied, "No." "Have you ever seen someone who is possessed by the spirit of madness?" The pagan answered, "Yes." "And what do you do for that person?" "We take roots, burn them so that the smoke rises about him and sprinkle him with water until the spirit of madness disappears." Rabban Yohanan said, "Listen to what you have said. When a person is defiled by contact with the dead, it is the same. He is possessed by a spirit of defilement, and as the verse says, 'And I will make . . . the unclean spirit vanish from the land'" (Zehariah 13:2).

When the pagan departed, Rabban Yohanan's students said,
"Our master, you put him off with a mere reed, but what will
you tell us?" Rabban Yohanan answered, "By your lives, I
swear the corpse does not defile, nor do the ashes and the water
cleanse! The ritual of the red cow is the Holy One's decree. As
the Holy One said, 'I have set this as a statute, I have made
this a decree. You may not transgress my decree!' 'This is the
ritual law that the Lord has commanded'" (Numbers 19:1).
— Pesikta de-Rav Kahana 4:7.

This fifth-century midrash created in the Land of Israel recounts an incident in which a non-Jew questioned a great Sage about the meaning of the ritual of the red cow. Rabban Yohanan ben Zakkai was the outstanding Pharisaic religious authority before the destruction of the Temple in 70 CE. He was responsible for establishing the great academy in Yavne that became the seat of Rabbinic authority immediately thereafter. Since the entire practice of lustration with the ashes of the red cow became obsolete when there was no Temple, this incident must have occurred prior to that event.

It was not uncommon then for non-Jews and pagans to inquire about Judaism and its practices. Sometimes they did so out of a genuine desire to understand the only monotheistic religion that existed; perhaps they were considering leaving behind their religions, complete with fantastic legends of the lives of multiple gods. Others asked out of curiosity and still others out of a desire to defame Judaism. In this story it sounds as if the pagan is disparaging Jewish practice, trying to demonstrate that it is mere sorcery, no different from common witchcraft. Yohanan's answer is to compare the ritual to what was then commonly done among pagans when someone seemed to be acting strangely. It was assumed that that person was possessed by a spirit, and similar actions were taken to drive out that spirit.

Yohanan's students do not accept that explanation and are certain that he does not believe it either. It is totally foreign to the beliefs and practices of Judaism. In response Rabban Yohanan does not offer any explanation as to why he said what he did. (Perhaps he believed there was no way that an idolater would have understood the truth.) Nor does he really explain the ritual to his students, because he has no simple explanation.

He does, however, say something of great importance. He tells them that there is no such thing as magic, no sorcery, no inherent supernatural powers in rituals. There is nothing in a dead body that automatically creates impurity and nothing in ashes that creates purity. This is simply God's decree. Had God wished it to be otherwise, it would have been that way.

Rabban Yohanan's message is *not* that it is wrong to try to understand the commandments or look for explanations of God's commands—that is done all the time, both in the Torah and in the writings of the Sages. Rather, he is denying that rituals such as these have any inherent powers. It is God alone who purifies us when we obey the rules that God has created. Superstition and witchcraft are false and have no part in Judaism.

In contrast, pagan religions believed in magic and sorcery because their gods were not considered all-powerful but were themselves subject to forces outside of themselves. If one knew the proper rituals and the correct spells, one could alter the will of the gods and force them to one's own will. The religion of Israel denied all of that. In Judaism humans can ask God but cannot coerce God. In the words of Balaam, "Lo, there is no augury in Jacob, no divining in Israel" (Numbers 23:22).

Rabban Yohanan goes even further in denying the efficacy of any rituals or spells. Everything is the will of God. When the laws and rituals in the Torah were first created, many of them were similar to practices already in existence in the religions of the Middle East. Sacrifices, for example, followed similar patterns already in existence. Similarly, the idea of a priesthood was not original. However, the Torah made many changes in these things because its basic assumptions about God and God's powers were so different. Priests in the Torah, for example, have no healing powers, nor can they perform miracles. Only God can do that. The ritual of the red cow follows forms that were then common: using various substances that were believed to have potency in driving out spirits of evil or impurity. In other religions, however, in contrast to what Rabban Yohanan said, it would have been believed that "the corpse *does* defile; the ashes and the water *do* cleanse."

D'rash: Personal Reflection

THE FINE LINE

Once I came home to my home in Jerusalem late at night to find that the mezuzah on my door had been taken off. The next day my neighbor told me that a group of young men had told her that they had looked at it, declared it unfit, took it off, and gave it to her, since we were not home. They left with her the message that if I did not fix it, terrible things would happen.

I did examine it, and, upon ascertaining that it was perfectly fine, I put it back on the doorpost, where it has remained to this day. I was upset that this group had tampered with my mezuzah without permission and had felt that it was perfectly all right for them to remove it. I was also angry that they wanted me to believe that an imperfect scroll in that container would endanger my home. I keep a mezuzah to remind me of God's commandments and to signify that this is a Jewish home—not out of a superstitious belief that it will protect me.

This incident reminded me that during one of the times when Israel was at war, a group of rabbis flew in an airplane around the borders reciting specific chants. These rabbis guaranteed that no enemy missiles could penetrate where they had cast their spells. I am glad that the Israeli Defense Forces have preferred to develop antimissile devices rather than depending on spells for our safety.

Superstition is common enough and relatively innocuous when it is little more than avoiding things we think may be harmful, like black cats and walking under ladders. But the mitzvot of Judaism are too important to be turned into nothing but superstitious practices.

Rabban Yohanan ben Zakkai left us with a significant lesson. He taught us that while there may be a superficial resemblance between some of our practices and the quasi-magical actions that superstition advocates, true belief does not grant that such actions have any power of their own. True belief relies on God alone. There may be a fine line between superstition and religion, but it is a line of great importance.

Balak

The Ways of Peace

NUMBERS 22:2–25:9

Just then one of the Israelites came and brought a Midianite
woman over to his companions, in the sight of Moses and of the
whole Israelite community who were weeping at the entrance
of the Tent of Meeting. When Phinehas, son of Eleazar son of
Aaron the priest, saw this, he left the assembly and, taking a
spear in his hand, he followed the Israelite into the chamber
and stabbed both of them, the Israelite and the woman, through
the belly. Then the plague against the Israelites was checked.
—Numbers 25:6–8

P'shat: Explanation

Unsuccessful in cursing the Israelites, Balaam devises another means
of defeating them: enticing them to engage in pagan orgies dedicated
to the god Baal-peor with Moabite women. The result is divine punishment by a devastating plague. When these orgies reach the point
of desecrating the sanctuary, Phinehas, the zealous Priest charged
with safeguarding the sanctity of the Tent, takes the law into his own
hands and kills the pair. This action seems extreme by our standards,
but in the context of the time, it is presented as a necessary action to
save the people. As a result, God praises Phinehas and grants him a
"covenant of peace" (Numbers 25:10–11).

Phinehas became a highly praised figure in Jewish tradition and
an example for others. The Sages, however, took a different stance.

D'rash: Exposition of the Sages

Hillel said: Be of the disciples of Aaron, loving
peace and pursuing peace, loving human beings
and bringing them close to the Torah.
—Tractate *Avot* 1:12

Rabbi Meir says: When Aaron would walk in the street
and chance to meet an evil or wicked person he would
greet him. If afterwards that person would think of
committing a transgression he would think: "Woe is me!
If I meet Aaron how can I lift my eyes to him? I would
be ashamed since he greeted me"—and he would not
sin. Similarly if two people quarreled, Aaron would
sit with one and tell him, "The other fellow is beating
his breast and tearing his clothing saying, 'Woe is me!
. . . I treated him badly!'" Aaron would stay with him
until he was pacified, then go and sit with the other
man [and tell him the same thing]. . . . When the two
would meet, they would embrace and kiss each other.
—*Avot de-Rabbi Natan* A 12

Although the Sages recognized that Phinehas's zealotry may have been needed at that particular moment and was therefore justified under the circumstances, they also realized the perils of zealotry. They understood it could easily lead to extreme actions going far beyond what Jewish law allowed. Fearful of people following Phinehas's example, they made Phinehas into an exception rather than the rule and frequently warned against fanaticism.

This fear underlies Hillel the Elder's praise of Moses's brother Aaron rather than Phinehas as a man of peace. Although Hillel never mentions Phinehas by name, from the context it is clear that he wished to replace him with another Priest, substituting the zealot with a man of peace and moderation.

Hillel (first century BCE–first century CE) was the most influential of the ancient Sages, the founder of an entire dynasty of leaders of the Sanhedrin and of a school of Sages known as Bet Hillel (the House of Hillel), whose liberal opinions predominated in Rabbinic Judaism over the stricter ideas of the rival Bet Shammai (the House of Shammai). With this statement he created a revolution in early Judaism, replacing the zealot Priest Phinehas with the patient Priest Aaron as the figure to be imitated. God may have made a covenant of peace with Phinehas, but Hillel teaches that Aaron, a model of love, patience, moderation, and peace, is the ideal religious leader.

This was a very bold step, since in the Torah Aaron is portrayed as less than the ideal leader. God holds him responsible and castigates him for the sin of the Golden Calf, whereas God praises Phinehas for his actions.

Notably, up until this point in history (e.g., consider the Maccabees in the second century BCE), Phinehas had been viewed as the ideal leader whose bold actions were to be emulated. Once Hillel proposed Aaron, Jewish religious leadership was never the same. Zealotry was replaced by peaceful persuasion, fanaticism by love.

Hillel's saying was directed to his own students who were preparing to become teachers of Torah. The ideal teacher, he said, is one who is characterized by two loves: the love of peace and the love of all humanity. Here, Hillel was not simply advocating a sentimental feeling of affection. Love, in his view, could not remain a passive ideal, a stance with no practical application. What good is loving peace if that love does not lead to action toward attaining peace? What good is an abstract love of human beings if it does not lead to a deed that demonstrates that love?

For this reason, in both of these cases Hillel began with the abstract emotion, "loving," and then followed it with an action. Love of peace must lead to pursuit of peace. Love of people leads the religious leader to bringing them closer to God's teaching: knowledge of Torah.

The fact that Hillel did not speak of Israelites or Jews but of "human beings" indicates that he viewed spreading the word of Torah to non-

Jews to be an ideal as well. In his time, Judaism was the only monotheistic religion, and many non-Jews were expressing an interest in Judaism as opposed to the paganism of their own culture. If Torah is the teaching of the Lord—the only God, Hillel believed—then what can one do to benefit human beings more than bringing them to that truth?

In this saying, Hillel does not explain what he means by peace. In ancient Jewish teachings, such as the words of the prophet Micah, the greatest dream is the elimination of warfare and the arrival of peace: "Nation shall not lift up sword against nation, neither shall they learn war anymore, but every person will sit under his grapevine or fig tree with no one to disturb him" (Micah 4:3–4). In *The Fathers According to Rabbi Nathan*, a third-century commentary on *Avot*, however, Hillel's statement was understood in a more personal way: as referring to relationships between individuals, between one person and another. According to the legends told there about Aaron, he made it his life's work to reconcile those who had quarreled. He went so far as to tell white lies for the sake of peace. He would tell a husband that his wife was sorry they had quarreled. The husband would then be willing to make up. So he would then tell the wife—truthfully—that her husband had agreed to be reconciled. They would then meet and resume their marriage. The result would be the birth of a child—many of whom, the legend recounts, would be called Aaron, since without him, they would never have come into the world (*Avot de-Rabbi Natan* A 12).

Aaron also never rebuked people who had done wrong but attempted to persuade them to change their ways. It is no accident that the qualities associated with Aaron are the same ones that characterized Hillel himself.

D'rash: Personal Reflection

AARON'S UNKNOWING DISCIPLE

When I was very young, not yet ten, I was extremely upset because my mother had quarreled with her best friend, a woman I liked very much. They stopped speaking to and seeing each other. This went on all too long, and I knew that both of them were unhappy about it. Although I had never heard the stories about Aaron the peacemaker, instinctively I followed his way: I went to the friend and said that my mother wanted to see her again, and then I told my mother that her friend intended to make up.

It worked. They reconciled, and for many years, until death separated them, they enjoyed the benefit of their close friendship and mutual support. I had become Aaron's disciple without knowing it. And many years later, when I learned Hillel's saying, "Be of the disciples of Aaron, loving peace and pursuing peace, loving human beings and bringing them close to the Torah," I immediately adopted it as my personal motto.

The love of peace and the love of human beings have stood at the core of my life's work ever since. A depiction of this saying adorns my study. I regard it as the words that should constantly guide me.

I cannot speak about other professions that may indeed face similar problems, but the rabbinate is a place where the maintenance of peace requires constant awareness. There are so many stories and anecdotes, for example, about relations between rabbis and cantors. So much depends upon all the individuals involved. Personal relationships with congregants can also be problematic.

I consider myself fortunate not to have had such problems. I have always preferred teamwork over asserting my professional hierarchy. With both colleagues and congregants, patience and tolerance are required—and, above all, mutual respect. As Aaron modelled, it is important to treat others well, to avoid conflicts whenever possible, and in fact to actively advance the cause of peace.

Hillel may have intended his words for Sages, teachers of Judaism, but they have the potential to be very meaningful to every one of us.

Pinḥas

Respecting Difference

NUMBERS 25:10–30:1

Moses spoke to the Lord, saying, "Let the Lord, source of the spirits of all flesh, appoint someone over the community who shall go out before them and come in before them, and who shall take them out and bring them in, so that the Lord's community may not be like sheep that have no shepherd." And the Lord answered Moses, "Single out Joshua son of Nun, an inspired man, and lay your hand upon him. Have him stand before Eleazar the priest and before the whole community, and commission him in their sight. Invest him with some of your authority, so that the whole Israelite community may obey."
—Numbers 27:15–20

P'shat: Explanation

When Moses is told to ascend to the heights in order to view the land because he will not be permitted to enter it, his immediate response is not to speak about his personal tragedy but to express his concern that the people need a new leader who will care for them. The imagery he uses of the sheep and the shepherd has become commonly accepted as a picture of what a leader should be: caring for the people and tending to them. Considering that Moses himself was a shepherd when he received the call to come to the aid of the Israelites in Egypt, it is not surprising that he chooses this specific imagery (Exodus 3:1). The worst things that could happen would be for the flock to be leaderless, totally lacking guidance, or to be guided by a leader who really does not care for and tend to them.

God gives an immediate answer, appointing Joshua, who had been assisting Moses, and calling him "inspired." God then instructs Moses to begin the process of transferring leadership by placing his hands upon Joshua. This is the origin of the process of investing rabbis with rabbinical authority, called *s'micha*—the laying on of hands.

Moses does not simply announce that Joshua is to be the leader; instead, he takes the needed steps to see that the transfer of power is done properly so there will be no vacuum into which an improper leader could step. Thus began the chain of leadership, leading eventually to rabbinical leadership today.

D'rash: Exposition of the Sages

If one sees crowds of people one should recite, "Blessed be God who discerns secrets," for just as their faces are not identical, so their thoughts are not identical. Each individual has his own thoughts. This is apparent from what Moses said at the hour of his death when he beseeched God saying, "Master of the universe—You know everyone's thoughts, therefore You know that the thoughts of Your children are not identical. When I leave them, therefore, I beg You to appoint a leader for them who can tolerate each one according to his own way of thinking." How do we know that? As he said, "Let the Lord, source of the spirits of all flesh, appoint someone over the community."
—Tanhuma Pinḥas 10

The Tanhuma, a late midrash possibly edited in the ninth century CE, quotes a saying of the earlier Sages, the *tannaim* (first century CE), concerning the proper blessing to be recited when seeing different types of people (*Berachot* 58a). The blessing stresses the fact that every person is an individual with unique physical properties and unique ideas and thoughts. No two bodies are identical, and no two minds are identical. This is a wonder to be praised and cherished.

The midrash then discusses the question of the precise leadership qualities Moses had in mind. It imagines a request Moses makes to God describing exactly what that leader should be like, taking as its inspiration Moses's reference to God as the "source of the *spirits* of all flesh," with the word *ha-ruhot* (the spirits) in the plural. From this the Sages determined that Moses requested a successor who could interact with each individual according to that person's own "spirit," that is, his or her own ideas and ways of thinking. Since God created each individual as a unique being, a good leader must be able to understand and respect these differences. The people need "a leader . . . who can tolerate each one according to his own way of thinking."

This is a remarkable passage. That the Sages so many hundreds of years ago should have been sensitive to the uniqueness of each human being's thought and ideas is not to be taken for granted. Furthermore, it is probably the most important theological statement concerning the uniqueness of the individual and the rights of each person to his or her own opinions. It is truly a bill of rights for human individuality. Rather than calling for adherence to uniformity and one way of thinking, it lauds diversity and sanctifies the integrity of each individual and of individual difference.

This midrash speaks to parents and teachers, as well as to leaders. Difference is not to be denied and not to be punished; rather, we bless God for it. That is what human life is all about.

D'rash: Personal Reflection

HONORING HUMAN DIFFERENCE

I was once faced with a difficult educational problem. After the principal of my congregation's Hebrew school retired, I had been called upon to serve temporarily as the educational director. Soon I discovered that a number of children were experiencing difficulty with our curriculum; some had dropped out altogether. Upon further investigation I found out that almost all of them were children who required special help and/or were in specific programs in their public schools for children with special needs. I also learned that some children in the congregation had never attended our school because of their special needs. Most of these youngsters had been diagnosed as having "learning disabilities."

I realized that it was wrong to neglect children like these. By not accepting them as unique individuals with their own ways of learning and meeting those needs, we were in effect denying them entry to their Jewish heritage—something that could be meaningful to them and add greatly to their self-esteem. I decided to learn more about learning disabilities and enrolled in a nearby university that specialized in it.

With the help of specially trained teachers, we eventually opened a program for these children, becoming one of the first synagogues to do so. Subsequently, I wrote a book, *The Other Child in Jewish Education*, urging Jewish educators and communities to address this issue and outlining *the* best practices for creating such a program, addressing both content and methodology. The midrash in Tanhuma Pinhas 10 is prominently cited in the book as proof that Jewish tradition calls upon us to respect individual difference. More than forty years later, this book is still used for this purpose.

Later, after moving to Israel, I became involved with creating a program of bar/bat mitzvah ceremonies for children with special needs sponsored by the Masorti movement. I wrote a responsum showing that these children were indeed eligible for bar/bat mitzvah, which some rabbinical authorities in Israel denied. This served as the basic justification for the program, which includes a year of studies culminating with a ceremony in a synagogue. No one who wished to participate in such a ceremony would be turned away.

Now, more than twenty years later, hundreds of children from all segments of Israeli life have benefited from this ongoing program. No matter what the child's abilities and problems, we have found ways for him or her to participate in an appropriate ceremony, much to the joy of the individual and the family.

Mattot

People before Wealth

NUMBERS 30:2–32:42

Moses said to them, "If you do this, if you go to battle as shock-troops, at the instance of the Lord, and every shock-fighter among you crosses the Jordan, at the instance of the Lord, until He has dispossessed His enemies before Him, and the land has been subdued, at the instance of the Lord, and then you return—you shall be clear before the Lord and before Israel; and this land shall be your holding under the Lord. But if you do not do so, you will have sinned against the Lord; and know that your sin will overtake you. Build towns for your children and sheepfolds for your flocks, but do what you have promised."
—Numbers 32:20–24

P'shat: Explanation

After declaring the laws regulating vows, this portion continues with the final two narratives in the history of the Israelites before they cross the Jordan River. The forty years of wandering have passed, although in the fifteen chapters of Numbers since that punishment was decreed we have been told very little of what happened in those years.

The first narrative relates the Israelites' final battle in the wilderness—the elimination of the Midianites who had brought about the Israelites' sin at Baal-peor (Numbers 25). In the second, the tribes of Reuben and Gad ask to remain on the eastern side of the Jordan because "the lands of Jazeer and Gilead [are] a region suitable for cattle" (Numbers 32:1). Moses—mistakenly—assumes that these tribes do not intend to join the fight to conquer the land of Canaan:

"Are your brothers to go to war while you stay here?" (Numbers 32:6). He sees this as nothing less than a sin—and no less serious than the one forty years earlier, when the people refused to continue on to the land upon hearing the spies' negative report.

The tribes of Reuben and Gad quickly assure Moses that they will fight at the forefront of the battle and only then return to their families on this side of the river. Thereupon Moses agrees. Interestingly, Moses does not ask God what the tribes can and cannot do; nor does God speak about it. Moses assumes that the tribes' proposal is acceptable to God. What would not be acceptable is shirking their duty to participate in the upcoming battle.

It is quite clear, however, that this settlement on the eastern side of the Jordan is not considered part of the Promised Land. Later on, the book of Joshua (22:10) reports that the tribes of Reuben and Gad built an altar there, although sacrifices are not to be offered anywhere but in the land of Canaan. When the other tribes accuse them of a great sin, they explain that they did not intend to offer sacrifices. The altar is purely symbolic, to indicate they are part of the Israelite community so that their children will not be told, "You have no share in the Lord" (Joshua 22:27).

Thus the first Diaspora community is established even before the invasion of Canaan—and problems between the Israelites within and beyond the land begin simultaneously.

D'rash: Exposition of the Sages

The Garmu family was expert at preparing the showbread. . . .
Fine bread was never seen in the possession of their
children so that people should not say, "They are eating
showbread!" Thus they fulfilled the verse, ". . . you shall be
clear before the Lord and before Israel" (Numbers 32:22).
The Abtinas family was expert in preparing the incense. . . . No
bride in their family ever wore perfume and if they married a
woman from elsewhere they forbade her to wear any so that

people should not say, "They are using perfume from the incense
for themselves!" Thus they fulfilled the verse, ". . . you shall be
clear before the Lord and before Israel" (Numbers 32:22).
— Yoma 38a

It is as important to be seen to be innocent by human beings
as by God, as it is said, ". . . you shall be clear before the Lord
and before Israel" (Numbers 32:22) and "you will find favor
and approbation in the eyes of God and man" (Proverbs 3:4).
— Sheqalim 3:2

The tribes of Reuben and Gad made that which was important
insignificant and that which was insignificant important.
They valued wealth above human life. For they said to
Moses, "We will build here sheepfolds for our flocks and
towns for our children" (Numbers 32:16). But Moses said
to them, "You should rather place that which is important
first— 'Build towns for your children' and only afterwards
'sheepfolds for your flocks . . .'" (Numbers 32:24). Said
the Holy One to them, "Since you valued your cattle more
than your people you will have no blessing from them!" . . .
Who is truly rich? One who is content with what he has,
as it is said, "You shall enjoy the fruit of your labors; you
shall be happy and you shall prosper" (Psalm 128:2).
— Numbers Rabbah 22:9

Three verses in the story of these tribes caught the interest of the
Sages, who used them not so much to illuminate the story itself but
to teach about the conduct of a moral life. In their careful perusal
of the Torah verses, they noticed a subtle difference between what
the tribes said about their plans and what Moses said in reply. The
tribes said, "We will build here sheepfolds for our flocks and towns
for our children" (Numbers 32:16), first mentioning their flocks, that
is, their valuable assets, and only then their own progeny. Accord-

ing to the Sages, Moses deliberately reversed this order in his reply: "Build towns for your children and sheepfolds for your flocks" (Numbers 32:24). He thus rebuked them: people are more important than wealth. Care for your children should be your first priority. If you are more concerned with multiplying your wealth, that is, caring for your flocks, than you are with the welfare of your families, you will have no blessing in your life.

For this one mistake, the Sages taught, these tribes were punished in the future. In the midrash this tale became the source of a well-known saying of Ben Zoma (first century CE): "Who is truly rich? One who is content with what he has" (*Avot* 4:1).

The other verse that intrigued the Sages was "you shall be clear before the Lord and before Israel" (Numbers 32:22). The Sages noted that Moses emphasized that the fulfillment of the tribes' promise would demonstrate their innocence to both "the Lord" and "Israel," that is, God and man, and not merely to one or the other. This became a general principle in Rabbinic ethics, as enunciated in the Mishnah *Sheqalim* 3:2: "It is as important to be seen to be innocent by human beings as by God."

Two historical instances were described in the Talmud to illustrate this. The showbread displayed in the Temple and the incense used there were based on very special formulas, carefully guarded secrets known only by the specific families who prepared them. As tradition had it, these families were careful to demonstrate to everyone—not only to God—that they only used these things for the Temple service and never for themselves. Therefore, those who prepared incense never wore perfume just in case people might think it came from the sacred incense, and those who prepared the bread never were seen with fine bread that could be thought to have been made with the same ingredients as the showbread. For this these families were praised.

This principle is applied frequently throughout Rabbinic literature. For example, the Sages advise those who hold positions of public trust such as administering charitable funds to be scrupulous in all their activities to avoid any possible suspicion concerning their misuse of those funds. As the saying has it, "Caesar's wife must be above suspicion."

D'rash: Personal Reflection

A MITZVAH FOR ITS OWN SAKE

When I became a congregational rabbi, one of my first decisions was not to accept any gratuities for services performed for my congregants. Although it was quite common for people to "tip the rabbi" for weddings, b'nai mitzvah ceremonies, and, heaven forbid, funerals and unveilings, I felt this practice was inappropriate for many reasons. For one thing, it was degrading for the rabbi to have his hand out for tips. For another, it placed the rabbi in an awkward position of being in that person's debt in the future. It also painted a picture of the rabbi as someone concerned more with money than with people.

But most of all it meant that I was being paid to perform a mitzvah rather than simply doing one for its own sake. Rather, like the families offering provisions for the Temple service who were careful not to be seen taking personal advantage of their position, I felt it important that I not be seen as gaining wealth for helping people in the performance of important life-cycle events. They are my congregants, and I am there to help them willingly. Let there be no suspicion that I am anything but "clear before the Lord and before Israel," innocent in the eyes of God and people.

I discovered, however, that many, perhaps even most, people really wanted to give something to the rabbi on those occasions and frequently would not take no for an answer. My solution was to create the Rabbi's Charity Fund and to tell people that while I would not accept anything for myself, if they wanted to they could contribute to that fund. I made it clear that the fund would support charitable causes, including scholarships for children to attend Jewish camps and help for families in need. Fund revenues would and in fact could not be used to benefit anyone in my family. The fund was supervised and administered by the congregation, so there could be no suspicion that it was being misused.

Over the years people became accustomed to the Rabbi's Charity Fund, many people benefited from it, and I felt content performing all these ceremonies simply as a part of what it means to be a rabbi.

Mase'ei

Defiling the Land

NUMBERS 33:1–36:13

*If anyone kills a person, the manslayer may be executed only
on the evidence of witnesses; the testimony of a single witness
against a person shall not suffice for a sentence of death. You
may not accept a ransom for the life of a murderer who is
guilty of a capital crime; he must be put to death. Neither
may you accept ransom in lieu of flight to a city of refuge,
enabling one to return to live on his land before the death of
the priest. You shall not pollute the land in which you live; for
blood pollutes the land, and the land can have no expiation for
blood that is shed on it, except by the blood of him who shed
it. You shall not defile the land in which you live, in which I
Myself abide, for I the Lord abide among the Israelite people.*
—Numbers 35:30–34

P'shat: Explanation

The last portion of the book of Numbers contains the laws concerning the establishment of cities of refuge to which one who has accidentally slain a person may flee in order to escape being killed by the victim's family blood avenger.

All the capital punishment laws in the Torah are based on the passage after the Flood stating that although it is permissible to slay animals for food, human bloodshed is forbidden: "Whosoever sheds the blood of man, by man shall his blood be shed; for in His image did God make man" (Genesis 9:6). This portion qualifies that general rule in two ways: it requires more than one witness in order to

226

sentence a person to death, and it clearly delineates the difference between unintentional slaying and intentional murder. If a court finds the former, that is, that the slaying was not deliberate, then the perpetrator is not to be put to death but allowed to find safety in a city of refuge. In the case of the latter, intentional murder, only one sentence is to be applied: capital punishment. There can be no monetary replacement—"ransom" or "expiation"—for such a crime. Nonetheless, the case requiring the imposition of such punishment must be proved beyond a doubt. It seems as if the Torah's abhorrence of bloodshed, expressed in the passage from Genesis, also requires that the punishment for doing so—which is also bloodshed—be carefully administered and limited.

The summation of this law reiterates a general principle found time and again in the Torah: killing human beings, shedding human blood, pollutes and defiles the land and will result in exile from it. As the prophet Ezekiel states after the Babylonian exile: "So I poured out my wrath on them for the blood which they shed upon their land. . . . I scattered them among the nations" (Ezekiel 36:18–19).

D'rash: Exposition of the Sages

"You shall not defile the land in which you live . . ." (Numbers 35:34). This teaches that bloodshed defiles the land and causes the Divine Presence to depart from it and that because of bloodshed the Temple was destroyed. It once happened that two Priests were running up the ramp [of the altar] and when one reached within four cubits of the top first, the other took a knife and stabbed him in the heart. . . . All who witnessed this burst into tears and then the father of the injured priest came and said to them, "Our brothers! He is an atonement for you—for my son is still in the throes of dying so that the knife has not become impure!" This shows that the impurity of their implements was of greater concern to them than bloodshed!
—Sifre Numbers Mase‘ei 3

A Sanhedrin that executes one person in seven years
is termed destructive. Rabbi Elazar ben Azaria says,
"One in seventy years!" Rabbi Tarphon and Rabbi Akiba
say, "Had we been in the Sanhedrin no one would ever
have been executed." Rabban Shimon ben Gamliel says,
"They would multiply spillers of blood in Israel."
—Makkot 1:11

Each morning the Temple altar had to be cleaned and its ashes from
the previous day's sacrifices removed. This was considered a great
privilege; all the Priests vied with one another for the honor. The
Mishnah relates that the race to reach the top once resulted in one
Priest pushing the other so that he broke his leg, after which it was
decided to establish a rotation system and determine in advance who
would do so (*Yoma* 3:1).

The story of one Priest killing the other in the race to clean the
altar, obviously a much more serious event, is related in both the
Tosefta and the Talmud, as well as in the passage from Sifre Numbers. Since it concerns an event in the days of the Second Temple,
it seems to be asserting that bloodshed was the sin that caused the
Second Temple (as well as the First Temple) to be destroyed. If the
story is true (we have no way of knowing), it is a terrible indictment
of the Priesthood of that time. First, the idea that one Priest would
deliberately kill another for such a reason is deeply troublesome. But
the statement of the father of the slain Priest is perhaps just as dis-
turbing. How could anyone, much less a father, be concerned with
the purity or impurity of a knife when the victim is in the throes of
dying?! What kind of priesthood would be more preoccupied with
matters of ritual purity than with human life?

There are many indications that the Priesthood during the Second
Temple period may have been less than pure and selfless. The Essenes
and the Dead Sea Sect considered it completely corrupt. This story
may reflect that assessment.

During the period when the laws of the Mishnah were being formulated, there was no Sanhedrin with the power to carry out executions. In that sense, the statements concerning execution found in
Mishnah Makkot are purely theoretical. They do, however, reflect a
continued stance by the Sages to restrict the use of the power to execute people. The statements of Rabbi Tarphon and Rabbi Akiba (late
first century CE) carry this to an extreme. In effect, they are saying
that they would always find ways to question the witnesses that would
invalidate their testimony. The end result would be nothing less than
eliminating capital punishment altogether. Rabban Shimon reacts
sharply, taking the stance still heard today that capital punishment
deters murder, and without it murderers would multiply.

In any case, for the Sages, as for the Torah, bloodshed is the ultimate sin, a sin so serious that God cannot abide it. Following the
teachings of the Torah and the Prophets, the Sages condemn bloodshed in the strongest possible terms and make it clear that no ritual
matter can possibly be as important as the preservation of human
life. Furthermore, the taking of human life, even if prescribed in the
Torah itself as a punishment, is a matter of great seriousness and is
not to be lightly—if ever—performed.

D'rash: Personal Reflection

INNOCENT BLOOD

We live in an era in which bloodshed—both real and pretend—
inundates our lives. We watched with horror as bodies tumbled from
the Twin Towers. We see terrorist massacres in city after city, bombs
exploding in Boston, London, Berlin, Paris, buses in flames in Jerusalem, mass shootings in schools. Our screens—large and small—
are also exposed to dramatic depictions of slayings night after night.
What does this do to us? Does it harden us so that we come to take
it for granted, or does it move us to believe that something should
be done to stop it?

I felt the effect of violent bloodshed once several years ago when we were driving north toward the Galilee to view some photographs being exhibited in a museum that I wanted to use in a book I was writing. We stopped for a red light at a well-known crossroads where there was a crowded bus depot filled with soldiers waiting for transportation back to their bases after the Shabbat break. The light changed, and as we moved forward there was a tremendous explosion. It shook our car. We stopped, as did all the traffic ahead of us. I was about to get out to see what had happened when we were told by someone—I don't remember if it was a policeman or a soldier—to drive on and clear the way for emergency vehicles. We continued on our way, terribly shaken. Later we heard the news that there had been a second explosion at the crossroads and that many soldiers had been killed or injured in the two blasts. Had the light not changed, we would have been there for the first explosion. Had we not been told to move on, I might have gone back and been there for the second explosion. As it was, all we had was some shattered lights in the rear of the car.

I never drive by the junction without reliving that experience and thinking of all the innocent lives that were lost, all the blood that was shed at that place.

V

Deuteronomy (Devarim)

Devarim

Words of Rebuke

DEUTERONOMY 1:1–3:22

These are the words that Moses addressed to all Israel on the other side of the Jordan. — Through the wilderness, in the Arabah near Suph, between Paran and Tophel, Laban, Hazeroth, and Di-zahab.
—Deuteronomy 1:1

P'shat: Explanation

Unlike the other four books of the Torah, in which the narrator is not identified, the book of Deuteronomy is presented as the record of a series of speeches by Moses delivered shortly before his death, just before the Israelites crossed over the Jordan to take possession of Canaan. Therefore, these words are the words of Moses, retelling the story of the Israelites' journey and preparing the people for the next steps, warning them against rebelling and promising them blessings and reward for loyalty to the covenant with God.

D'rash: Exposition of the Sages

"These are the words that Moses addressed." Are these the only words he addressed? Did he not write the entire Torah? . . . ["Words," devarim, indicates that] these were words of rebuke. . . .
Rabbi Tarphon says: By the Temple service I swear that I doubt if there is anyone in this generation worthy of rebuking others. Rabbi Eleazar ben Azaria says: By the

233

Temple service I swear that I doubt if there is anyone in this generation who is able to receive rebuke. Rabbi Akiva says: By the Temple service I swear that I doubt if there is anyone in this generation who knows how to rebuke others. Rabbi Yohanan ben Nuri says: I call heaven and earth to witness that Rabbi Akiva received rebuke from me before Rabban Gamliel more than five times when I complained about him and yet I know that he loved me even more each time!
—Sifre Deuteronomy 1

The Sages viewed the opening words of Deuteronomy as problematic. "These are the words that Moses addressed to all Israel" could be interpreted as meaning that Moses spoke "these" words in Deuteronomy and no other words. That would imply that Moses did not say the words in the rest of the Torah, which would contradict one of Rabbinic Judaism's basic tenets: the Torah in toto is the work of Moses.

The Rabbis' solution was to prove (in many sources not quoted here) that often in Scripture, the Hebrew word *devarim* (words) refers specifically to words of rebuke. Therefore, the first verse really means, "These are the *words of rebuke* that Moses addressed to all Israel." Thus the Sages characterized the entire book of Deuteronomy as words of rebuke to the people Israel.

The three Rabbis' statements that follow all concern the question, Under what circumstances should one undertake to rebuke another person? Leviticus 19:17 tells us that we have an obligation to reprove others: "Reprove your kinsman but incur no guilt because of him." Just two verses later (Leviticus 19:19) we are also taught: "Love your fellow as yourself." The Sages see this adjacency as indicating that only if we love our fellow should we feel free to rebuke him. Otherwise, the rebuke is not emanating from the pure motivation of our desire to help him improve himself.

Moses loved the people of Israel. Time after time, when God was angry with them and even threatened their destruction, Moses defended them. Therefore, the Sages believed he had earned the right to be open and frank with the people before departing from them. This was his last opportunity to influence them. As Jacob had done with his sons, Moses too waited until the end of his life before rebuking them so severely.

Each of the three Rabbis then addresses a problematic aspect of rebuke as it pertains to the rest of us.

Rabbi Tarphon teaches that only one who is worthy has the right to tell others what is wrong. The threshold for such worthiness must have been very high, because Tarphon did not believe that anyone of his generation—all those living in the era after the Temple's destruction, including himself—could meet it.

According to Rabbi Eleazar ben Azaria, it is equally important that those being rebuked are capable of understanding the motivation of the rebuke and willing to consider what is being said enough to benefit from it. The ancient Israelites were like that, he upholds, but the Rabbis' own generation is not.

Rabbi Akiva adds that in addition to being worthy enough to rebuke, one also has to know how to conduct the rebuke. There is an art to it, a way of presenting criticism so that it can be accepted. Not everyone can do this, and according to Akiva, such an art did not exist in his time.

Interestingly, Akiva himself was not known for castigating others. In all of his teachings, commentaries, and parables, he never speaks belittlingly about the Jewish people or castigates them for wrongdoing. On the contrary, Akiva is always accepting of others and inclined to overlook others' faults while accepting criticism aimed at himself.

That is what Yohanan ben Nuri's story illustrates. Ben Nuri supervised and disciplined the students at the Yavneh academy, headed by Rabban Gamliel II. When Akiva was a student at Yavneh, sometime in the 80s CE, he was evidently brought up for discipline four or five times—unfortunately, we are never told for what actions. Ben Nuri notes that Akiva did not resent these rebukes, which speaks well for him.

D'rash: Personal Reflection

CONTROLLING CRITICISM

From time to time, all of us who are parents have faced the dilemma of how to deal with a child who is misbehaving in a serious way. Do we get angry and threaten the child? Do we say everything on our mind? I think one would have to be a saint to constantly keep calm and never lose one's temper.

Here it is good to remember that the basis for rebuke is love. If that love exists and has been demonstrated, criticism—especially of an action and not a person's essence, and particularly when delivered so as not to belittle and shame—is more easily accepted and can be effective.

The same principle is true when teachers rebuke children. Having been a teacher, I know how easy it is to become angry with a student and how easy it is then to rebuke the student or become sarcastic. That happened once to my teenage daughters when we came to live in Israel. It was not easy for them to adjust to such a different school and to cope with not being on the same language level as others. Most of their teachers were understanding, but one man seemed to delight in making fun of their Hebrew and embarrassing them in class time after time. My daughters are now adults, grandmothers, in fact, but they have never forgotten that man. They cringe whenever they happen to see him.

As a congregational rabbi I was often faced with the dilemma of how to sermonize about things I thought were wrong in the congregation, in the Jewish community, and/or in the nation at large. First, I had to decide if I had the right to rebuke. Who was I to judge others? Then, I needed to weigh if the congregation was prepared to be rebuked. Might speaking out be helpful, or might it do more harm?

For the most part, I tried to be positive and not negative with the community. Sometimes, though, I determined that not to speak my mind would be to betray the things I truly believed. I would not avoid controversy. Rather, I would carefully choose what I felt was worth the battle and find a way to be fair in speaking of it. Above all, I needed to always remember that the command to rebuke comes only after the command to love one's fellow human being.

Now, reflecting back, I'm certain that at times I made the wrong decision, but I hope I demonstrated enough care and concern for my community that I was forgiven an occasional mistake.

Va-'ethannan

The Grace of God

DEUTERONOMY 3:23-7:11

I pleaded with the Lord at that time, saying, "O Lord God, You who let Your servant see the first works of Your greatness and Your mighty hand, You whose powerful deeds no god in heaven or on earth can equal! Let me, I pray, cross over and see the good land on the other side of the Jordan, that good hill country, and the Lebanon."
—Deuteronomy 3:23-25

P'shat: Explanation

Standing on the threshold of the Land of Promise as the Israelites prepare to cross over the Jordan, Moses, in desperation, tries one last time to persuade God to permit him to enter the land. His plea to God is a moment of great pathos. The word he uses to describe his prayer—*va-'ethanan* (I pleaded)—is not simply a request or a "prayer." Rather, Moses throws himself on God's mercy, begs for God to be gracious—*hanun*.

Unfortunately for Moses, his request is not granted. God permits him to ascend a mountain and look at the land, but he cannot enter it.

D'rash: Exposition of the Sages

Israel had two excellent leaders, Moses and David, King of Israel. The entire world could have been sustained by the merit of their good deeds, yet they never asked anything of God except as an expression of God's freely-given grace. If these two—who

*could have sustained the entire world by the merit of their good
deeds ... never asked anything of God except as an expression
of God's freely-given grace, certainly anyone who is not worth
even one thousand-thousand-thousandth or ten-thousand-ten-
thousandth part of their students should never ask anything
of God except as an expression of God's freely-given grace!*
—Sifre Deuteronomy 26

This Rabbinic saying addresses a very basic question, On what grounds
are we to make a request of God? Are we to say to the Holy One, "I am
worthy, I have performed so many good deeds, I have been loyal to
You and never transgressed—or almost never—and therefore answer
my prayer positively"?

Worthiness would seem to be an appropriate basis for petitioning
God. After all, the Torah itself says time and again that if we observe
the commandments, we will be rewarded, and if we do not, we will
be punished.

Yet the Rabbis are very clear about this: Moses and David *were* worthy. Indeed, for more than forty years Moses had been God's servant,
devoting all his actions to God's service. His and David's good deeds
were so numerous that they sustained the entire world—or could have.

Yet when Moses asks God for permission to enter the land, he
does not say, "Let me enter, because after all I have done I deserve
it!" Rather, he pleads with God to do so because of God's gracious
nature. The word he uses, *va-'ethanan* (I pleaded), reminds the Sages
of the Hebrew word *hinom* (freely). They conclude that Moses did not
ask God to reward him for his actions but for God to grant him grace
freely because of God's goodness. Similarly, David never makes a claim
on God; he, too, entreats God, relying solely on God's benevolence.

The Sages thus established that if Moses and David, who had so
much merit, never invoked it when petitioning God, then the rest of
us, who cannot begin to compare in worth to them, certainly should
not approach God this way. Instead, we should act as they did—asking
God for what we need from the basis of God's graciousness.

This does not mean that one's deeds are unimportant. On the contrary: the Sages taught that to be a Jew is to follow God's commands, acting ethically in all our dealings with our fellow human beings. In effect, in Judaism there is nothing more important than our deeds. Yet our good actions should not be done in expectation of reward but undertaken simply because they are the right things to do.

This insight has been woven inextricably into Jewish prayer. Each morning Jews begin their prayers, "Not upon our merit do we rely when we come in supplication before You, but upon Your great mercy." We also recite an entire prayer called Taḥanun from the same Hebrew root meaning "gracious," calling humbly upon God to show us God's grace. We follow the example of Moses in this week's portion: "*Va-ethannan*—I pleaded with the Lord at that time."

When we join with others in prayer, our services encompass three kinds of prayers to God: praise, thanksgiving, and requests. Notably, both praise and thanksgiving are considered higher forms of worship than requests. Indeed, Jewish tradition has said that in the Messianic Age, prayers connected with praise and requests will be eliminated, and only prayers of thanksgiving will remain. In the meantime, however, while eliminating requests would greatly reduce the number of our prayers and the length of our worship services, this would also deny us the very human desire to express our wants and needs to the Almighty.

The Sages teach us to avoid in our prayers any implication that we deserve God's blessings. Therefore, we should not connect our requests with accounts of our good deeds, and we should avoid asking to be rewarded for doing what we should be doing in any case.

D'rash: Personal Reflection

THE ART OF PRAYER

Although Hebrew liturgy contains praise and thanksgiving as well as requests, requests are the true core of our services. When we pray we are always asking God to give us something that matters to us: grant us a year of good crops, a year of prosperity, a time of peace, healing, and so forth. Our prayer book tends to keep requests to a minimum and confine them to important matters. Of course, individuals may always ask for whatever they want, and some of our requests may be more appropriate than others.

When I was a chaplain in the United States Air Force, one of the strangest things I was ever asked to do was to give a prayer at a wrestling match between the representatives of two squadrons. What was I to say? "Let *our* man win"? "Keep them from killing each other"? I managed to find some excuse as to why I could not be there that evening.

In truth, prayer is a difficult art. Do we really believe that God, the Supreme Power, hears each human prayer and decides whether to grant the request or not? If not, why do we pray? Perhaps because if we do believe in the existence of such a Power, it is important for us to feel that by reaching out to God, we might obtain the guidance and strength to work toward goals that will make our lives meaningful. Prayer also draws our attention to the wonders of life and allows us to demonstrate our appreciation of the world. Prayer is an opportunity to divorce ourselves from the routines of our lives in order to contemplate what is truly vital. Certainly God does not need our prayers, but we do.

Why not simply say whatever is in our hearts rather than attend organized services and repeat the words of traditional prayers that are often difficult to understand? One reason is that the prayer book is the best introduction to Judaism and Jewish belief that exists. We are not only individuals; we are also members of a collective group, the Jewish people, with a shared history and destiny. These prayers serve as a common basis and a common heritage.

Because prayer is difficult and the prayer book is not simple to understand, I have always felt it is important to provide people with a guide to help them appreciate and participate in communal prayer with deeper understanding. Prayer has to be taken seriously if it is to be meaningful. I undertook to write such a book, and *Entering Jew-*

ish Prayer now serves as an introduction to worshippers as well as a text in colleges and seminaries. Later, the Rabbinical Assembly asked me to write a commentary on the Conservative siddur; *Or Ḥadash: A Commentary on Siddur Sim Shalom* was the first time this had ever been done.

When you write books like this, you often wonder if they have any impact. Well, once when I was traveling in the Far East, I spent Shabbat in Singapore. I went to the local synagogue near my hotel. There I discovered an Orthodox congregation with a Moroccan Chabad rabbi following Sephardic traditions and worshipping in a lovely old building financed long ago by the Sasoon family. It could hardly have been more different from the synagogues for which I wrote the siddur commentary.

I sat down in the men's section while my wife was up in the balcony. After a while a man sat down next to me and took out his siddur. His prayer book was the commentary I had written! This was probably the last place in the world I would have expected to see it.

My curiosity aroused, I said to him, "Pardon me—what is that siddur you are using? Where did you get it?" He replied that he was from New Jersey but had been living and working in Singapore for five years. His son was now preparing for his bar mitzvah, and he— the father—wanted to teach him about the prayers. When he was back visiting in New Jersey he had gone into a Jewish bookstore and asked the proprietor for a book that would help him understand the prayers, and the man had recommended this particular commentary. "Is it helpful?" I asked. "Oh yes," he answered. "It's really given me just what I need to know to teach my son." "Do you know who wrote it?" I asked. "Not really," he said and then glanced at the book and read off my name, after which I introduced myself. We both enjoyed the coincidence, and I felt that this was a good indication that the work had been worthwhile.

ʿEkev

Searching for Truth

DEUTERONOMY 7:12–11:25

For the Lord your God is God supreme and Lord supreme,
the great, the mighty, and the awesome God, who shows
no favor and takes no bribe, but upholds the cause of
the fatherless and the widow, and loves the stranger,
providing him with food and clothing. You too must love
the stranger, for you were strangers in the land of Egypt.
—Deuteronomy 10:17–19

P'shat: Explanation

Biblical scholars have long posited that Deuteronomy is the product of a specific group of ideologues who used the format of Moses's farewell speech to convey their understanding of what had happened to the Israelites in their formative years and God's role in their journey. In comparison to earlier books of the Torah, Deuteronomy gave its writers an opportunity to portray God in less anthropomorphic and more abstract ways.

Of the five books, Deuteronomy is the most philosophical and theological. It devotes considerably more time to speaking about God. This particular portion, ʿEkev, is especially God-dominated. According to the scholars, by assuming that Moses is holding forth in a long discourse rather than simply recounting events, the writers capitalize on an opportunity to emphasize their concept of the Lord: YHVH is the specific name of the God of Israel.

The term "the Lord your God," which emphasizes that YHVH alone is the people's God, appears here time and time again in reference to what "the Lord your God" did for you either in freeing you from Egypt, in leading you through the difficulties of the wilderness, or in forgiving the people in the many cases when Israel angered the Lord and Moses pacified God.

The section also describes what "the Lord your God" demands of the people: to love the Lord your God. This phrase is found seven times in chapter 10, verses 12–22 alone. Note that in Hebrew, "your" is in the singular; this is a very personal stipulation addressed to each and every individual.

The essence of the Lord is described in the first verse of this passage in four words: *ha-El*, the God, that is, the only being who is truly God; *ha-gadol*, the Great One; *ha-gibor*, the Mighty One; and *ha-nora*, the Awesome One. All of these emphasize might and power, a being far above human glory and before whom the only proper attitude is reverence.

But lest you think that the Lord is therefore distant and uncaring, the text immediately follows with a depiction of the Lord's attributes, that is, how the Lord relates to humanity. Concerned with fairness and justice, the Lord cares for those most in need within society, the people with little power or influence.

The passage concludes by instructing Israel to follow in the ways of God—what has been termed "the imitation of God." If the Lord loves the needy, so must you.

This section is a lesson in both what to believe and what to do as a result.

D'rash: Exposition of the Sages

Rabbi Pinhas the Priest ben Hama taught: Moses established the appropriate form of prayer: "The great, the mighty, and the awesome God." Jeremiah said, "The great and mighty God" (Jeremiah 32:18)—eliminating "awesome." "Awesome" refers to

the Temple which was destroyed. Where is the awe if
enemies come into God's house and are not in awe?
Daniel said, "The great and awesome God" (Daniel
9:4)—eliminating "mighty." His children have been
captured and imprisoned, so where is God's might?
The Men of the Great Assembly restored greatness to the One
to whom it is due, as it is said, "The great, the mighty, and
the awesome God" (Nehemiah 9:32). Why? They explained:
God is high above any praise humans use to exalt Him.
Said Rabbi Yaakov ben Rabbi Eleazar: Jeremiah
and Daniel knew that God loves truth. Therefore
they did not need to flatter Him.
—Midrash Psalm 19:2

Moses's brief description of the Lord—"The great, the mighty, and the awesome God"—has taken on the role of a creedal declaration, becoming part of the first blessing of the *Amidah*, Judaism's central prayer. It is also quoted several other times in the daily liturgy, a clear indication that the Sages who created the liturgy considered it very important.

Rabbi Pinhas, a fourth-century *amora* born in the Land of Israel, noticed that the same three attributes are found in two other books of the Bible, but in each case one attribute is missing. He explains this by saying that each of the authors felt compelled to omit a given quality because God had not demonstrated that particular attribute in the preceding historical events. How could one call the Lord "awesome" when the Temple had been destroyed? How could one call the Lord "mighty" when God's children had been captured and exiled? When all three attributes appear again, in Nehemiah, it is, Rabbi Pinhas says, because God's greatness is far beyond the human ability to articulate it.

Rabbi Yaakov, however, adds a different thought. He insists that what Jeremiah and Daniel did was correct, because the Lord loves truth above all. If God did not demonstrate might or awe, there was no reason to say that God had done so. Flattery is not appropriate where God is concerned.

There is something both liberating and daring about this statement. It encourages us to raise questions about God and about God's relationship to life events. It teaches that as far as Judaism is concerned, Jews need not be afraid to speak the truth or to ask painful questions.

D'rash: Personal Reflection

SEARCHING FOR TRUTH

This midrash with its emphasis on speaking the truth about God encourages us to question and seek the truth even if it is uncomfortable.

When I began my rabbinical school studies at the Jewish Theological Seminary in New York, I was impressed to discover a faculty devoted to furthering both the observance of Jewish law and its students' freedom of thought and inquiry. My fellow students and I were totally free to question the origin and meaning of Jewish beliefs, dogmas, and practices. Indeed, we were encouraged to probe into and formulate a theology of Judaism that we could actually believe. We studied Bible with professors who made radical proposals for emendations to the text and called into question the historicity of events but who insisted that at Torah readings we pronounce every letter and every traditional vowel correctly. We studied Talmud and Jewish law with experts who picked apart and reconstructed texts and could trace changes and developments in Jewish laws and practices but who still insisted on the maintenance of Jewish practice. Nor were our instructors all of one mind about many subjects. We were taught by people as different as Abraham Joshua Heschel and Mordecai Kaplan and had to make up our own minds about which direction to go.

Kaplan, of course, was the great iconoclast. Challenging everything, he was totally intolerant of sloppy thinking or illogical conclusions.

We could not emerge from his classes without having had to clarify our thoughts and beliefs and therefore being the better for it.

Speaking for myself, I can say that I accepted many of his concepts, certainly that Judaism is a civilization—or, as he later amended that—a religious civilization. But while agreeing with many of his challenges to a traditional concept of the Deity, I could not accept his naturalist theology, in which he saw God as the personification of various processes, "the Power that made for salvation," as he put it, rather than as a being beyond nature. Such a definition seemed to me to lack any possibility of action or purpose and to totally eliminate the idea of a personal God. But he did indeed force me to think.

As a result, several years after receiving my rabbinical degree, I challenged his ideas. In "A God to Match the Universe," an article published in the official organ of his movement, *The Reconstructionist* (March 5, 1965), I accepted many of Kaplan's critiques of the traditional concept of God but contended that what he substituted for it was simply insufficient. In my view, the concept of God had to include a Reality beyond nature. "In place of a God who acts upon the universe in supernatural ways," I suggested, "we must conceive of God as manifested in the evolution of the universe and of man as working through the forces of history and human nature in a way much more complex and much more difficult to understand ... a God who does move, work, plan, and initiate, even if it is in ways we cannot explain."

In the next issue, Kaplan himself responded in his usual forceful and cogent way. Neither of us flattered God. Both of us sought to find the truth.

Re'eh

DEUTERONOMY 11:26–16:17

Do not worship the Lord your God in like manner, but seek only the site that the Lord your God will choose amidst all your tribes as His habitation, to establish His name there. There you are to go, and there you are to bring your burnt offerings and other sacrifices, your tithes and contributions, your votive and free-will offerings, and the firstlings of your herds and flocks. Together with your households, you shall feast there before the Lord your God, happy in all the undertakings in which the Lord your God has blessed you. You shall not act at all as we now act here, every man as he pleases, because you have not yet come to the allotted haven that the Lord your God is giving you. . . . Take care not to sacrifice your burnt offerings in any place you like, but only in the place that the Lord will choose in one of your tribal territories.

—Deuteronomy 12:4–9,13–14

P'shat: Explanation

These verses are nothing less than revolutionary. They present Moses as instructing the Israelites: When you enter the land, you are not to follow the worship practices of the Canaanite inhabitants. Specifically, you are not permitted to bring sacrifices in a multiplicity of sacred sites. Rather, you are to have only one sanctuary, to be established in an unnamed place chosen by God. There and only there are you to come with your offerings. There and only there are you to rejoice before God at the festivals designated and described later in this Torah portion.

The reason for the centralization of the cult is not stated. As the end result, however, eventually Jerusalem and its Temple became the center of Jewish worship and reverence for all time — all this without Jerusalem even being mentioned in the Torah.

This command was particularly revolutionary because worship in multiple sanctuaries was accepted as the norm throughout the rest of the Torah and remained in effect for hundreds of years after the people's entry into the land. Even though only one sanctuary (for many years in Shilo) housed the Ark of the Covenant, other sacred sites were scattered throughout the land, and no one demanded their destruction.

The idea of a sanctuary in Jerusalem did not appear until the time of David. Even then, although it was the royal sanctuary and, especially after Solomon built the Temple, the central and most important one, it was not exclusive. While King Hezekiah ruled (715–687 BCE) there was one brief and unsuccessful attempt to centralize all worship in Jerusalem (2 Kings 18:3–7); it would take another half-century or so, until King Josiah's reign (640–609 BCE), for all other sacrificial sites to be destroyed. A copy of Deuteronomy — or at least a part of it — had been discovered in the Temple, prompting Josiah to undertake this revolution (2 Kings 22:8–23,25).

No one knows for certain when and where Deuteronomy was actually written and if the writers did or did not view Jerusalem as the ideal locus for centralized worship. Nonetheless, because of these verses, from the time of Josiah until the Temple was destroyed not long thereafter in 586 BCE, and again when the Temple was reestablished in the fifth century BCE, no official Temple or shrine was built elsewhere. Jerusalem became the Jewish people's sacred city and the Temple Mount the most holy place in the Jewish world for all time.

Another unexpected consequence was the creation of the synagogue. Since a great many Jews lived too far from the Temple (such as outside the Land of Israel during the Babylonian exile and later throughout the Roman Empire), they needed places of worship near their settlements. Thus a new institution was created—a synagogue, a place of worship where no sacrifices would occur, where Torah study and prayer would be paramount.

The history of Judaism and of worship changed forever because of these verses.

D'rash: Exposition of the Sages

"But seek only the site that the Lord your God will choose
amidst all your tribes as His habitation." Inquire of a prophet.
You might think you have to wait until a prophet tells you,
therefore it says, "but seek"—seek out and find the place. Then
the prophet will inform you. That is what David did, as it is
said, "I will not give sleep to my eyes or slumber to my eyelids
until I find a place for the Lord, an abode for the Mighty One of
Jacob" (Psalm 132:5). For how long [will the present situation
be permitted]? "... because you have not yet come to the allotted
haven...." A non-permanent altar was permitted from the
time of resting in the land until the time of allotment. As it is
said, "This is My resting place for all time; here I will dwell
for I desire it" (Psalm 132:14). "Resting place refers to Shilo,
while allotted haven refers to Jerusalem," so says Rabbi Judah.
—Sifre Deuteronomy 62,66

For the Sages living at the time of the Second Temple or following its destruction, there was no question that the place in which God would forever dwell was Jerusalem.

Moses, however, never mentioned the city. Thus the Rabbis wondered how the Israelites knew where to build the one central sanctuary. To them the answer was obvious: ask a prophet. That's what King David did. He would not rest until he knew where to locate the final place for the Ark and the shrine.

The Sages wrestled with another difficulty: When did this law come into effect? After all, as everyone knew, for centuries the final resting place had not been found, and for some two hundred years the Ark had rested in a tent in Shilo.

The Sages concluded that the law requiring one permanent sanctuary was not in effect when the Israelites arrived in the land—a period the Rabbis called "the time of resting." The stipulation did not become law until the people came into possession of Jerusalem, "the allotted haven." Thus, until then a temporary altar was still permitted.

In a sense, through their interpretations the Sages gave final approval to King David's choice of Jerusalem as the site for the main sanctuary. Jerusalem, they asserted, was what God had always intended and indeed what Moses had commanded in Deuteronomy. Shilo was a legitimate sanctuary, but only temporarily, until Jerusalem came into David's hands. From then on it was Jerusalem and only Jerusalem forever.

D'rash: Personal Reflection

THE VISION OF JERUSALEM

I have lived in Jerusalem for more than half of my life. I was here as a student in the days when Jerusalem was a divided city, when Jews were cut off from its ancient section and its most sacred sites. I have seen it grow and expand and become Israel's largest city. I am well aware of its problems and its difficulties, but I still succumb to its magic and am thrilled every time I drive up the hill in my neighborhood of East Talpiot and see the panorama of the city rise in front of me—the new buildings to the left, Mount Scopus and the Mount of Olives to the right, the walls of the Old City, the Western Wall, the golden Dome of the Rock straight ahead. The very thought that the hilltop ahead may be the place where Abraham and Isaac halted on their way to Mount Moriah, the knowledge that this was the city conquered by David and glorified by Solomon, the place where great prophets walked and taught, where Ezra proclaimed the sanctity of the Torah, all this and so much more excite the imagination. No wonder Jerusalem has always had a special place in my heart.

My connection to Jerusalem was strengthened and given even greater meaning several years ago when Israel undertook a year of celebration marking three thousand years since the founding of Jerusalem as David's capital. The American committee for the celebration commissioned a book about Jerusalem for that occasion, and in 1994 I was asked to write it. Imagine my delight at being given the opportunity to spend a year or more in libraries reading everything I could find written by Jews about Jerusalem.

I thought then that I knew a great deal about Jerusalem, but I learned much more about the city and its importance in Jewish tradition than I expected. I gained a true appreciation of what Jerusalem had come to represent in Judaism. It was the symbol of God's Presence, of the moral and ethical society God desired us to create. Even more important than its past, it also represented the hope of a peaceful future for all of humankind. I was especially pleased when the legendary mayor of Jerusalem, Teddy Kollek, agreed to write the book's preface and even gave me a lapel pin of a lion, the symbol of the city, which I wear with pride.

When the book, *The Jerusalem Anthology*, was published, I signed two special copies bound in leather for Prime Minister Yitzhak Rabin and President Bill Clinton. Rabin's copy was presented to him at the opening event of the year-long celebration, held in October 1995 in the magnificent rotunda of the Capitol in Washington, DC, in the presence of the vice president, senators, Supreme Court judges, and many others. I was privileged to attend.

The main speaker was Yitzhak Rabin. Rabin was not usually an eloquent speaker, especially in English, but on that occasion he spoke beautifully, movingly, and very personally about his own childhood in Jerusalem.

President Clinton was given the book at a banquet, and I later received a gracious thank-you letter from him. But I never received one from Rabin. The reason for that is all too well known and painful. This event was his last public appearance in America. He left immediately thereafter, returned to Israel, and within a matter of days was assassinated at a peace rally in Tel Aviv on November 4, 1995. And with him died the hopes we had at that time for true peace in Jerusalem and all of Israel.

Yet such dreams and hopes should never die. I still pray that we will all see the time when Jerusalem will indeed be what its name implies—a city of true peace. In the words of the prophet Isaiah about his dream of the future of Jerusalem, "For instruction shall come forth from Zion, the word of the Lord from Jerusalem. . . . Nation shall not take up sword against nation; They shall never again know war" (Isaiah 2:3–4).

Shofetim

Justice for All

You shall appoint magistrates and officials for your tribes, in all the settlements that the Lord your God is giving you, and they shall govern the people with due justice. You shall not judge unfairly; you shall show no partiality; you shall not take bribes, for bribes blind the eyes of the discerning and upset the plea of the just. Justice, justice shall you pursue, that you may thrive and occupy the land that the Lord your God is giving you.
—Deuteronomy 16:18–22

P'shat: Explanation

Moses is preparing Israel to become an independent nation on the people's own land, with all the responsibility that implies. Here Moses addresses many of their newfound needs: a leader, an army, rules of warfare.

But first and foremost is the need for enforcement of justice. Officials who will enforce the laws—magistrates—have to be appointed, as do judges, who will hear cases and decide upon each individual's guilt or innocence, throughout the land. How is this to be done?

Some forty years earlier, when the people began their journey, Moses had created a system of justice. "I charged your magistrates at that time as follows, 'Hear out your fellow man, and decide justly between any man and a fellow Israelite or a stranger. You shall not be partial in judgment: hear out low and high alike'" (Deuteronomy 1:16–17). Now Moses commands the people to create such a justice

254

system in their new land, throughout all their settlements. And again, his first demand is that justice be impartial.

He warns them against permitting their judges to become corrupt through accepting bribes (a concern that resonates to this day). Note the repetition of the word "justice" — "Justice, justice shall you pursue" — to emphasize that justice is the key to good governance. Furthermore, it is so important that the people must pursue it — they are not to be passive and not to take it for granted. It is so important that if justice does not exist, the people will not thrive and will not remain in the land God is giving them.

Elsewhere, Moses has warned the people that their possession of the land is dependent upon their obedience to God's commands. Here, he singles out one specific matter of supreme importance — and it is not adherence to ritual but adherence to impartial justice for all who live in the land.

D'rash: Exposition of the Sages

> It was taught: When there is a case between an Israelite and a heathen, if you can rule for the Israelite using Jewish law, do so and say, "This is our law." If you can rule in his favor using heathen law, do so and say, "This is your law." If you cannot do either, then use subterfuges to rule against the heathen. This is the rule of Rabbi Ishmael, but Rabbi Akiva says we should not use subterfuges because of the Sanctification of God's Name. ... It was taught by Rabbi Akiva, "Robbery of a heathen is forbidden [by the Torah]."
> — Bava Kamma 113a

> Rabbi Ishmael interpreted the verse "Hear the causes between your brethren and judge righteously" (Deut. 1:16) to mean that judging righteously applied only to your fellow Jew — i.e. "your brethren." Therefore, in the case of a Jew and non-Jew he would always rule in favor of the Jew regardless of

*whether they chose to be judged according to the rules of Israel
or those of the nations. Rabban Shimon ben Gamliel, on the
other hand said that one must rule according to whichever
system the litigants agree upon and follow that law.*
— Sifre Deuteronomy 16

The political situations faced by the early Sages (the end of the first
century and beginning of the second century CE) and the Israelites
as depicted in Deuteronomy were completely different. Deuteronomy is addressing an independent nation ruling over its own land
and the population of that land. By contrast, when the Sages lived,
there was no Jewish sovereignty; the land had become a province of
Rome, and the only official courts and judges were those appointed
by Rome. Unofficial Jewish courts judged by Jewish law. Since Jews
and non-Jews—pagans—lived in mixed communities and did business together, sometimes cases arose in which one litigant was Jewish and the other pagan. At such times the litigants could decide to
come before a Jewish court and task the Jewish court to follow either
Jewish or Roman law.

Relations between Jews and non-Jews were complicated. On the
one hand, they had to live together and do business together. On the
other, most Jews certainly resented the Romans, who were there as
conquerors and not as friendly neighbors. Furthermore, Jews in general felt that paganism and its practices were without value and that
some pagans were untrustworthy. With some justification, many Sages
despised the Romans and viewed all non-Jews as supporters of Rome.

Some Jews had personal reasons for resenting the Romans. As
one example, according to tradition (*Gittin* 58a), the Romans had
enslaved Rabbi Ishmael (quoted in the above passage) when he was a
youth. That may explain why Rabbi Ishmael declares that the Torah's
demands for justice and just courts apply only to Jews; non-Jews can
be tricked, and Jewish judges should always favor Jews. The Torah
itself justifies this stance, he contends.

Yet his contemporary and frequent opponent in matters of law and interpretation, Rabbi Akiva, himself no friend of Rome, disagrees. Justice is justice, Rabbi Akiva affirms, and a court must always be just. Going even further, Rabbi Akiva asserts that the Torah forbids cheating non-Jews and that doing so is a double sin, since it also involves the desecration of God's Name, whereas being honest and just brings praise to the Name of the Lord.

D'rash: Personal Reflection

ATTITUDES TOWARD NON-JEWS

The fact that such an important Rabbinic authority as Rabbi Ishmael could rule that it is not only permissible but required to pervert justice in favor of a Jew and thus to deprive a non-Jew of justice indicates that within official Jewish tradition there are those who treat non-Jews in ways we would not want non-Jews to treat us.

Even today, in the twenty-first century, some extremist rabbis teach these concepts, instructing their students that non-Jews are less worthy, even less human, than Jews. This might not have bothered me too much if it were just a question of theory and not of practice, but, living in Israel, I've seen that some Jews have been sufficiently influenced by these teachings to take actions against non-Jews and non-Jewish houses of worship, damaging buildings, sometimes injuring others, and even causing deaths. There have also been prejudiced rulings. For example, one Israeli rabbinical authority ruled that the Torah forbids renting rooms or apartments to Arab students near the universities where they study. Whatever happened to "justice, justice"? What about the Torah's teaching that all human beings are equal, all created in the divine image, all descended from one human pair, and therefore all brothers and sisters?

As I mentioned before, I decided this must not go unnoticed and therefore wrote a responsum on the status of Gentiles in Jewish law today. It deals extensively with the question of how we should handle negative or discriminatory statements regarding non-Jews in traditional Jewish literature. I was particularly interested in the educational aspect of the subject because of experiences my children had had in a religious school where teachers had made no attempt to explain the context of these negative statements when teaching Rabbinic texts and had not stopped their students from making negative statements about Arabs during school trips.

Surveying the classic Jewish literature on the subject, I was able to show that although negative statements about non-Jews do appear in the literature of the Sages and in medieval and later mystical writings, including Hasidic works, the Torah itself takes a uniformly positive attitude toward non-Jews. The Torah definitely accords non-Jews the status of human beings created in God's image and does not legally discriminate against them. Furthermore, the negative statements in Rabbinic writings are far outweighed by the positive statements. The greatest authorities, such as Rabbi Akiva, were opposed to such discrimination and undertook to eliminate any discriminatory rulings from Jewish law.

The responsum concluded:

Living in an interconnected world when enlightened religious leaders of all faiths are seeking ways of reconciliation, we as Jews, whether living in the Diaspora with equal rights, or in Israel where we have the responsibility of caring for the rights of our fellow citizens of minority groups, cannot allow ourselves to be influenced by teachings that disseminate hatred and disdain for human beings of whatever nation or faith. Rather, following the rulings of Rabban Gamliel, Rabbi Akiva, and the later teachings of the medieval authority the Meiri and others, we declare that all rules discriminating against Gentiles in matters of a civil nature and moral actions are no longer to be considered authoritative in Judaism, not only because of the harm they cause to the image of Judaism and to relations with non-Jews, but because they are intrinsically immoral and deter us from attaining the honest virtues to which we aspire as Jews.

Furthermore, the responsum urged Jewish educators everywhere to revise their curricular material to positively address these issues.

I was particularly pleased when a group of Israeli educators took this seriously enough to engage in dialogue with me about methods for dealing with this in their schools.

Ki Tetse'

Cruelty versus Kindness

*If, along the road, you chance upon a bird's nest, in any tree or
on the ground, with fledglings or eggs and the mother sitting
over the fledglings or on the eggs, do not take the mother
together with her young. Let the mother go, and take only the
young, in order that you may fare well and have a long life.*
—Deuteronomy 22:10

P'shat: Explanation

This Torah portion constitutes another collection of individual laws
that are to be put into effect once the Israelites have their own land.
Some of these laws are serious and severe, such as those concerning
a "wayward and defiant son" (Deuteronomy 21:18–21) and against
adultery (Deuteronomy 22:22). Others seem less important, such as
permission to eat grapes from someone else's field (Deuteronomy
23:25) and prohibiting the muzzling of an ox when it is threshing
(Deuteronomy 25:4).

The law cited above is extremely unusual and totally unrelated to
any of the others. Why are we suddenly to be so concerned about birds
and birds' nests? Not only that, but of all the laws in this collection,
only this one carries a reward: if you do this, you will "fare well and
have a long life." The negative consequence, should one not take the
stipulated action, is implied.

Notably, this particular reward is promised upon obedience of only
one other law in the Torah: the commandment to honor one's parents.
Deuteronomy 5:16 so concludes, that you may long endure, and that

you may fare well in the land that the Lord your God is assigning you."
Is the Torah really equating the bird's nest law with the command to
honor one's parents? So it seems. Both are concerned with parents
and their offspring, even if in one case the parents are human and in
the other they are birds of the air.

This, too, is one of three Torah commandments addressing humane
treatment of animals. The others are the prohibition against slaughtering an animal and its young on the same day (Leviticus 22:28) and
against boiling a kid in its mother's milk, which appears three times
in the Torah (Deuteronomy 14:21; Exodus 23:19, 34:26). The commonalities in all three—the relationship between a creature and its
young—cannot be coincidental.

Will the mother bird feel less pain if she is sent away before the
young are taken? It is doubtful. Will the kid feel less pain if it is boiled
in the milk of some other animal? Equally doubtful. Nonetheless, even
if abiding by the prohibitions does not have a merciful effect upon the
creatures involved, there is something inherently cruel about doing
those things. The merciful effect is upon us as human beings, who
are being sensitized against cruelty.

D'rash: Exposition of the Sages

[Elisha ben Abuya] was once sitting and studying in the
valley of Ginosar when he saw a man climb to the top of a
palm tree where he took the mother bird with her fledglings
and then descended peacefully. The next day he saw another
man climb to the top of the palm tree where he took the
fledglings and sent away the mother bird, descended and
was bitten by a serpent and died. He [Elisha] said, "It is
written 'in order that you may fare well and have a long
life!' Where is the happiness he deserved? Where is his long
life?" He [Elisha] was unaware of the interpretation that
Rabbi Jacob had given that "in order that you may fare well"

refers to the world to come where all is well, and "have a
long life" refers to the future when all lasts for a long time.
—Jerusalem Talmud *Haggiga* 2:1,77b

Elisha ben Abuya, a contemporary of Rabbi Akiva, was one of four
Sages who, under Akiva's guidance, practiced mystical exercises known
as "entering into paradise," that is, attempting to reach the highest
heavens and be in the Divine Presence. Except for Akiva, all the others suffered bad consequences. Elisha became a heretic. Exactly what
engendered his abandonment of Jewish observance and belief in God
is the subject of different traditions, one of which is described above.

The essence of the story is that Elisha witnessed instances of a
wicked person who prospers and a good person who suffers—in
this case, actually dies. This is the opposite of what religion generally
teaches—that those who observe the commandments are rewarded
and those who disobey are punished. And this case is even more
extreme, since the Torah specifically states that obeying this commandment will result in the follower's long life, but exactly the opposite happens.

Thus, observing that the world does not follow the reward-and-
punishment pattern he had been led to believe in, Elisha abandons his
beliefs. The traditional definition of an atheist is one who says, "There
is no Judge, and there is no justice"; that is what Elisha determined.

The Talmud story adds that Elisha did not know of the alternate
interpretation of the assured reward, namely, that it did not refer to a
reward in this world but to a subsequent reward in the world to come.
It is unlikely, however, that this would have satisfied him.

Rabbi Jacob recognizes that the literal interpretation of that verse
cannot be true, so he looks for another way to understand it. Other
Sages also recognize that all too often the righteous suffer and the
wicked prosper, and they seek out ways to understand this. Eventually, though, they too come to the conclusion that there are no easy
answers to this dilemma and that belief in God and God's goodness
must become a matter of faith in the eventual triumph of good in

this world. More importantly, one must take the two positions that we cannot possibly understand everything that happens in our vast and complicated universe, and goodness is its own reward.

The problem that confronted Elisha and all believing monotheists remains to be solved: how to account for suffering and evil in a world created by a good, just, and merciful God.

Still today, many believing Jews cling to the belief that suffering is a punishment for sin and prosperity a reward for righteousness. Whenever calamity strikes, they explain it by pointing to some dereliction in religious observance.

Fortunately, long ago Judaism questioned that belief. The second-century *tanna* Rabbi Yannai taught, "It is not in our power to explain the prosperity of the wicked or the suffering of the righteous" (Pirkei Avot 4:15). Centuries before, the book of Job told of a righteous man who suffers terrible calamity. Visiting him, ostensibly to comfort him, his "friends" try to convince him to admit that somehow he sinned, and so his suffering was deserved. Job, however, clings to his innocence at all costs: "Until I die I will maintain my integrity. I persist in my righteousness and will not yield" (Job 27:5–6). In the end God appears and proclaims that indeed Job was correct, and the others were mistaken: "You have not spoken the truth about Me as did My servant Job" (Job 42:7). Job was righteous, and his suffering was undeserved.

God's speech to Job does not really solve the problem; instead, it questions if human beings are capable of understanding the order of the magnificent universe God created, a place where order, including moral order, does exist.

Another book, Ruth, presents a similar case of a just person, Naomi, a female Job, who suffers terrible calamity. The book of Ruth, however, shows that there is a human response to suffering: *hesed*, acts of human kindness. One human being can give assistance to another, thereby enabling the afflicted individual to overcome suffering and return to life. Here, Ruth performs the service of *hesed* for Naomi, her mother-in-law, by accompanying her on a journey Naomi had planned to make alone from Moab to Bethlehem, bereft of her two sons. Later, a landowner and farmer, Boaz, helps them both by providing them with sustenance. Further on, Boaz and Ruth marry. The child born to them, Obed, recompenses Naomi for her lost children and returns her to a happy life.

D'rash: Personal Reflection

NO EASY ANSWERS

As a rabbi I was often present for members of my community who were experiencing undeserved suffering.

I remember with pain one particular instance. A family with whom I was closely involved not only as their rabbi but as a friend suffered a terrible loss. They were Holocaust survivors who had been blessed with daughters but who also wanted a son. Finally, a son was born to them. When this long-awaited child was still very young, he died suddenly from unexplained causes.

What was I to do? What was I to say? I decided that neither words of comfort nor attempts at theological explanations were appropriate. To utter clichés I did not believe would only worsen the situation. All I could offer them was to be with them, to do whatever was needed to be done, to give a simple eulogy lauding them and the love they had given to their child. I offered them love and joined in their mourning, seeing to it that they had all possible support from their friends and community. If they asked questions, I tried to answer them honestly whenever possible and to speak the truth—that some questions have no answers.

Drawing from some of the concepts discussed earlier, I also tried to assure the family that their suffering was not a punishment from God; instead, all human life is replete with both happiness and sorrow. Illness and death are not related to one's merit or lack thereof. On the other hand, it is hard to understand the world and life without a belief in something more than ourselves and above nature— something that we call God.

Their loss remained with them forever, but they went on with their lives and continued to be believing Jews and observant in whatever ways they could.

The questioning of faith and belief is always legitimate, even if there are no ultimate answers. In the end, the best we can offer is human kindness, which brings with it help and consolation.

Ki Tavo'

Coming to the Land

DEUTERONOMY 26:1–29:8

*When you enter the land that the Lord your God is giving
you as a heritage, and you possess it and settle in it, you shall
take some of every first fruit of the soil, which you harvest
from the land that the Lord your God is giving you, put it in
a basket, and go to the place where the Lord your God will
choose to establish His name. You shall go to the priest in
charge at that time and say to him, "I acknowledge this day
before the Lord your God that I have entered the land that
the Lord swore to our fathers to assign to us." . . . You shall
then recite as follows before the Lord your God: "My father
was a fugitive Aramean. He went down to Egypt with meager
numbers and sojourned there; but there he became a great
and very populous nation. The Egyptians dealt harshly with
us and oppressed us; they imposed heavy labor upon us. We
cried to the Lord, the God of our fathers, and the Lord heard
our plea and saw our plight, our misery and our oppression.
The Lord freed us from Egypt by a mighty hand, by an
outstretched arm and awesome power, and by signs and
portents. He brought us to this place and gave us this land,
a land flowing with milk and honey. Wherefore I now bring
the first fruits of the soil which You, O Lord, have given me."*

—Deuteronomy 26:1–3,5–10

P'shat: Explanation

Most of these verses may be extremely familiar to readers because they are recited as the very heart of the Passover seder. They originated, however, not in connection with Passover but with the ceremony of the First Fruits—*Bikkurim*—declaring each individual's thanksgiving for the privilege of being in the land and harvesting its fruits. During the ceremony, which could be performed anytime from Shavuot to Sukkot, each Israelite would lay the fruits of the land out before God, as it were, in acknowledgment and appreciation of the bounty received. The individual would then acknowledge that God's promises to Abraham, Isaac, and Jacob both to bring their descendants to the Land of Canaan and to grant that land to them had been fulfilled—the fruits were the tangible proof of that.

Each person then recited verses that amounted to a condensed version of the Israelites' journey as related over many chapters in the Torah—the descent into Egypt, the growth of the nation, Israel's enslavement, God's intervention to free the people, bringing them to the land "flowing with milk and honey." This recitation was truly a *Reader's Digest* rendition of the history of the Israelites from Abraham through Joshua. So when the Sages were searching for a brief and cogent way to tell the story of the Exodus, this recitation was the obvious choice. At the seder only four verses are recited, beginning with "My father" and ending with "signs and portents."

Notably, in the First Fruits ceremony when the Temple still existed, the Israelites recited a fifth verse, which speaks of coming to the land and leads into bringing the produce of the land, but this last verse is not found in the Haggadah. One possible explanation is that when the Haggadah was compiled, the land was no longer in Jewish hands. Jews were living there, but under Roman control. Therefore, to recite the fifth verse would have been to describe a part of the promise that was not then realized. If that is the case, perhaps consideration should be given to reinstating the verse at the Passover seder now that Jewish sovereignty has been restored.

On the other hand, the rationale for the deleted verse may have been that the Exodus rather than the coming to the land is the subject of the seder. The opposite is true of the First Fruits declaration, in which coming to the Land of Canaan and possessing it are being celebrated.

D'rash: Exposition of the Sages

*How were the first fruits brought up [to Jerusalem]?
... Early in the morning the leader of the group would say,
"Come let us go up to Zion, to the Lord our God!" (Jeremiah
31:6).... They were led by an ox with horns covered with
gold and an olive wreath on its head. The flute was played
before them. When they were close to Jerusalem they sent
a messenger to announce their coming and displayed their
offering. Representatives of the Temple went out to meet
them.... They would be greeted in accord with the size of
their group. The artisans of Jerusalem would greet them
saying, "Brothers of such and such a place, we welcome you
with delight!" The flute would be played before them as
they proceeded to the Temple Mount. When they reached
the Temple Mount each would place the basket on his
shoulder—even if he were King Agrippa—and walk to the
Temple Court. There the Levites would sing, "I extol you,
O Lord, for you have lifted me up, and not let my enemies
rejoice over me" (Psalm 30:2).... With the basket still on
his shoulder he would recite the entire passage beginning
"I acknowledge this day before the Lord your God ..."*
—Bikkurim 3:2,4,6

*"... that I have entered the land that the Lord swore to
our fathers to assign to us." Thus including proselytes
who bring [their first fruits] and also make this*

declaration since to Abraham it was said, "... For I
make you the father of a multitude of nations" (Genesis
17:6). He was the father of all who enter under the
wings of the Presence of God, and Abraham was
promised that his progeny would inherit the land.
—Midrash Ha-Gadol Ki Tavo to the verse

This Mishnah tractate, edited ca. 200 CE, 130 years after the Second Temple's destruction, records this detailed description of groups arriving at the Jerusalem Temple in joyous procession, their first fruits offerings in hand. From a simple individual ceremony, the First Fruits ritual had evolved into a considerably more elaborate affair involving large groups of people, processions, and music—very much a public celebration.

The Sages recorded this rich description, preserving its many details, so that when the Temple was restored they could reproduce the ceremony in all its glory. The account also includes exactly what the Sages thought should be done and who could do it. They were especially concerned that it be inclusive; everyone, rich and poor, educated and uneducated, should experience it.

Reading it helps us to appreciate what a joyous undertaking this was. The ceremony was not performed in a simple, perfunctory way, just to fulfill a duty, but with music and glorious ornamentation as an expression of joy and gratitude not merely for the fruit but for the land itself. Individuals came as part of a group, but each individual brought his own basket and made his own declaration acknowledging that he personally had come to the land God had promised Abraham. Of course, by that time no one participating had actually come to the land—that wording was more appropriate for those who had actually come from the desert with Moses and entered under Joshua's leadership, since the verse says "*I* have entered the land" (emphasis mine). Nevertheless, hundreds of years later, each person was encouraged to feel as if he too had made that journey and entered the land promised to his ancestors.

The midrash adds that even those not of Jewish birth who had joined the Jewish people through conversion would say these same words, because once converted they were considered to be the true children of Abraham to whom the promise was made.

D'rash: Personal Reflection

CELEBRATING COMING TO THE LAND

When I drive back from the coastal area near Tel Aviv up through the Judean hills to Jerusalem, following the way these processions would have come, I often try to picture them in my mind. What would it have been like to participate in this ceremony, actually carrying produce that one had grown and offering it as a concrete symbol of having a land of one's own? Although I obviously did not make that journey from Egyptian slavery through the wilderness to freedom, as one who did come on *aliyah* to the Land of Israel I can at least identify with that experience. Just as at Passover each person is enjoined to feel as if he or she had personally participated in the Exodus, perhaps those who live in Israel today should also have a ceremony that would reproduce the wonder of coming to the land.

As I see it, from the description in the Torah and the later elaborations, this ceremony was intended for one thing: to emphasize the centrality of the Land of Israel to Judaism and the Jewish people. The coming to and settling in the land, enabling it to bring forth its produce, are the cause for celebration: "And you shall enjoy, together with the Levite and the stranger in your midst, all the bounty that the Lord your God has bestowed upon you and your household" (Deuteronomy 26:11).

The role that the land plays in Judaism is often underestimated and misunderstood by non-Jews, since there is really nothing comparable in other religions. Once I was asked to present a paper entitled "The Role of the Land in Jewish Tradition" at an interfaith conference. I attempted to show that the land is a major component of Judaism and of our lives as Jews, whether we live in Israel or not. Since the audience was composed of Christian clergy whose knowledge of the Hebrew Bible is usually quite comprehensive, I pointed out that the narrative of the Torah beginning with Abraham and continuing through Deuteronomy is, after all, basically the story of how the Israelites were granted the land, journeyed to it, and then entered it. I also noted that many of the Torah's laws are specific to the land and not applicable outside of it. I specifically described the First Fruits ceremony mandated by the Torah and elaborated by later authorities, calling attention to the fact that it was a religious ceremony designed to remind the Jewish people that coming to and settling in the land were the entire purpose of the divine promise made to the Patriarchs. The realization of the ideals of the Torah could only be fully implemented in a land of our own.

Furthermore, I explained, one of the most important words in both Judaism and Christianity is "redemption," yet its meaning is very different for both faiths. Whereas in Christianity redemption means saving the individual from sin and its consequences, in Judaism redemption usually means saving the Jewish people from exile and bringing them back to their own land.

From the ensuing discussion, I gathered that for many participants this was a revelation, a new way of looking at the Torah and its narrative. At the very least, it was considered important enough that the group sponsoring the conference included this lecture in a publication they later disseminated.

Other Jewish holidays celebrate the Exodus, the Creation, the Revelation. Entering the land has no holiday of its own, but it has this ceremony and this declaration. Unfortunately, the ceremony itself is no longer practiced, but its meaning should not be forgotten. To eliminate the land from Judaism is to remove its heart.

Nitsavim

Not in the Heavens

DEUTERONOMY 29:9–30:20

Surely, this Instruction which I enjoin upon you this day is not too baffling for you, nor is it beyond reach. It is not in the heavens, that you should say, "Who among us can go up to the heavens and get it for us and impart it to us, that we may observe it?" Neither is it beyond the sea, that you should say, "Who among us can cross to the other side of the sea and get it for us and impart it to us, that we may observe it?" No, the thing is very close to you, in your mouth and in your heart, to observe it.

—Deuteronomy 30:11–14

P'shat: Explanation

Moses is nearing the conclusion of his speech to the people. He has just warned them once again that their remaining in the new land is dependent upon their adherence to all of God's laws and statutes. Now, speaking with a touch of sarcasm, Moses emphasizes that the Israelites have no excuse not to obey the commands, as might be the case if the instructions had not been fully communicated or were difficult to understand. On the contrary, the people have them in hand. They received the laws directly—their parents heard God speak of some laws, and Moses has conveyed all the rest. The instructions are not esoteric. The people do not have to ascend to the heavens or undertake a difficult journey overseas to comprehend them. The instructions are already within their hearts and minds, so they can easily be observed.

One novelty of the religion of Israel was that it did not require the worshipper to undergo mysterious rites in order to understand it. Also, unlike most other religions of the time, one did not have to be a philosopher to know what to do in order to follow God's will. Nor was such knowledge confined to a select group of Priests who alone could fathom the will of the gods. For the first time everything was laid out before an entire people.

Uniquely as well, the laws of the Torah were written and available to all. Parents were commanded to teach them to their children. This explains why the ability to read was so prevalent among the Israelites. Throughout the ages Jewish education and literacy were important not only for the priesthood and the elite but for the masses too.

This had an enormous influence on Jews through the ages. In medieval times, when only members of the Christian clergy were literate—and not all of them—Jews were capable of reading and understanding their Scripture as well as the language of their country. If Jews were known as "the people of the book," it was not only because they prized the Torah but because books and literacy were integral to the lives of all Jews.

D'rash: Exposition of the Sages

Rabbi Eliezer declared the oven of Akhnai pure while the Sages declared it impure. On that day Rabbi Eliezer brought all the possible arguments but the others did not accept them. He then said to them, "If the law is as I say let this carob tree prove it!" The carob tree then moved one hundred cubits from its place. They retorted, "No proof can be brought from a carob tree." Again he said, "If the law is as I say let the stream of water prove it!" The stream of water then flowed backwards. They retorted, "No proof can be brought from a stream of water." He then said to them, "If the law is as I say let the walls of the study house prove it!" The walls then inclined as if to fall.... They remain that way till today. He then said to them, "If the

*law is as I say let Heaven itself prove it!" A Heavenly Voice
then proclaimed, "Why do you argue with Rabbi Eliezer?
The law always agrees with him!" Rabbi Joshua then arose
and exclaimed, "It is not in the heavens!" . . . The Torah has
already been given so we do not heed a Heavenly Voice. . . .
Rather, "one must incline after the majority" (Exodus 23:2).*
—Bava Mezia 59b

*Moses said to them, "Do not say that another Moses will come
and bring us a different Torah from heaven. I tell you now, 'It
is not in the heavens'—no part of Torah remains in heaven."*
—Deuteronomy Rabbah 8:6

This wonderful legendary account of a dispute between the great
Rabbi Eliezer ben Hyrcanus and the other Sages, many of them his
pupils, has had a tremendous influence upon the development of
Jewish law. Eliezer, the outstanding pupil of Rabban Yohanan ben
Zakai and the teacher of Rabbi Akiva, was the leading legal authority of his time (the end of the first century CE and the beginning of
the second century). Nevertheless, in this seemingly minor dispute
concerning the ritual purity of an oven, the majority of the Sages dis-
agree with his decision—and following the dispute, they decide that
in this and in all other matters, the majority rules. This latter decision is based upon an interpretation of a few words in Exodus 23:2
taken out of context (as the Sages often do) and understood to mean
"follow the majority."

Even more importantly, this story elucidates that decisions about
Jewish law are not to be determined on the basis of miracles or through
heavenly oracles but by logical reasoning alone and via majority vote.
Wonder workers or pseudo-miracle workers are to have no role in
legal decisions.

Furthermore, the text goes so far as to say that even if we are to
hear a voice from heaven that might actually reflect divine will, we
are to pay it no attention, because, as Moses had said, "It is not in

the heavens." Whereas Moses had used those words to teach that divine instruction was given to the people and therefore was easily within reach, the Sages give Moses's statement a different meaning: we are no longer to look to heaven for instruction. Once the Torah was proclaimed, the authority moved from the realm of the heavenly to the realm of earth—to the power of the human mind to interpret it. Thus, we humans will no longer wait for a divine voice to tell us what is to be done. Whatever God wanted to give us is already here. From now on it is up to us humans—aka the Sages—to interpret it properly.

Furthermore, the Sages understood "it is not in the heavens" to mean that revelation was complete. If others were to say, "We have a new instruction that supersedes what you have," Jews were not to accept it. This, in fact, was an argument against a Jewish-Christian group active at the time that spoke about a "New Covenant" in contrast to the "Old Covenant." At a later time this argument was also applied to Mohammed's teachings.

D'rash: Personal Reflection

IN PRAISE OF REASON

My own reaction to the story of this Rabbinic dispute is to be ever so thankful that Judaism did not go in the direction of one central figure who could determine Jewish law or fall under the spell of a leader with supposedly supernatural powers. How easy it might have been to accept an outstanding Sage as infallible, invest him with the power to decide everything, and grant that his rulings were incontrovertible. Alternatively, we could have gone the way of appointing someone to lead us who seemed to have supernatural powers, but we did not. Instead we said, "It is not in the heavens." Where would we be now had our Sages not invoked this principle but instead heeded the voice and concluded that they had no choice but to accept Rabbi Eliezer's opinion even though they disagreed with it?

Va-yelekh

Caring for the Flock

DEUTERONOMY 31:1–30

Moses went and spoke these things to all Israel. He said to them: I am now one hundred and twenty years old, I can no longer come and go. Moreover the Lord has said to me, "You shall not go across yonder Jordan." The Lord your God Himself will cross over before you; and He Himself will wipe out those nations from your path and you shall dispossess them. Joshua is the one who shall cross before you, as the Lord has spoken. . . .

Then Moses called Joshua and said to him in the sight of all Israel: "Be strong and resolute, for it is you who shall go with this people into the land that the Lord swore to their fathers to give them, and it is you who shall apportion it to them. And the Lord Himself will go before you. He will be with you: He will not fail you or forsake you. Fear not and be not dismayed!"

—Deuteronomy 31:1–3,7–8

P'shat: Explanation

As the time of his death draws near, Moses takes further steps to prepare the people for what is to come. His successor has already been chosen (Numbers 27:15–18). Now he announces that he will die. He is old, he has no strength left, and, if all this is not enough, God has forbidden him to cross the Jordan.

Moses is making it absolutely clear to the people that there is no possibility of his continuing as their leader. Joshua is to be their leader.

He then speaks to Joshua publicly, in effect, handing Joshua the reins of power, delineating his tasks, and emphasizing that Joshua must be strong and not fear. He gives the command not to fear twice, first to the people — "Be strong and resolute, be not in fear or in dread of them [the Canaanites]; for the Lord your God Himself marches with you" (Deuteronomy 31:6) — and then to Joshua. Even though Moses knows that Joshua has been divinely appointed, he also realizes that the people may feel that no one can really replace Moses. Therefore, he tells the people that ultimately God will see to it that they enter the land and are victorious. If God is with them, it makes no difference who their leader is.

Moses repeats this injunction almost word for word to Joshua. Joshua too must feel apprehensive about taking on this responsibility. He too needs the assurance that God is with them.

One can imagine what a critical moment this is for the people. Facing their greatest challenge, the invasion of the land and the battle against the Canaanites, they are also confronted with the loss of their leader of more than forty years. The man who led them in their struggle against Pharaoh, who mediated between them and God to attain forgiveness for them when they sinned, will no longer be guiding them. It would only be natural for them to fear what is to come, especially under a new and untried leader.

Perhaps these words will give them courage. If God is with them, as Moses says, then they need not fear.

D'rash: Exposition of the Sages

The Holy One said to Moses, "Give Joshua a spokesman, and let him question, respond, and teach while you are still alive, so that when you depart, Israel will not say to him, 'When your Master was alive you never spoke and now you do?!'"
At that moment Moses was filled with strength with which he fortified Joshua in the sight of all Israel, as it is said, "Then Moses called Joshua and said to him in the sight of all Israel: 'Be strong and resolute. . . .'" He said to him, "This people that I am giving you — they are like young kids, just

infants. Do not be too strict with them about their actions, for even their Master [God] has not been strict with them about their deeds," as it is said, "I fell in love with Israel for he was still a child" (Hosea 11:1). Rabbi Nehemiah says, "[Moses said to Joshua] I am not permitted, but if I were, I would bring them in to dwell near the tents of the shepherds."

—Sifre Deuteronomy 305

When looking at Jewish illustrations from the Middle Ages portraying biblical figures or the early Sages, images typically found in the Passover Haggadah or prayer books, it is obvious that the style of clothing and surroundings draws from the time when the images were created rather than the period in which these people actually lived. This is no different from the Christian art of the period.

This same anachronism is also found in the Sages' interpretations of the Torah text. They frequently describe biblical figures taking actions that were typical of their own time—the early centuries of the Common Era—rather than of the biblical era. Thus, Isaac is said to be studying in a *beit midrash* (house of study), and Abraham and Sarah are described as teaching converts.

Here, too, in expanding the story of Moses's transferring his authority to Joshua, Moses is depicted as a Rabbinic Sage who is training a younger disciple to become a Rabbi. In the account, God tells Moses to give Joshua a spokesman, just as any Sage has. Whenever a Sage would teach, someone served as a loudspeaker, repeating aloud the words of the Sage so they could be heard in a large space. When a student became a Sage, he would "question, respond, and teach," as God instructs Moses to have Joshua do while Moses is still alive. So in this midrash, Joshua is becoming what the Sages said Moses was, namely, Rabbenu, our Teacher, our Rabbi, rather than the warrior he was in reality, as depicted in the Torah.

When commenting on Moses's charge to Joshua to be strong, the Sages incorporated into it their interpretation of the following verse: "Go follow the tracks of the sheep, and graze your kids by the tents of the shepherds" (Song of Songs 1:8). When God first appoints Joshua, God likens him to a shepherd who is to tend his flock (see Numbers 27:17–18). In the Song of Songs verse, the shepherd is described as tending "kids," young animals. The midrash then applies this metaphor to the Israelites. Kids, as opposed to sheep, are very young and have to be treated differently. Thus Moses advises Joshua—the new shepherd of Israel—to be gentle, tolerant, and not too strict with the people. Moses adds that God too has treated the people this way; God has not been terribly harsh with them. The verse from Hosea quoted above, "I fell in love with Israel for he was still a child," strengthens this idea by calling Israel a child who is the object of God's love. The standard for treating children who have erred is different from that for adults, much more lenient and forgiving.

The Sages were very daring in saying this, since Israel is called to account and punished for misconduct often enough in the Torah. Perhaps the Rabbis based their reading of leniency on the fact that God could have destroyed Israel as punishment for some of the people's sins but ultimately allowed Israel to continue.

I am inclined to think, however, that the interpretation was influenced by the Sages' depictions of Moses and Joshua as their contemporaries. Moses says to Joshua what one of the Sages might have said to his disciple: As a teacher and a religious leader, do not be overly strict. Remember your people—your flock—are not hardened criminals. They are not sophisticated but need to be led gently into observance of the Torah. If God can forgive them and love them, so should you.

D'rash: Personal Reflection

PREACHING LOVE, FORGIVENESS, AND COMPASSION

Although no name is attached to the midrash of Moses telling Joshua to treat the Israelites gently because they are young and innocent, the chapters of the *Sifrei* in which it appears are generally attributed to Rabbi Akiva and his school.

When doing research for a book about Akiva I was struck by how he constantly avoids using harsh words and being judgmental about people. He does not lecture about sin; rather, he speaks about God as loving and forgiving. For example, he taught, "If there are 999 angels that testify to a person's guilt and only one who declares him innocent, the Holy One will rule according to his merit" (Jerusalem Talmud *Kiddushin* 1:10). When instructing his students about Jewish law, he explained, "The Sages did not say these things to be stringent but to be lenient!" (*Niddah* 8:3). And, as is well known, Akiva taught that the most fundamental rule of the Torah, upon which all else is based, is expressed in Leviticus 19:18: "Love your fellow as yourself" (*Sifra* 89b). So I can imagine the teaching in the midrash—"This people that I am giving you are like young kids, just infants. Do not be too strict with them about their actions"—coming easily from Akiva's lips.

Unfortunately, not all rabbinical authorities follow Akiva's way or pay attention to what—according to the midrash—Moses said to Joshua. At one point I attended the only synagogue that then existed in my Jerusalem neighborhood. The local rabbi delivered learned sermons—but they all had the same message: this is what you have been doing wrong and are not permitted to do. Weekly, there was always something new to add to the list of stringencies.

Finally, one week his subject was the well-known teaching, "All Israel has a place in the world to come" (Sanhedrin 10:1). That sounded promising. The only trouble was, he then went on to list all the exceptions to that rule—and by the time he finished excluding people, there did not seem to be very many people left to populate that world.

At this point my wife, friends, and I left and started another synagogue where we would not have to be admonished week after week but could instead feel the love and compassion the Sages ascribed to Moses in his final words to Joshua.

Ha'azinu

Destruction, Vengeance, and Vindication

DEUTERONOMY 32:1–52

So Jeshurun grew fat and kicked—
You grew fat and gross and coarse—
He forsook the God who made him
And spurned the Rock of his support.
They incensed Him with abominations.
They sacrificed to demons, no-gods,
Gods they had never known,
New ones, who came but lately,
Who stirred not your fathers' fears.
You neglected the Rock that begot you,
Forgot the God who brought you forth. . . .
How could one have routed a thousand
Or two put ten thousand to flight,
Unless their Rock had sold them,
The Lord had given them up? . . .
For the Lord will vindicate His people
And take revenge for His servants. . . .
Vengeance will I wreak on My foes. . . .
O nations, acclaim His people!
For He'll avenge the blood of His servants,
Wreak vengeance on His foes, and cleanse
  His people's land.
    —Deuteronomy 32:15–18,36,41,43

P'shat: Explanation

The compilers of Deuteronomy incorporated one of the finest examples of biblical poetry into Moses's speech to Israel. It was to serve as a warning to the people to make certain that neither they nor their children would ignore Moses's teachings when they entered the land. The song itself, as Moses calls it, is couched in prophetic form, foretelling the future but describing it as if these things have already occurred. It is as if the Israelites have already rebelled against their Rock—the God who brought them into being, nourished them, and gave them a good, rich land. They spurn God, choosing to worship "no-gods." As punishment, with God's permission a "no-folk" vanquishes them (Deuteronomy 32:21).

The horrors they will suffer at the hands of their enemies are frightening. Still, God will not allow their enemies to decimate them, lest these nations mistakenly think that they and not God have this power. In the end, God will wreak vengeance on these destroyers and "cleanse His people's land."

Since none of this has happened when Moses is proclaiming it—the people have not yet even come to the land, not yet prospered, not yet rebelled, not yet been set upon by an enemy—one might expect this song to exhort the people to resist the temptations of false gods and remain faithful to their Rock, thereby avoiding disaster. However, this exhortation does not appear in the song—only in the few words Moses adds after reciting it. As a result, many scholars believe that the song was written long after the era of Moses at a time when all of this was actually happening. Exactly when that would have been is not known.

The essential message—abandoning Moses's teaching will bring disaster—is not new. It has been conveyed elsewhere in Deuteronomy through blessings and curses and the words of Moses in chapters 29 and 30. Nevertheless, there is a difference between prose and poetry. The power of language in this song, with its emphasis on vengeance against the nations, adds an urgency that earlier words could not convey. Justifiably, it was included in this book and became famous.

D'rash: Exposition of the Sages

How great is this song, for it refers to the present,
the past, and the future to come, as well as to
both this world and the world to come!
It once happened during the revolt in Judea that a mounted
Decurion [a Roman officer] pursued an Israelite to kill
him. He could not catch him, but after a while he was just
about to reach him when a serpent emerged and stung the
Israelite's heel. The Israelite then said to the Decurion,
"Do not think that we have been delivered to your hands
because you are mighty—it is only that 'Except their
Rock had given them over'" (Deuteronomy 32:20).
"For their rock is not as our Rock." The power that You
gave them is not the same as the power You gave us.
When You give us power, we act mercifully toward
them. When You give them power, they act with
cruelty to us. They kill us, burn us, and crucify us.
"Vengeance in Mine, and recompense." I will punish them, I
Myself, not by an angel or a messenger. . . . When the Holy One
brings calamity upon the nations, He will shake the earth.
"For He'll avenge the blood of His servants, wreak vengeance
on His foes. . . ." There will be two acts of vengeance, one
for the blood and one for the violence. The violence that
the nations of the world have perpetrated against Israel
will be considered as if they had shed innocent blood.
—Sifre Deuteronomy 322,323,325,333

The Sages wrote this detailed exposition of the song in the period following the Second Temple's destruction (first through second centuries CE). To those who experienced those events and their consequences, this song seemed to relate to their times and not simply to some ancient prophecies and happenings. Their need to understand how Rome could have possibly defeated Judea spurred them to connect these verses to the failure of the great revolt and the destruction of Jerusalem.

Some comments express the people's despair in the face of Roman cruelty. Was this fair and just? Why were the Romans able to defeat the Jews? What had they done wrong? How should they respond to their enemies' claims and taunts that Rome had succeeded because of its great strength and that the God of Israel had been proven powerless? What could they say to the newly emerging Christian sect, which contended that the defeat of the Jews was a sign that God had rejected them because they refused to accept the new Messiah?

The story of the Roman officer who tried to kill a Jew but did not because a serpent bit the Jew first illustrates the idea that if God was not punishing Israel, Rome never could have succeeded. Not Rome but God was all-powerful. Furthermore, the Jews' defeat did not mean that God was rejecting Israel, since the time would come when the people would exact great revenge against their enemies with God's help. Although the Jews had sinned against God and were being punished, the nations were unnecessarily cruel. Therefore, the Jewish blood that had been shed was considered to be innocent blood, and it was just a matter of time before Israel would once again dwell in peace.

D'rash: Personal Reflection

OVERCOMING ADVERSITY

I am constantly amazed by how the Jewish people have recovered from disasters that have threatened to annihilate us. During the Second Temple period the Jews returned from the Babylonian exile and created a great and flourishing entity in Judea. When the Romans destroyed Judea, the Jews who remained in the land created the renewed and expanded Judaism we know today. When the Jews suffered an overwhelming defeat in the Bar Kokhba rebellion (135 CE), they recovered, and Jewish life flourished in the Land of Israel yet again, as it also did in the lands of exile. Now, after the Shoah, we have been able to create a Jewish state for the first time in two thousand years. What is more, the world Jewish population has reached nearly eighteen million, the number of Jews before the Nazis declared their intention of eliminating us completely, and is now on track to exceed eighteen million in the future.

I am also amazed by Jewish triumph over tragedy on a personal scale—such as survivors of the Holocaust who, against all odds, have become creative members of society and are contributing meaningfully to the Jewish future.

Let me mention just one such person I have had the honor of knowing. He was liberated at the end of his teenage years, somehow surviving years of suffering in Auschwitz and the loss of his family. He went on to pursue a career in Jewish education, first in Canada and then in the United States, where he led Jewish schools and motivated and influenced hundreds of Jewish youngsters. At one point when we were working together, he suggested we create a film strip called *The Holocaust* for use in high schools, the first such audiovisual aid on the subject. I worked with him on the script, he found the pictures, and the film was put into use. Later he decided it was important to spread knowledge of the Shoah to college-age youth— Jews and non-Jews—by creating classes in the subject in university history departments. Backed by the financial resources of friends he inspired, he set up such an institute and created these classes in hundreds of universities throughout North America and even overseas. He has dedicated his life and work to this enormous enterprise solely as a volunteer because he believes that knowledge of the Shoah must be disseminated.

As one who led a privileged life while he and so many others were being systematically destroyed, I can only wonder at his ability to survive, to flourish, and to create. I stand in awe of him and all those who have done just that.

Ve-zo't ha-berakhah

The Death of Moses

DEUTERONOMY 33:1–34:12

*So Moses the servant of the Lord died there, in the land
of Moab, at the command of the Lord. He buried him
there in the valley in the land of Moab, near Beth-peor;
and no one knows his burial place to this day. Moses
was a hundred and twenty years old when he died; his
eyes were undimmed and his vigor unabated. And the
Israelites bewailed Moses in the steppes of Moab for thirty
days. . . . Never again did there arise in Israel a prophet
like Moses—whom the Lord singled out, face to face.*
—Deuteronomy 34:5–8,10

P'shat: Explanation

The story of the death of Moses is unique in the Torah, just as Moses
himself was unique. As the text itself says, there never again was
a prophet like him who had anywhere near the same closeness to
God. This relationship is apparent in God's personal involvement in
Moses's death.

At 120 years of age Moses may be an old man, but he has not lost any
of his physical powers. He does not die because of illness or advanced
age but because God so wills it: his death comes at God's command.
True, it is a punishment: God deprives him of his last wish, to enter
the land of Canaan, but the punishment is mitigated by God's taking
him to high ground where he can at least see the land and depart this
world under God's tender care. And once Moses dies, God alone performs the burial, in a place known to God alone.

The Torah is careful to let us know that Moses was not perfect. No human being is. But at the same time, the text makes clear that Moses was as close to perfection as one can be. He is deserving not of worship—that is reserved for God alone—but of reverence and respect above all others.

D'rash: Exposition of the Sages

The Holy One said to the Angel of Death, "Go and bring Me the soul of Moses." He went and stood before him and said, "Moses—give me your soul!" He (Moses) said to him, "You do not have the right to stand where I dwell and you dare say to me, 'Give me your soul'?!" He (Moses) rebuked him and he departed humiliated. The Angel of Death went and reported this to the Mighty One. Once again the Holy One said to him, "Go and bring Me his soul." So he went to (Moses's) dwelling and sought him but he did not find him. He went to the sea and said to it, "Moses—have you seen him?" It replied, "Since the day when he made Israel pass through me I have not seen him." So he went to the mountains and hills. He said to them, "Moses—have you seen him?" They replied, "Since the day when Israel received the Torah on Mount Sinai we have not seen him." So he went to Gehennom [the underworld inhabited by the dead]. He said to her, "Moses—have you seen him?" She said to him, "I have heard his name but I have never seen him." So he went to the heavenly angels. He said to them, "Moses—have you seen him?" They said to him, "Go unto human beings." He went to the Israelites. He said to them, "Moses—have you seen him?" They said to him, "God understands his way. God has hidden him away for the life of the world to come and no one knows of his place. . . ." Because of Moses' death Joshua wept and mourned for him for many days until the Holy One said to Joshua, "How long can you go on mourning? Does the death of Moses affect

you alone? Does not his death really affect Me the most?!
For from the day he died there has been great mourning
unto Me . . . but he is assured of life in the world to come."
— Sifre Deuteronomy 305

Well aware of Moses's uniqueness, the Sages created this myth about his death that demonstrates just how unusual Moses was—a myth that is not without humor.

The Angel of Death has power over everyone. In the end, no one escapes his clutches, good and bad alike. But the story pokes fun at him. Moses dismisses him as a creature of no importance. God sends him twice on a wild goose chase, and in the end he cannot even begin to fulfill his mission because he cannot even track Moses down. It is not Death but God who actually takes Moses's soul and God alone who cares for it, lovingly hiding it away, awaiting its return to life in the future world.

At the same time, the legend manages to not so subtly remind us of the two greatest things Moses accomplished—splitting the sea, the last act in attaining Israel's freedom, and giving the Torah on Sinai—by having Death visit each of them. Death then descends into *Geihinnom*, but *Geihinnom* has never even seen him. The last part of the legend, when God speaks so boldly to Joshua and takes the mourning for Moses upon God alone, is an unequaled tribute to Moses.

What provoked the Sages to tell such a fantastic story? On the one hand, it asserts Moses's uniqueness—emblematized by God's special relationship to him—along with his unequaled greatness—the one who outwits Death itself. On the other, it also demonstrates that Moses is ultimately only a human being, and all human beings perish, but there is the promise of a life in the world to come.

I wonder if, by these parables, which were commonly used in sermons, the Sages were also commenting in an oblique way about the differences between depictions of the central figures of Judaism and Christianity. Christianity, emerging at that time, taught that Jesus was not only the Messiah but actually divine, one of the three manifestations of God: the father, the son, and the Holy Spirit. The story of his resurrection denoted that he came back to life and would cause others to come back as well through their belief in him. Here, the Sages are teaching that even the greatest Jewish figure—Moses—was never divine, though he too defeated death. By these assertions, they may have been intimating that there was no need for a new savior. Furthermore, no one would ever measure up to Moses's greatness, much less surpass it.

D'rash: Personal Reflection

AN UNUSUAL FUNERAL

The Torah begins with the transcendent description of God creating the universe. It concludes with the tender account of God burying Moses in an unknown grave. Some would see this as a terrible comedown, but my viewpoint is the opposite: God has become the caring God of the individual and not merely the unknown force beyond nature. In Jewish tradition, no act of loving-kindness is greater than that of burying the dead. When we do this we are imitating God.

Conducting a funeral and burial may be the most significant and most difficult part of the congregational rabbinate. Confronting the task of comforting a mourning family and helping each of its members through this critical period is daunting, yet a rabbi faces it time and again, as I did during the fifteen years I served congregations in the United States and have occasionally done since coming to Israel.

I have never forgotten the very first funeral I conducted as a rabbi. I was serving as a chaplain at an airbase in South Dakota. Since no other rabbis were anywhere in the area, I was frequently called upon to help Jewish civilians as well. In this case an elderly Jewish woman had died in Deadwood, which was within traveling distance of my base, and her brother called to ask me to conduct the funeral at the Jewish section of the local cemetery, which was renowned for the graves of some notorious figures from the Old West days. I had never met the family and knew nothing about them.

When I arrived I sat down with the brother and younger sister of the deceased, the only family she had, in order to learn about her. The first thing I discovered was that for some time these three had been the only Jews in Deadwood, although at a much earlier time the community had been flourishing, with its own synagogue. That had disappeared long ago. All the other Jews in the community had been buried in the cemetery.

I was then informed that the funeral would begin with an Eastern Star ritual conducted by the ladies of that organization, the female component of the Masons. The deceased had been an active member of this group. I was somewhat uncomfortable with that, so I told the brother and sister that I would wait until that ceremony was finished and then go in and conduct a Jewish funeral. I quickly realized, however, that when living in that community, belonging to such an organization was a vital part of one's existence.

The deceased, they told me, had been a lawyer, not a usual profession for a woman born sometime in the 1880s in the Far West, but then everything about this family was unusual. Her father had been a mining engineer, which is how they came to live in Deadwood, known for its silver mines. An emigrant from Germany, he had been an active member of the Deadwood Jewish community, raised his three children to be proud Jews, and insisted that the two girls as well as the boy be educated in Judaism, be university graduates, and establish professions, which they had. None of them had married. There had been a dearth of suitable Jewish partners. Yes, at one time many Jewish families had lived in Deadwood, but there were none today, because all of them had intermarried. The main street was filled with stores with Jewish names, but only the names, not the families, were Jewish. With the death of their older sister, these two siblings were the only living Jews in Deadwood.

The Eastern Star service began, and I watched it from the doorway to the next room. It consisted mostly of placing various flowers on the casket accompanied by words with obviously symbolic meanings. The ceremony seemed strange to me but not offensive. When they finished, I went in, said the appropriate prayers in Hebrew with English translations, and gave a eulogy.

I felt certain that what I did was as strange to the assembled group as their service had been to me. I also conducted the burial service and shoveled dirt in the grave according to Jewish custom. That was sixty years ago. I assume that the last two Jewish graves in the Jewish section of the Deadwood, South Dakota, cemetery were filled in many years ago.

When we returned to the family's home after the service, the brother and sister proudly showed me the Jewish books their father had collected, among them prayer books in old Gothic German script he had brought from Germany and a series of English-language first editions of early publications of the Jewish Publication Society (JPS). Their father had arranged to have the volumes sent to him all the way from JPS's Philadelphia headquarters so that his children growing up in the Far West would learn about their Jewish heritage. They insisted on giving me those books, saying they did not want them to go to waste when the two of them were gone. They were certain I would appreciate having them.

They were right. Seeing those books, I gained an appreciation for the way in which this family had remained loyal to Judaism in a place and time when it was not easy for them to do so. Giving their sister a proper Jewish burial was the least I could do to show my respect. It was an honor for me to do so.

VI

Holidays

Rosh Hashanah

Sound the Shofar

GENESIS 21:1–22:24

They arrived at the place of which God had told him. Abraham built an altar there; he laid out the wood; he bound his son Isaac; he laid him on the altar, on top of the wood. And Abraham picked up the knife to slay his son. Then an angel of the Lord called to him from heaven: "Abraham! Abraham!" and he answered, "Here I am." And he said, "Do not raise your hand against the boy, or do anything to him. For now I know that you fear God, since you have not withheld your son, your favored one, from Me." When Abraham looked up, his eye fell upon a ram, caught in the thicket by its horns. So Abraham went and took the ram and offered it up as a burnt offering in place of his son. . . . "By Myself I swear," the Lord declared: "Because you have done this and have not withheld your son, your favored one, I will bestow My blessing upon you and make your descendants as numerous as the stars of heaven and the sands on the seashore; and your descendants shall seize the gates of their foes."
—Genesis 22:9–13,16–17

P'shat: Explanation

This is the climax of the story read on Rosh Hashanah commonly known today as "The Binding of Isaac" but more accurately titled "The Test of Abraham," since it begins with the verse, "God put Abraham to the test" (Genesis 22:1). Abraham is told to take the son God had promised him would be the father of his myriad descendants, who would inherit the land, the son born so miraculously to Abraham and Sarah in their old age, and "offer him as a burnt offering." Would Abraham do that, or would he refuse? He could have easily argued that this command was the direct contradiction of everything God had promised him. Indeed, Abraham was known to argue with God. But he did not hesitate. Rather, he is depicted as actually raising his knife to slay the lad.

The human sacrifice is not wanted, however, and Abraham offers an animal instead. As a reward, God declares that Abraham's descendants will be numerous and conquer the land.

What was the purpose of such a heart-rending tale that raises so many questions? Various ideas have been suggested. Perhaps it was intended to prove once and for all that God does not desire human sacrifice, as many pagan rites required; animal sacrifice was sufficient. Perhaps it was meant to explain why God favored Abraham's descendants and made them great—this was a reward for Abraham's obedience. Whatever the case, the climax of the story is God's declaration: God is bestowing a special blessing upon Abraham's progeny that includes their supremacy over their enemies.

The fact that God gave an unconditional reward to Abraham is mentioned time and time again throughout the Torah, especially at times when doubt might have arisen because of the Israelites' conduct. If God ever considered annihilating the people because of their misconduct, the argument could be made that God had promised Abraham this reward. Even if the Israelites do not deserve this reward, God cannot go back on that promise.

The question then arises, What is the connection between this story and the holiday of Rosh Hashanah? On the surface that is not immediately clear.

D'rash: Exposition of the Sages

Abraham said to the Holy One, "Master of the universe, a man tests another when he does not know his true character,

but You know everyone's nature. Why then did You have to do
this?" God said to him, "For now I know that you fear God."
Immediately the Holy One opened the heavens and said, "By
Myself I swear. . . ." Abraham said, "You have sworn, now I
shall swear that I shall not leave this altar until I tell You all
that I wish to say." God said to him, "Speak." "Did You not
say to me, 'Look toward heaven and count the stars, if you are
able to count them. . . . So shall your offspring be'?" (Genesis
15:5). God said to him, "Yes." Abraham said, "From whom?"
God said to him, "From Isaac." He said to God, "I could have
said to You, 'Yesterday You told me that, and now You tell me
"Offer him there as a burnt offering"?!' (Genesis 22:2). But I
suppressed my inclination and did not say that. Now when
Isaac's descendants sin and are in trouble, remember unto
them the binding of Isaac. Consider it as if his ashes were
strewn before You on the altar and forgive them and redeem
them from their troubles." Said the Holy One, "In the future
Isaac's descendants will certainly sin before Me and on Rosh
Hashanah I shall judge them. If they want Me to find some
merit for them and remember the binding of Isaac, let them
sound the shofar—the ram's horn—before Me and I will
save them and redeem them from their transgressions."
—Midrash Tanhuma Va-yera' 23, Rosh Hashanah 16a

In the Sages' retelling, this biblical story has been totally recast. Isaac
is no longer a passive figure but a full participant throughout the incident, willingly allowing himself to be martyred. For his part, Abraham does not simply submit to God's will; he does what he did in the
story of Sodom and Gomorrah: he challenges God and demands a
reward for his restraint.

Furthermore, the reward Abraham seeks is totally different from
the one described in the Torah. Abraham dismisses that promise of
the land and a blessing (or takes it for granted) and instead asks God
to redeem Isaac's descendants from trouble when they sin.

God acquiesces and specifies that when they sin, and they certainly will, Isaac's descendants will require "redemption from their transgressions" on Rosh Hashanah, the Day of Judgment. They will receive a positive judgment if they invoke the merit of the binding of Isaac. How is this to be done? Through taking the horn of the ram that had been caught in the thicket and sounding it before the Lord.

This story is read from the Torah on Rosh Hashanah and referred to often in the liturgy of that day not because of the simple meaning of the text but because of the Sages' interpretation of it. They made the sounding of the shofar, made from a ram's horn, a reminder of the binding of Isaac, and they tied the story to a universal theme of sin and redemption from transgression.

Notably, many of the questions that have been raised concerning God's testing of Abraham come to the fore in this midrash as well. Why should God require such a test? Doesn't God know whether or not Abraham truly reveres God? In that light, isn't the test superfluous and even cruel? What is the purpose of it all?

Another crucial question is, Why did the Sages introduce such a drastic change in the reward? Nowhere in the biblical story is there any mention of trouble, sin, and redemption.

The biblical story originated in ancient times in an era when Israel was enjoying the gift of living on its own land, prospering and multiplying — as God had promised. In those days, Rosh Hashanah was not yet considered a day of judgment but a celebration of creation and of God's sovereignty.

The Sages' retelling of the story, however, took place after the Second Temple period, when the Jews' situation had changed drastically. At this time, both the Temple and Jerusalem had been destroyed, and the Jews were in exile. The people were experiencing martyrdom — and Isaac became the perfect symbol of that martyrdom and suffering.

Therefore, as Abraham states clearly in this midrash, the people had other needs to ask of God: forgiveness for their sins and help in their time of trouble. As retold in the midrash, this story grants both to them.

This new approach to the story of Abraham's test thus provided a meaningful context for the times—and also for sounding the shofar, the only command associated with Rosh Hashanah in the Torah. Sounding the shofar, the horn of the ram Abraham sacrificed, would send a nonverbal plea to God: remember how Abraham suppressed his merciful feelings toward his son; remember how Isaac and all the martyrs of Israel who came after him were willing to die for the sanctification of Your Name; and suppress Your attribute of justice, replacing it with mercy when You judge Your people on Rosh Hashanah.

D'rash: Personal Reflection

EVERYONE MAKES MISTAKES

I have always felt that the sounding of the shofar is the high point of the Rosh Hashanah service. There is something very moving about a sound that does not come from a sophisticated musical instrument but from a primitive horn whose distinctive wail conjures up thousands of years of Jewish history. It somehow reflects the deepest yearning of the human soul for redemption, for closeness to the being who is beyond all else and yet deep within each of us.

Personally, whenever I hear it, I also recall an incident that occurred one Rosh Hashanah when I was leading services and a highly distinguished scholar was calling out the notes for the shofar blower. Unfortunately, at one point he made a mistake and called an incorrect note. The person blowing the shofar hesitated—he could not sound the note called because it was the wrong one, and he could not sound the right one because it had not been called. Not realizing his mistake, the scholar simply repeated his error. Although I felt very uncomfortable about embarrassing him, I had no choice but to simply go over to him as quietly and unobtrusively as possible and point to the correct note in the prayer book. He immediately corrected himself, and the service continued.

When the service was over and we were walking out together, the scholar turned to me and said, "That was a very good thing that happened." "Why?" I inquired. "Because," he said, "sometime in the future you will make a mistake, and rather than feeling bad about it, you will remember my mistake and say to yourself, 'If he could make a mistake, anybody can make a mistake!'"

And, sure enough, whenever I make a mistake—and we all make mistakes, even great scholars—I remember what happened that year and simply move on.

Rosh Hashanah is a time when we ask God to forgive us. It is also a time when we should learn not to expect perfection of ourselves and forgive ourselves too.

Yom Kippur

Sending Our Sins Away

LEVITICUS 16

*Aaron shall lay both his hands upon the head of the live
goat and confess over it all the iniquities and transgressions
of the Israelites, whatever their sins, putting them
on the head of the goat; and it shall be sent off to the
wilderness through a designated man. Thus the goat
shall carry on it all their iniquities to an inaccessible
region; and the goat shall be set free in the wilderness.*
—Leviticus 16:21–22

P'shat: Explanation

An entire chapter of Leviticus is devoted to the ritual for the Day
of Atonement, Yom Kippur. Of the thirty-four verses in the chapter, only the last five detail how the Israelites are to observe the day,
namely, by practicing self-denial and cessation from work. All the
other verses describe the actions of the High Priest, the central figure in the rites of the day.

He had an elaborate ritual to follow, special garments to wear, and
various sacrifices to bring. In addition, he was to sprinkle blood and
bring incense, all intended to purge the sanctuary "of the uncleanness
and transgression of the Israelites" (Leviticus 16:16). As directed by the
text, he performed these acts once a year, on the tenth day of the seventh month, so that the sanctuary would be ritually pure for the great
feast of Sukkot (held on the fifteenth of the month, five days later).

One of the important rituals described in the two verses above concerns a goat that was designated to be sent off into the wilderness in

order to carry all the iniquities and transgressions of the people. (This goat would come to be known in Old English as the "scapegoat"—really the "escape goat," since it would run away into the wilderness and not be sacrificed.) Before the escape, the High Priest would confess the people's iniquities, place his hands on the goat's head, and thus transfer the transgressions to the animal.

This was a "rite of riddance," a symbolic way of ridding the people of all their sins. No one else besides the High Priest was asked to confess; all the burden of expiation of sin was his. His words of confession were not specified.

This is the way in which Yom Kippur was observed in the days of the First Temple.

D'rash: Exposition of the Sages

The Priest stands and puts his two hands upon [the goat] and makes confession, and thus would he say: Please Lord! I have transgressed, I have done wrong. I have sinned before You. I and my household. Please Lord! Atone for the transgressions, the wrongs and the sins that I have transgressed, done wrong and sinned before You, I and my household, as it is written in the Torah of Moses Your servant, "For on this day atonement shall be made for you to cleanse you of all your sins; you shall be clean before the Lord" (Leviticus 16:30). And the priests and the people who stood there when they heard the Name [Lord] uttered by the High Priest in holiness and purity would bow, kneel, and prostrate themselves and say, "Blessed is the Name of His glorious Majesty forever!"
—Yoma 3:8–9

One is commanded to confess when it becomes dark on the eve of Yom Kippur. However, the Sages said that one should confess before eating (the last meal before the fast), lest

one become distracted while eating and drinking . . . and
then . . . one must confess after eating and drinking . . . and
then . . . one must confess during the evening service . . .
and at the morning service . . . and at the additional
service . . . and at the afternoon service . . . and at the Neilah
service since one may have sinned anytime during the
day. . . . Rabbi Judah ben Petira says that one must specify
each sin. . . . Rabbi Akiva says, "It is not necessary."
—Tosefta *Yoma* 4:14

During and after the days of the Second Temple, the confession of sin became much more central to the Yom Kippur ritual. The Mishnah gives an exact formula for what the High Priest is to say and then repeats that he is to make a confession first for himself and his family (as above), then for the whole house of Aaron (*Yoma* 4:2), and finally for the entire people of Israel (*Yoma* 6:2). He is to use the exact Name of God (YHVH), which we no longer know how to pronounce, and the people are to respond to hearing it by prostrating themselves each time and praising the Lord.

The original, brief, private ritual for the High Priest alone no longer exists. Now it is a long and solemn ceremony attended by massive crowds of Israelites who also participate in it. It has become a public ceremony for the entire nation.

The Tosefta, an early Rabbinic compilation of teachings not included in the Mishnah, goes much further, mandating that starting from the time of the Second Temple's destruction, each individual is to confess his or her sins not merely once but no fewer than seven times on Yom Kippur. Some Sages stipulate that the people must specify their exact sins, although Rabbi Akiva does not require this.

Eventually, the content of the confession was not left up to the individual but formulated in two different ways: one brief and general and the other long and very specific. The confession now became the center of the Yom Kippur service.

D'rash: Personal Reflection

AN UNFORGETTABLE YOM KIPPUR

Without question the Yom Kippur I can never forget was on October 6, 1973, when Egypt and Syria unexpectedly attacked Israel. Having made *aliyah* in August, my wife and I were living in the Mevaseret Tzion absorption center, run by the Jewish Agency. There was absolutely no thought in our or anyone else's minds of the possibility of war. The euphoria of the great victory in the Six-Day War had blinded us all to the reality that awaited us.

A group of Americans living at the center had asked me to conduct High Holy Day services for them. Everything went very well on Rosh Hashanah, and there was no reason to think anything different would occur on Yom Kippur.

My sermon on Kol Nidre night was based upon the Rabbinic text that teaches that one should repent and confess one day before one's death. When the question is raised, "How does one know when that is?" the answer given is, "You can't know; therefore, one should repent every day." Throughout my talk I repeatedly used the mantra "You never know what is going to happen tomorrow." Little did I know how true that was.

On Yom Kippur, because of our isolated location (and absorption center officials were off for the holiday), we didn't know war had broken out until the sirens went off in the late morning and we had turned on our radios to find out what was happening. We were supposed to go into the bomb shelters but discovered they were padlocked. When we broke in we found them to be almost unusable—but who had thought they would be needed? We cleared them out and went inside. There seemed to be no reason to be there, since there was no attack on Jerusalem.

We recited *Mincha*, the afternoon prayer, while standing on the roof of the shelter. It is impossible to describe our feelings while saying those prayers. Our confessions were full of pathos, but our minds were not so much on our sins as on the possible peril to our lives and to the existence of the State of Israel, where we had come to live.

By late afternoon, officials from the absorption center had arrived and instructed us to go to our homes. We said a quick *Neilah*—long before the proper time—and then went to our houses, turned on the TV, and watched a pale Golda Meir address the nation, giving us assurances that neither she nor we really believed.

The end of Yom Kippur is usually an uplifting experience—an affirmation of our faith and belief; the sounding of the shofar, which is an assertion of good tidings; the singing of "Next Year in Jerusalem." There was none of that—instead, we wondered if next year there would be a Jerusalem at all.

In the end Israel survived and so did we, but not without a great cost. It was a Yom Kippur never to be forgotten.

Sukkot

The *Festival Par Excellence*

LEVITICUS 22:26–23:44

*The Lord spoke to Moses, saying: Speak to the Israelite people
and say to them: These are My fixed times, the fixed times of
the Lord, which you shall proclaim as sacred occasions. . . .
On the fifteenth day of this seventh month there shall be a
Feast of Booths to the Lord, seven days. The first day shall be a
sacred occasion; you shall not work at your occupations; seven
days you shall bring offerings of fire to the Lord. . . . On the
first day you shall take the product of hadar trees, branches
of palm trees, boughs of leafy trees, and willows of the brook,
and you shall rejoice before the Lord your God seven days. . . .
You shall live in booths, in order that future generations may
know that I made the Israelite people live in booths when I
brought them out of the land of Egypt, I the Lord your God.*
—Leviticus 23:1–2,34–36,40–43

P'shat: Explanation

The reading for the first day of Sukkot features the list of all the sacred
days of the Hebrew year, including, of course, the festival of Sukkot,
which lasts for seven days. The first day is the only one on which work
is prohibited, but the main observances of the festival, namely, living in booths and using branches and fruit (in unspecified ways), are
observed the entire week. Two of the four plants mentioned are trees:
willows and palms. The fruit of the hadar tree is not specified but
later was identified as the *etrog*. Leafy trees are not identified either
but later were taken to mean the myrtle. These seem to be examples

of the beautiful greenery growing in the Land of Israel. Carrying them may have been symbolic of the fertility of the land.

Dwelling in booths is also specified and may have its origins in the fact that Sukkot was an ancient harvest festival: these huts were the temporary structures erected in the fields and used as shelter during the harvest.

As with Pesach, an existing agricultural festival was now given a historical context. For Pesach, it was the Exodus. For Sukkot, it became a recollection of the journey in the wilderness — "I made the Israelite people live in booths [*sukkot*] when I brought them out of the land of Egypt." Sukkot is also the name of the first stop on the people's journey — "The Israelites journeyed from Rameses to Sukkot" (Exodus 12:37). This verse could mean either that God protected the Israelites by having them dwell in huts (*sukkot*) in the wilderness, or that God let them stop in the place named Sukkot on their journey, or both.

Notably, however, nowhere in the Torah's story of Israel's journeys is mention made of the people dwelling in actual booths, although something of the sort would seem to have been a normal thing to do when the people stayed in one place for prolonged periods of time.

There are five commandments regarding Sukkot: resting on the first day, bringing sacrifices for seven days, holding four different growing things, rejoicing, and dwelling in booths. Because of this plethora of activities, Sukkot is the most colorful festival of the year, the one involving the most physical objects, and the most joyful one too. Therefore, it has always been known as *he-Ḥag*, "*the* pilgrimage festival," the most significant festival of them all.

D'rash: Exposition of the Sages

"... the product of hadar trees ..." This refers to Abraham,
whom the Holy One glorified — hidro — with a good old age, as
it is said, "Abraham was now old, advanced in years, and the
Lord had blessed Abraham in all things" (Genesis 24:1), and it
says, "... and glorify — v'hadarta — the old" (Leviticus 19:32).
"... branches — kapot — of palm trees ..." This refers to Isaac,

who was tied—kafut—and bound upon the altar. "... boughs
of leafy trees..." This refers to Jacob. Just as the myrtle has
many leaves, so Jacob had many children. "... willows of the
brook..." This refers to Joseph. Just as the willow withers
before the other three, so Joseph died before his brothers.
Another interpretation: "... the product of hadar trees..." This
refers to Sarah, whom the Holy One glorified—hidra—with
a good old age, as it is said, "Now Abraham and Sarah were
old..." (Genesis 18:11). "... branches—kapot—of palm trees..."
This refers to Rebecca. Just as the palm tree has both eatable
fruit and thorns, so Rebecca had a righteous son and an evil
one. "... boughs of leafy trees..." This refers to Leah. Just as the
myrtle has many leaves, so Leah had many children. "... willows
of the brook..." This refers to Rachel. Just as the willow withers
before the other three, so Rachel died before her sister.

—Leviticus Rabbah 30:10

Another interpretation. These refer to Israelites. Just as the
etrog has both pleasant taste and lovely fragrance, so among
the Israelites there are those who are both learned in Torah and
perform good deeds. "... branches of palm trees..." Just as the
dates of the palm tree have a pleasant taste but lack any fragrance,
so there are Israelites who are learned in Torah but do not perform
good deeds. "... boughs of leafy trees..." Just as the myrtle has
a lovely fragrance but has no taste, so there are Israelites who
perform good deeds but are not learned in Torah. "... willows of
the brook..." Just as the willow has neither pleasant taste nor
lovely fragrance, so there are Israelites who are neither learned in
Torah nor perform good deeds. What should the Holy One do about
them? It is impossible to do away with them. Therefore the Holy
One binds them all together into one group so that these atone for
those!... When? When they are one group. Therefore Moses warns
Israel, "On the first day you shall take them [i.e., all of them]."

—Leviticus Rabbah 30:12

Since the Torah offers no rationale for the four items that the Israelites are to take during Sukkot, the Sages found many different ways to explain them, making them symbolic of various people or groups. The midrashim cited above are just two examples of this; there are many more.

The first midrash connects these items with the Patriarchs and the Matriarchs, finding suitable verses that match them up with incidents in their lives. The second one makes them symbolic of different groups within the people Israel. It designates these items' two main features—taste and fragrance—and compares them to two important human qualities—learning and performance of good deeds. There are four species of plants and four types of Israelites. The best group, of course, consists of people who are both learned and active in doing good things. The worst are those who are neither.

The example is based on the verse's implication that all four plants are to be taken and held together, not separately. Indeed, in Jewish practice the three branches are bound together as the *lulav*, and the *etrog* is held next to it. Therefore, the answer to the question of how to deal with the fact that some Israelites are less than perfect is to put them all together so that the better group makes up for or justifies the existence of the poorer one. This reflects a basic value frequently found in the Sages' writings: Israel must be *agudah ahat*—one unity—if it is to survive and prosper. Disunity always results in disintegration and defeat. Unity makes for strength and triumph. We support and we help one another.

D'rash: Personal Reflection

A UNITED COMMUNITY

The four species (*lulav* and *etrog*) is a powerful symbol of Jewish unity. In our times this symbol could be applied to the different groups that comprise world Jewry. That could mean different ethnic groups—Ashkenazi, Sefardi, Ethiopian—or different religious groups—ultra-

Orthodox, Orthodox, Conservative, Reform, Reconstructionism, and so on. It could mean secular and religious, the Diaspora and Israel. In Israel it could also mean cutting across the political parties—too many to mention. The ideal is "one unity." The reality is that the divisions are so many that unity is difficult to achieve, but that does not mean it isn't worth striving for.

The closest I have ever come to experiencing a united Jewish community was during my first pulpit in Denver. I was delighted to become part of the Denver Rabbinical Association (DRA), composed of all the rabbis of the major congregations: Orthodox, Conservative, and Reform. True feelings of camaraderie existed among all the rabbis in the association. We may not have agreed on many theological matters, but there was mutual respect and the sincere desire to create one larger Jewish community in Denver.

Meeting together regularly over the years, the group succeeded in adopting many different policies that applied to the entire community. For example, to insure that the religious aspects of weddings would always be the central concern, the DRA established a rule that all weddings were to be held in synagogues; as a result, no Denver rabbi officiated anywhere else. Also, when questions arose concerning Sabbath observance at the Jewish Community Center (i.e., what activities were to be permitted or forbidden on Shabbat), the group created an agreed-upon policy, thus avoiding conflict.

Furthermore, because of the close collaboration among the rabbis, at certain times over the year, such as Israel Independence Day and Holocaust Memorial Day, all the Denver congregations came together for a joint celebration. The different rabbis and synagogues took turns hosting and chairing these events. I remember what a good feeling it was one year when I chaired the Israel event, which was held in an Orthodox synagogue.

Obviously, none of this could have happened without the rabbis' willingness to put aside differences. In time I discovered that the secret of our success was really the personality of the leading Orthodox rabbi, Rabbi Manuel Laderman. He was true to his Orthodox beliefs and also flexible and accepting of others. He set an example that others followed.

When I left that community and served elsewhere, I was disappointed to see that the Denver pattern was not the norm; denominational differences seemed to dominate Jewish community life. Coming to Israel, where the combination of politics and religion causes greater rifts, Jewish unity seems even further away.

It was therefore heartening when, at the beginning of the twenty-first century, four Jerusalem synagogues—two Masorti (Conservative), one Reform, and one Orthodox—formed a consortium and held events together, such as commemorations of outstanding leaders who had passed away and celebrations of significant Israeli events. As a result, feelings of respect for differing ways of observing Judaism, rather than the more common feelings of antagonism, are widespread in the community.

It was not accidental that all four of these congregations originated with American *olim*. The American Jewish community has never had one official rabbinate or one governmentally supported version of Judaism; instead, it has established a paradigm of pluralism, something sorely lacking in Israel. With these inroads, the ideal of Jewish unity and mutual respect in Israel remains alive, as does the hope that it can someday be achieved.

Shemini Atzeret

Tarry a While

DEUTERONOMY 14:22–16:17, NUMBERS 29:35–30:1

*After the ingathering from your threshing floor and your vat,
you shall hold the Feast of Booths for seven days. You shall
rejoice in your festival, with your son and daughter, your male
and female slave, the Levite, the stranger, the fatherless, and
the widow in your communities. You shall hold a festival for
the Lord your God seven days, in the place that the Lord your
God will choose; for the Lord your God will bless all your crops
and all your undertakings, and you shall have nothing but joy.*
—Deuteronomy 16:13–15

*On the eighth day you shall hold a solemn gathering for
yourselves; you shall not work at your occupations.*
—Numbers 29:35

P'shat: Explanation

On festivals we always read from two different books of the Torah.
The first, the main reading, is somehow related to the particular festival; the second, a brief additional reading from the book of Numbers, always specifies the sacrifices that are to be offered on that
particular day. Oddly enough, on Shemini Atzeret the reading from
the first book, taken from Deuteronomy, never mentions that day at
all. It describes the seven days of Sukkot and stops at that. The brief
reading from Numbers, on the other hand, specifies the sacrifices to
be brought "on the eighth day" and calls it "a solemn gathering" — in

312

Hebrew, *atzeret*. From this the name of the holiday—Shemini Atzeret, the Gathering on the Eighth Day—was derived.

The calendar of Jewish festivals is recorded in four books of the Torah: Exodus, Leviticus, Numbers, and Deuteronomy. Shemini Atzeret is not mentioned in the accounts in Exodus and Deuteronomy. In Leviticus, on the other hand, we read: "On the eighth day you shall observe a sacred occasion and bring an offering by fire to the Lord; it is a solemn gathering; you shall not work at your occupations" (Leviticus 23:36). It is difficult to understand why this reading, rather than the Deuteronomy text, is not used on the day.

One possible explanation is that the Deuteronomy section was chosen as the reading because it alone emphasizes the importance of caring for the needy in our communities. As it says, "You shall rejoice in your festival, with your son and daughter, your male and female slave, the Levite, the stranger, the fatherless, and the widow in your communities" (Deuteronomy 16:14). This theme is also mentioned earlier in the reading concerning tithes, "And the stranger, the fatherless, and the widow in your settlements shall come and eat their fill, so that the Lord your God may bless you in all the enterprises you undertake" (Deuteronomy 14:29), and in several other places. It is wonderful to have holidays dedicated to rejoicing, but the celebration of our own blessings must not cause us to forget to share our happiness with others who are less fortunate and need our help.

D'rash: Exposition of the Sages

"On the eighth day you shall hold a solemn gathering. . . ." It is written: They answer my love with accusation . . . (Psalm 109:4). Thus you find that on the Festival [Sukkot], Israel sacrifices seventy bulls on behalf of the seventy nations [of the world]. The Israelites say, "Lord of the universe, behold we offer seventy bulls on their behalf, for which they should love us, but instead they hate us," as it is said, "They answer my love with accusation. . . ." Therefore the Holy One says to them,

"Now bring an offering on your own behalf!"—"On the eighth day you shall hold a solemn gathering for yourselves ... one bull, one ram ..." (Numbers 29:35–36). "One ram ...": This may be likened to a sovereign who made a banquet lasting seven days and invited all the inhabitants of the province for the entire seven days of the banquet. But when the seven days were over he said to his beloved confidant, "We have done our duty for the people of the province, now let us make do with whatever food you can find, a pound of meat or vegetables." Thus did the Holy One say to Israel, "On the eighth day you shall hold a solemn gathering for yourselves. . . ." Make do with whatever you can find, ". . . one bull, one ram."
—Numbers Rabbah 21:24

Said the Holy One, "My children, on the seven days of Sukkot we occupy ourselves completely with our guests [the seventy nations of the world]. On the eighth day let us—Me and you—remain alone together."
—Pesikta de-Rav Kahana 28

Although the Torah frequently speaks of three pilgrimage festivals, Pesach, Shavuot, and Sukkot, there are really four, since Shemini Atzeret is a holiday in its own right. It is not the last day of Sukkot but rather an appendage to it. Functionally it is to Sukkot what Shavuot is to Pesach. Shavuot is also called an *atzeret*. It comes seven weeks after Pesach, while Shemini Atzeret comes seven days after the beginning of Sukkot—an appendage.

Unlike the other three, it also has no connection to either the agricultural year or a historical event. It seems like a holiday without a reason or purpose. This concerned the Sages. They asked, "Why is there an appendage altogether? Why is it needed? What purpose does it serve?"

Their answer is based upon their understanding of the meaning of the seventy sacrificial offerings given on Sukkot. Since the number of nations in the world was also thought to be seventy, the Sages reasoned that Sukkot was the time when the people Israel brought offerings to God on behalf of all the nations of the world. The connection between Sukkot and the nations of the world was strengthened by the fact that when the prophet Zechariah described a time in the future when all nations, not only Israel, would come to worship the Lord, the only holiday he mentioned was Sukkot: "All those nations that came up against Jerusalem shall make a pilgrimage year by year to bow low to the King Lord of Hosts and to observe the Feast of Booths" (Zechariah 14:16).

The Sages said that the eighth day, the day after Sukkot, was different from Sukkot. It had no connection to the other nations. It was for Israel alone, to demonstrate the special relationship between Israel and God. Like the beloved confidant in the parable told in the midrash, when the host was finished with entertaining all the guests, he—in this case, the Lord—wants his friend to tarry a while so that they can spend a day together, just the two of them. As the Psalmist put it, Israel is "the people close to Him" (Psalm 148:14), a testament to their unique relationship.

At the same time, this midrash also contains a harsh critique of the nations. They reward Israel's act of sacrificing on their behalf—an act of love and friendship—by hating Israel. God's response to this complaint is to grant the people of Israel an extra festive day for their own benefit—and, as an added bonus, on this day the sacrificial demands are minimal. This day, Shemini Atzeret, is devoted to the special relationship between God and Israel, God's special friend. That is its purpose and justification.

D'rash: Personal Reflection

THE HATRED OF THE NATIONS

Considering that the Sages were writing at a time when Jews were suffering from persecution and oppression wherever they lived, it is not surprising that they spoke so harshly of the hatred of the nations. Nor is it surprising that today, in our post-Holocaust era, that same feeling of resentment against many nations often exists as well. The fact that perhaps the most cultured and civilized nation in the world, the nation that gave the world great music, literature, and drama, could evince such hatred and go to such extremes to rid itself and the world of Jews, and that so many of its citizens could have cooperated in those atrocities or stood silent while they were perpetrated, seems utterly impossible to understand. That other nations cooperated so easily seems to testify to a degree of unprecedented hatred toward Jews. And whereas other nations, including the great American democracy, did not take an active part in persecuting Jews, they lacked any concern for saving Jewish lives, callously turning away refugee ships and denying entry to those fleeing persecution and death. One wonders, who really cared for the Jews?

Yes, there were brave individuals who stood against the tide, people who risked their own lives to save Jewish lives, "the righteous of the nations," as Yad Vashem calls them, and they deserve all the honor and love we can give. These individuals also imbue us with hope that not everyone is against us. I have met such people and admire them greatly. Yet their numbers were all too small.

As one who grew up when Hitler was in power and lived through that entire era, albeit in the safe shelter of America and with no known relatives who went through the Shoah, I too had no sympathy for Germany or Germans. It could even be said that I returned their hatred. I would never knowingly buy anything made in Germany and certainly never drive a German car. Nor would I set foot in Germany.

I vividly recall returning from America to Israel sometime in the 1980s when, at the last minute because of an airline strike, I was put on a chartered plane that made an unannounced stop at a German airport. Looking out the window, I saw that German police carrying machine guns had surrounded our plane. Even though I knew they were there to protect and not to harm us, shudders went through my entire body. When airline officials announced on the public address system that all passengers had to deplane and wait in the airport terminal, I refused, because I would not tread on the cursed ground of Germany. The crew insisted that I leave, but I was adamant. Finally, they had no choice but to allow me to remain on board.

But times change. In 2005 I was living in England and was a member of the European Rabbinical Assembly, which was having a conference in Berlin organized by the rabbis who served congregations in Berlin and elsewhere in Germany and partly subsidized by the German government. I was invited to attend and, with trepidation, decided to do so.

In the end I did not regret my decision. I was impressed by the German officials we met who demonstrated sincere commitment to supporting Jewish institutions in Germany and to teaching the truth about the Holocaust to Germans. I was moved by the many signs describing what had been done to Jews that had been erected at various sites around the city. I also realized that, for the most part, the people I met and the crowds I saw on the streets could not possibly have taken any part in the Shoah because they hadn't been born yet. I could not blame them for what had been done as long as they acknowledged it and carried it as part of a burden of German history.

There is no question of forgiving Germany. There can be no forgiveness for the Shoah. And I am not naive: I recognize that today as well, antisemitism exists in Germany—as it does throughout Europe and in America. Yet there is a difference between the Germany of yesterday and the Germany of today: the current German government fights against rather than with the antisemites. Germany today demonstrates that hatred of Jews need not be part of official government policy everywhere for all time.

Simḥat Torah

The Never-Ending Cycle

DEUTERONOMY 33:1–34:12, GENESIS 1:1–2:3

*So Moses the servant of the Lord died there, in the land of
Moab, at the command of the Lord. He [God] buried him in the
valley of the land of Moab, near Beth-peor; and no one knows
his burial place to this day.... Never again did there arise in
Israel a prophet like Moses—whom the Lord singled out, face
to face, for the various signs and portents that the Lord sent
him to display in the land of Egypt, against Pharaoh and all
his courtiers and his whole country, and for all the great might
and awesome power that Moses displayed before all Israel.*
—Deuteronomy 34:5–6,10–12

*When God began to create heaven and earth—the earth
being unformed and void, with darkness over the surface of
the deep and a wind from God sweeping over the water—
God said, "Let there be light"; and there was light.*
—Genesis 1:1–3

P'shat: Explanation

The end and the beginning—in that order—are what we read on
Simḥat Torah. It is as if the Torah has no beginning and no end but
simply goes on forever. Thus the last verses (quoted above) lead directly
into the first verses.

Simḥat Torah is unlike any other festival mentioned in the Torah.
For one thing, the Torah never mentions any day by that name. It
does not exist. In the Diaspora it is celebrated on the second day

318

of Shemini Atzeret. In Israel, where the original biblical calendar is followed and the additional second days of festivals are not celebrated, Simḥat Torah is observed on Shemini Atzeret itself. They are one and the same.

Simḥat Torah developed in Babylonia in the Geonic period (late in the first millennium) as a celebration of the end of the yearly cycle of Torah readings and the beginning of the new cycle. The one-year cycle of Torah readings was the custom in Babylonia. At that time in the Land of Israel, however, the Torah was read once in three years, and the end of the cycle did not always fall on the same date, as it did in Babylonia.

The entire last section of the Torah, Ve-zo't ha-berakhah, is read only on Simḥat Torah and not on a Shabbat and is followed immediately by the opening part of the first section, Bere'shit. The entire portion of Bere'shit is read on the Shabbat following Simḥat Torah. Unlike Shavuot, which became a celebration of receiving the Torah, Simḥat Torah celebrates having read the entire Torah, finishing one cycle and beginning a new one. We celebrate that achievement with joyful song and dance, calling everyone up for an *aliyah* to the Torah and carrying the Torah scrolls around the synagogue. The importance of the Torah to Judaism and the Jewish people is emphasized in this unique way.

I think it is safe to say that for all the importance that sacred writings play in other religions, none has quite the central place as the Torah has within Judaism. The idea of reading the sacred text out loud publicly so that everyone would know what it says, rather than it being the secret possession of priests and religious leaders alone, goes back to early biblical times. There was the custom of *Hakhel*: reading it, or substantial parts of it, aloud once every seven years "in the presence of all Israel . . . men, women, children" (Deuteronomy 31:11–12). In 444 BCE, during the time of Ezra, when Jews had returned from exile in Babylon, the entire Torah was read aloud and explained to the assembled populace (Nehemiah 8). And when synagogues emerged during Second Temple times, it became customary to read and explain the Torah there every Shabbat. It was even more important than prayer.

Because on Simḥat Torah we begin by reading the last section of the Torah and then follow with the first section, we experience the Torah from a different point of view. Usually we think of it as moving from the cosmic vision of an exalted being who created the universe to a more narrow concern with the history of one nation, the Israelites, and the death of one person, Moses. But beginning with that and then reading of creation delivers a different message: the God who cares for Moses is the same God who created and governs the entire universe. Particularism and universalism, care for the individual and for the cosmos, are not opposites but two sections of a whole — inseparable parts of the divine concern. As the Sages said, wherever you find God's exalted nature, there too you find God's humility: God's care for humankind.

D'rash: Exposition of the Sages

"He [God] buried him in the valley of the land of Moab, near Beth-peor. . . ." Why did Moses merit having the Holy One perform his burial? It was because when the time arrived for the redemption of Israel from Egypt all the Israelites busied themselves with gathering silver and gold [from the Egyptians] while Moses toiled for three days and nights to find Joseph's coffin since they would not be able to leave Egypt without Joseph's body. Why? Because before he died Joseph had made them swear to do so (Genesis 50:25). . . . [When Moses found the coffin] he placed it upon his shoulders and carried it while all the Israelites followed him. The Israelites were carrying the gold and silver that they took from the Egyptians while Moses carried the coffin of Joseph. The Holy One said to him, "You may think that what you have done is insignificant, but — by your life! — this act of loving kindness that you have done is a great one, for you did not

care about silver and gold for yourself. Therefore I Myself
will perform that same act of loving kindness for you!"
—Deuteronomy Rabbah 11:7

Rabbi Simlai explained: The Torah begins and ends with acts
of loving kindness. It begins with acts of loving kindness, as it is
said, "And the Lord God made garments of skins for Adam and
his wife, and clothed them" (Genesis 3:21). It ends with acts of
loving kindness, as it is said, "He [God] buried him in the valley
of the land of Moab, near Beth-peor . . ." (Deuteronomy 34:6).
—Sotah 14a

The very last action God performs in the Torah is to bury Moses. The
Sages noted and commented on this fact. No one else is ever said to
have been buried by God; why did Moses warrant such an honor?

Remembering that the text says, "And Moses took with him the
bones of Joseph" (Exodus 13:19), the Sages connected these two
unusual events. After all, Moses was the leader of Israel. Why should
he have taken it upon himself to find and take Joseph's bones? Surely
someone else could have found and carried them. The Sages contrasted
this with the Israelites' busyness in taking silver and gold from the
Egyptians as recompense for their years of slavery.

In Judaism caring for the dead is considered perhaps the most
extreme act of *hesed* (loving-kindness), for the one who gives receives
nothing in return. The dead cannot express thanks for what you have
done. The Sages conclude that because Moses took it upon himself
to perform this act, God rewards him by declaring that God will do
the very same thing for Moses, and does.

Rabbi Simlai notices that the Torah begins with God performing
another act of *hesed*: clothing the naked. The Torah's mention of the
Holy One making garments for Adam and Eve is also unusual. That
the Supreme Being, the Master of the Universe, would undertake the
humble act of sewing garments is surely not to be taken for granted.
There is no other such incident in the Torah.

Burying the dead and clothing the naked are two of the many acts of loving-kindness frequently mentioned in the Torah, and so, Rabbi Simlai says, they frame the entire Torah, indicating that this is what the Torah is all about. We are to follow God's actions and perform similar acts for others. This too is the message of Simḥat Torah.

D'rash: Personal Reflection

MOSCOW 1976

The evening of Simḥat Torah outside the synagogue in Moscow was one of the most moving times of my USSR mission of 1976, when the Israeli government secretly sent me to meet with refuseniks. The massive gathering of Jews in Moscow that night has become legendary in the story of Russian Jewry's struggle for freedom. The police had cordoned off the street, and it was jammed with people, an estimated fifteen to twenty thousand. There was no way of knowing, because the authorities never officially acknowledged the event. It had snowed earlier that day, and some had feared that people would not come, but obviously nothing could keep them away.

Not everyone there was a refusenik, I was told, but anyone who still wanted to be a Jew or meet other Jews would not have thought of missing it. There was a greater feeling of freedom there than ever before. Many groups of young people were playing Israeli music on guitars, accordions, and other instruments. Some had brought amplifiers. All of this was happening openly in the streets of Moscow. The KGB was there as well, but the singing and dancing were unceasing. *Simcha*—joy—was the prevailing feeling.

One young man told me he had just received permission to leave and would be going to Israel very soon. He was wearing a pin with the letter *mem* on it. I asked him what it meant; he said it stood for *moreh* (teacher), because he was a Hebrew teacher. "They'll have to find another one now," he said. Someone else asked if I could arrange to bring more books on Jewish culture into the country. "Please," he said, "tell people not to be so timid. Some things do get through. We cannot neglect Jewish culture!" I suggested he come to a lecture I was giving a few nights later, but he said he could not because he was going to Siberia to meet a well-known Jewish activist who had been exiled there. "I must go and see how he is. It is important that someone sees what is happening." He also spoke of another Jew who was still in prison, hoping that he might be exchanged for someone held by the Americans.

Even with all the joy of the evening, the stark reality of Jewish life in the USSR could not be ignored. This reality brought a chill colder than that of the Moscow winter night. Whenever Simḥat Torah comes around, that night in Moscow lingers in my memory.

Hanukkah

Light versus Might

ZECHARIAH 2:14–4:7

This is the word of the Lord to Zerubbabel: Not by might,
nor by power, but by My spirit—said the Lord of Hosts.
—Zechariah 4:6

P'shat: Explanation

Hanukkah was the last of all the Jewish festivals to be added to the
Jewish year in Rabbinic times. It is also the only one that does not
appear anywhere in Scripture. Whole books were written about it in
ancient times, the books of Maccabees, but the Sages did not view
these books as sacred, possibly because they were written in Greek.
Hanukkah is also not featured in the Mishnah, the earliest collection
of the Sages' writings.

On the Shabbat of Hanukkah the haftarah reading is taken from
the prophet Zechariah. Living at the time of the Jewish return from
the Babylonian exile in the sixth century BCE, when the Jews experienced difficulties in reestablishing their independence and rebuilding
the Temple, the prophet spoke of the symbolism of the great candelabrum that had illuminated the Temple and made it the symbol of
God's great power. Therefore, he counseled hope and not despair
and taught that the divine spirit was greater than physical strength.

D'rash: Exposition of the Sages

What is Hanukkah? As the Sages taught: On the 25th of
Kislev eight days of Hanukkah begin, during which we do not

324

*give funeral orations or fast. That is because when the Greeks
entered the Temple, they rendered all the oil in the Temple
unclean. When the Maccabean Royal House overcame them
and was triumphant, they searched but found only one jar
of oil that had the seal of the High Priest. It contained only
one day's worth of oil. A miracle occurred concerning it, for
they were able to kindle lights with it for eight days. The
following year they appointed those days as festival days
with the recitation of Hallel and prayers of thanksgiving.*
— Shabbat 21b

This is the story the Sages told to explain why we light lamps on the eight days of Hanukkah. The books of Maccabees, on the other hand, record that on the 25th of Kislev the Maccabees rededicated the Temple "and celebrated the rededication of the altar for eight days and offered burnt offerings with joy and offered a sacrifice of deliverance and praise" (1 Maccabees 4:56–57). They also say that "they burned incense and lighted lamps . . . and they celebrated it for eight days with gladness like the festival of Sukkot remembering how on Sukkot they had still been wandering in the mountains like wild animals. . . . And they passed a public ordinance decreeing that the whole Jewish nation should observe these days every year" (2 Maccabees 10:6–8). These apocryphal books mention lighting lamps but say nothing about either a problem concerning the oil or a miracle with it.

Similarly, the paragraph inserted in the *Amidah* on Hanukkah echoes the books of Maccabees, explaining that we are thanking God for the miracles and deliverance that occurred when the Hashmonaim (Maccabees) overcame the Greeks. Coming into the Temple, the Maccabees "cleansed and purified the Sanctuary and kindled lights there. They set aside these eight days for giving thanks and chanting praise to You." Again, nothing is said about miraculous lights.

Furthermore, everyone must have known this story, so why did the Sages ask the question, What is Hanukkah? The real question seems not to be, Why do we celebrate Hanukkah? but two other, related questions, Why do we celebrate Hanukkah for eight days? and Why light lights for all eight days? One possible explanation, to imitate the eight days of Sukkot, was obviously not satisfactory for the Sages, so they told the story of the miraculous oil. Why? After all, in the case of Purim, the Sages seem to have felt no need to introduce any supernatural miracle. It was enough that the Jews overcame their enemy Haman and were not exterminated as he had planned.

Some have speculated that the Sages added the story of a supernatural miraculous event—as if the triumph over the Greeks was not miracle enough—out of a desire to play down the significance of the Maccabees. In the end the Hashmonaim dynasty turned out to be anything but glorious: the Hasmoneans took upon themselves the mantle of majesty, which belonged only to the House of David, and proved as cruel and corrupt as any Oriental kingdom. Theirs certainly could not be considered a legitimate substitute for the true kingship of the House of David.

I'm not certain if the miracle of the oil was inserted to play down the Maccabees. After all, they are mentioned in the story itself. Perhaps the real intent was to play down the role of military might and stress even more the power of the Almighty. Too much emphasis on military might may have seemed dangerous to the Sages after the disastrous failure in 70 CE of the Great Revolt, which many of the Sages seem to have opposed. Certainly, the great Rabban Yohanan ben Zakkai saw it as nothing but folly that would lead—as it did—to utter destruction. Better to concentrate on light and God as the source of light—as the prophet had said long before, "Not by might, nor by power, but by My spirit—said the Lord of Hosts" (Zechariah 4:6). Since this verse comes as part of the prophet's vision of the menorah as a symbol of God's spirit, it may have inspired the idea of the miracle of the oil continuing to burn in the menorah.

Certainly, strength is needed, but it must be exercised with discretion and not celebrated as the be-all and end-all of life.

The story of the oil is patterned after the folklore miracle stories told about the prophet Elijah, such as the jar of flour and the jug of oil that did not "give out" or "fail" but continued to multiply (1 Kings 17:14–16). Similar stories were told in Christian tradition, with loaves and fishes multiplying and water turning to wine.

On one level, then, the miraculous oil can be seen merely as an appealing, pious folktale. But perhaps the Sages had something else in mind. The flame, the symbol of God's presence and the triumph of goodness over evil, light over darkness, has a powerful place in Jewish tradition. Hanukkah, therefore, symbolizes not only a victory over our enemies but also the kindling of the light of God, of Torah, and of decency. This light must continue to illuminate us and must never be extinguished. If the light does not lead to illumination, victory is an illusion. That is the deeper message of Hanukkah.

D'rash: Personal Reflection

TOO MUCH LIGHT

My wife and I once spent Hanukkah in Tierra del Fuego, at the very southern tip of South America. There, at that time of year, the height of summer, there is no sunset. It never gets dark. And so we had a problem: When were we supposed to light the Hanukkah lights? We finally lit them just before going to sleep.

But the problem was not merely when to light the Hanukkah menorah but also whether we should do so at all. When there is no darkness, kindling lights becomes an exercise in futility. Lighting lights becomes significant only when darkness sets in.

It is not accidental that throughout the world, the time of darkness has become a time to light lights. Christmas lights play such a prominent role in that holiday. Many cultures have a similar practice that probably originated in sympathetic magic. To encourage the sun to shine longer, the people would light fires. They believed this would help to restore the sun's brilliance.

Lighting lights when the days are short and dark is also a very human thing to do. It is well known that the gloom of darkness causes depression and may even increase suicides in far northern regions. It makes sense, then, that Jews would have wanted to light lights at Hanukkah time, in the winter season, in order to dispel the darkness and brighten their lives.

Pagans did the same thing. And so I believe the Sages told the story of the miraculous oil because they wanted to make certain that kindling lights was not viewed as a mere imitation of pagan practices but was truly tied to the events of Hanukkah.

We all need light in our lives. Humans have both physical and physiological needs for light in the winter season, and there is also a psychological need for something to brighten our lives whenever things seem dark. This is as true today when we are depressed about events in our larger world as it was in the times of the Sages. We all need to be reassured that there is hope that things will improve, just as there is hope that there will be increased light in the days to come. That is also the reason why Hillel's way of lighting the lights of the Hanukkah menorah—increasing the number of lit candles each day—became the standard practice, instead of Shammai's method of decreasing the number each day until there were none. Increasing light is optimistic; decreasing it is pessimistic. One gives us hope; the other takes it away.

Experiencing no darkness in Tierra del Fuego helped me to really realize the beauty and the profundity of the story of the cruse of oil, even if it is only a legend. Although lighting candles in the absence of darkness seemed a strange thing to do, we can do so in the awareness that there is always a need to bring the light of God's presence and moral teaching into a world in which these are lacking. Our struggle is not against physical darkness but against moral and spiritual darkness. When there is darkness, let there be light. When there is evil, let there be good. When there is suffering and need, let us bring God's light into the world through our deeds.

Light can be increased in the world, but only when we take actions to improve the world and thus fight against the darkness that threatens our treasured values. We are to think of this when we kindle the lights of Hanukkah.

Purim

Why Not Bow Down?

THE BOOK OF ESTHER

Some time afterward, King Ahasuerus promoted Haman
son of Hammedatha the Agagite; he advanced him and
seated him higher than any of his fellow officials. All the
king's courtiers in the palace gate knelt and bowed low
to Haman, for such was the king's order concerning him;
but Mordecai would not kneel or bow low. Then the king's
courtiers who were in the palace gate said to Mordecai,
"Why do you disobey the king's order?" . . . He explained
to them that he was a Jew. . . . Haman was filled with
rage. But he disdained to lay hands on Mordecai alone. . . .
Haman plotted to do away with all the Jews, Mordecai's
people, throughout the kingdom of Ahasuerus.
—Esther 3:1–6

P'shat: Explanation

The entire book of Esther, usually referred to simply as "the Megillah," *the* scroll, is read in both the evening and the morning on Purim. It is an unusual book. It presents itself as an account of important events written by Mordecai and sent to the Jews throughout Persia, instructing them to observe these days of Purim, an obligation they took upon themselves (Esther 9:20–23). The book's purpose, then, is to explain why Purim is observed. Even more unusual is the fact that the book never mentions God and never refers to any religious observance, not even a prayer of thanksgiving. The common explanation among scholars is that it was written to explain and justify the Persian Jews' observance of a carnival-like holiday; actually, it is a Jewish version of a Persian myth about the triumph of the good gods Marduk and Ishtar over the evil god Human. It is a historical fiction, correctly depicting the ways of the Persian court and the lives of Jews under Persian rule, but it is not a factual record of historical events.

The story turns upon the verses cited above that explain why Haman hated the Jews and plotted "to destroy, massacre, and exterminate all the Jews, young and old, children and women, on a single day . . . and to plunder their possessions" (Esther 3:14). Problematically, Mordecai's refusal to bow down to Haman—the cause of all the trouble—seems at first to be without any reason. Hebrews often bowed down to non-Jews, as Moses bowed to Jethro (Exodus 18:7). There is no prohibition against it. When Mordecai says that it is because he is "a Jew," the text does not explain why being a Jew kept Mordecai from showing respect to Haman, the king's appointee.

By way of explanation, some biblical scholars point to how Haman is introduced in the text. We are told that he is "the son of Hammedatha the Agagite." This is not a piece of useless information. Agagite refers to King Agag, ruler of the Amalekites at the time of King Saul (1 Samuel 15:8). Samuel had commanded Saul to slay King Agag together with all the Amalekites in retaliation for the Amalekites' cowardly attack on the Israelites when they fled Egypt: "Now go, attack Amalek, and proscribe all that belongs to him. Spare no one, but kill all alike" (1 Samuel 15:3). In the Torah the Amalekites are the symbol of evil, the eternal enemies of the Israelites, the foes God swore to exterminate: "The Lord will be at war with Amalek throughout the ages" (Exodus 17:16). Of course, then, Mordecai will not bow down to Haman, of the seed of Agag the Amalekite king. A Jew does not bow down to Amalek! Mordecai's disrespect is thus not without cause. It is part of the deep-seated enmity between Israel and Amalek, played out yet again here in the story of Purim.

D'rash: Exposition of the Sages

But Mordecai would not kneel or bow low. Was Mordecai
looking for a quarrel or to be disobedient to the king's order?
When Ahasuerus ordered people to bow down to Haman,
Haman placed an idolatrous image on his breast so that
everyone would bow down to an idol. When Haman saw
that Mordecai refused to bow down to it, he was filled with
rage. Mordecai said to him, "There is One who is above
all who are worshipped. How can I abandon Him and
bow down to an idol?" That is why Mordecai is called a
Jew—Yehudi—because like Abraham he proclaimed the
yehidi—the oneness (uniqueness) of God! He sanctified
God's name and caused many others to acknowledge
God's greatness, as we read, "And many of the people
of the land professed to be Jews . . ." (Esther 8:17).
—Esther Rabbah 6:2

Because the book of Esther is so totally devoid of religious concern, lacking even a mention of God, when the book was translated into other languages, including in ancient times, attempts were made to insert prayers and observances of Jewish rituals. Similarly bothered, the Sages often filled in the lacunae in their midrashic comments.

In the section quoted here, they offer a religious explanation for Mordecai's refusal to bow down to Haman. Knowing that Jews are not forbidden to bow down to gentile officials but are forbidden to bow down to idols, the Sages supply the fact that Haman wore the image of an idol and expected everyone to acknowledge that idol. Mordecai, as a Jew, refused to do so and explained that his religion forbade such a thing. This would explain why Haman wanted to kill all the Jews: they had refused to acknowledge the gods of Persia.

The Sages also comment on the fact that Mordecai is identified as being a Jew—Yehudi. That is an unusual word, since at that time "Israelite" was the more common expression. The Sages indicate that

Mordecai was not from the tribe of Judah—Yehudi could also mean a Judaite—so they suggest reading the word slightly differently, as *yehidi*, meaning "unique" or "one"; this would refer to Mordecai's teaching the oneness of God. Thus they depict Mordecai as doing what the midrash said Abraham did: converting people to the belief in one God. They then use the later verse relaying that many Persians suddenly became Jews or began to act like Jews in order to avoid being killed as proof of something quite different, namely, that Mordecai taught the Persians about the one God and converted many of them to Jewish belief. The lack of religious teaching in Esther is thus overcome.

D'rash: Personal Reflection

THE MEGILLAH AS HISTORY

Once, in the spring of 1956, I experienced a completely different reading of the Megillah.

Up to that point, because I had studied the biblical books using the academic discipline of biblical criticism, I had always understood Esther as historical fiction. Aside from this, in keeping with Jewish practice, the usual readings of the Megillah I had attended were rather raucous and humorous affairs. The name of Haman the villain was drowned out by noisemakers and/or shouting, and people were in costume and ready for a carnival.

I was therefore in for a shock when one of my professors at the Hebrew University in Jerusalem, Ezra Melamed, invited me to the Megillah reading at the synagogue he served as rabbi and spiritual leader. Congregation Anshei Shushan—the People of Shushan—was comprised of Persian Jews who had come from the Iranian city they identified with the ancient biblical Shushan, where the book of Esther takes place. In the early part of the twentieth century, they had left behind their ancestors' graves, as well as the traditional burial sites of Esther and Mordecai, to journey to then Palestine with Professor Melamed's father, their rabbi. Now Professor Melamed had inherited this position.

The members of this congregation considered the story in the book of Esther to be their ancestral history. They took it all very seriously. Purim was their story. One did not make light of one's story of salvation.

They had their own customs and even their own special foods for Purim. Hamantaschen were unknown to them. As their name indicates, these cookies were an Ashkenazi recipe. The members of this congregation ate some very flat cake instead. The synagogue was in an old part of new Jerusalem, a section of winding streets and small houses. It was not elaborate or large. There was a women's balcony, where my wife sat. There were absolutely no costumes and no Purim noisemakers. The rule was that no noise at all could be made during the reading. Every word was sacred and was to be heard, even the accursed name of Haman. Professor Melamed himself read the Megillah. He used a cantillation melody, but not the one I knew, and, truth be told, he declaimed rather than sang it and gave a dramatic reading worthy of Laurence Olivier. I am only sorry I had no way of recording it.

I listened, enthralled and anxious to know how it would all come out. I remember one particularly very exciting section. When Esther described Haman's evil plan, Melamed very dramatically shouted out the king's question, "Who is he and where is he who would dare to do this?" (Esther 7:5), then spat out Esther's answer, "The adversary and the enemy is this evil Haman!" (Esther 7:6), pointing him out. A collective gasp arose from the congregation. Soon after, once the king was reminded that Haman had prepared a fifty-cubit-high stake to execute Mordecai, came those words of doom: "Impale him on it!" At that point a woman shouted out from the balcony, "Kakh l'Natzer!" (So too for Nasser), the Egyptian ruler at that time, a sworn enemy of Israel.

Today, Professor Melamed, of blessed memory, is long gone, and I don't know if or where that synagogue still exists. And even though my rational mind tells me that it's only a story and we should all hoot and shout and have a good time when we hear it, there is a spot somewhere in me that recalls this time at Purim when I heard the book of Esther read as real history by people who believed every word.

Pesach

Festival of Freedom

EXODUS 12:21-51

*And they baked unleavened cakes of the dough that they had
taken out of Egypt, for it was not leavened, since they had
been driven out of Egypt and could not delay; nor had they
prepared any provisions for themselves. The length of time
that the Israelites lived in Egypt was four hundred and thirty
years; at the end of the four hundred and thirtieth year, to the
very day, all the ranks of the Lord departed from the land of
Egypt. That was for the Lord a night of vigil to bring them
out of the land of Egypt; that same night is the Lord's, one
of vigil for all the children of Israel throughout the ages.*
—Exodus 12:39-42

P'shat: Explanation

The Torah reading for the first day of Pesach describes the events
beginning on the last night when the Israelites were in Egypt. They
slaughter the lamb and eat it, and God brings the tenth and final
plague upon Egypt—the slaying of the firstborn—which, finally,
impels Pharaoh to let them go. Taking with them the treasures the
Egyptians give them, a token recompense for their hundreds of years
of free labor, the people journey from Rameses to a place called Sukkot, one day's journey, and eat the unleavened bread they have made
from the dough they also brought with them. Thus we have the two
main symbols of the holiday—*pesach*, the paschal Lamb, and *matzah*,
the unleavened bread—which are to be eaten every year in commemoration of the Israelites' triumphal exit.

The event is summarized in the verses cited above, a ritualistic formulation that twice repeats the length of time the people have been in Egypt and twice proclaims that this was a special night of vigil for the Lord. Strangely enough, the period of time — 430 years — does not seem to accord with the words spoken to Abraham predicting the enslavement and redemption: "And they shall be enslaved and oppressed four hundred years . . . and they shall return here in the fourth generation" (Genesis 15:13,16). Nor do the numbers 430 and the fourth-generation coincide. The Sages calculated that 400 years represented the time from the birth of Isaac until the Exodus, while the words to Abraham were said 30 years before that, making 430. In any case, the actual number of years of enslavement had to be much fewer than that. Biblical chronology is often a puzzle.

D'rash: Exposition of the Sages

"Nor had they prepared any provisions for themselves."
This informs us of how praiseworthy Israel was, for they
did not say to Moses, "How can we go into the wilderness
without provisions for the journey?!" Rather, they trusted
him and followed Moses, as it is said, "Thus said the Lord:
I accounted to your favor the devotion of your youth. Your
love as a bride — how you followed Me in the wilderness,
in a land not sown" (Jeremiah 2:2). What was their
reward? "Israel was holy to the Lord . . ." (Jeremiah 2:3).
". . . at the end of the four hundred and thirtieth year, to
the very day. . . ." This informs us that as soon as the time
that had been designated came, God did not hold them
back for even a second. [Indeed] it was on the fifteenth
of Nisan that God spoke to Abraham our father.
". . . at the end of the four hundred and thirtieth year, to the
very day, all the ranks of the Lord departed from the land of
Egypt." ["Ranks of the Lord"] refers to the ministering angels.

So it is that you find that whenever Israel was enslaved,
the Divine Presence, as it were, was enslaved with them.
—*Mekhilta Pisha* 14

The Sages often attempted to understand why a particular unusual or seemingly superfluous word or phrase appeared in the Torah. This would then serve as the impetus for developing a new idea or understanding, just as a grain of sand serves as the impetus for growing a pearl.

One example is the Hebrew word translated as "ranks" (*tzivot*), which has many meanings. It is often translated as "hosts of." In this verse it probably refers to the Israelites themselves; they are the hosts of God.

Sometimes, though, it refers to the heavenly hosts, the angels, and that is the way the Sages understand it in this midrash. Therefore, the verse is taken to imply that at the same time that Israel was redeemed and freed from Egypt, the entire heavenly family, which would include God, was also redeemed, leaving Egypt. This new concept provided hope for Jews who were then living either in exile or in Israel under the yoke of Roman rule and oppression. The thought that God was with them in their suffering and would be redeemed with them gave them strength.

Similarly, the phrase "to the very day" seemed unusual and unnecessary. The Sages then taught that it was there to emphasize God's faithfulness to the divine promise of redemption. God spoke to Abraham on the 15th of Nisan, promising redemption in 430 years. *On that very same day*—and to the very instant—430 years later, the people were redeemed. Thus Israel could hope that promises of future redemption would also be promptly fulfilled.

Why, the Sages wondered, did the Torah need to tell us that the Israelites had not made any provisions for the journey? It was, they decided, in order to inform us that the people had perfect faith and trust: they went out into the wilderness, as Jeremiah later put it, a place where no food was to be had, simply at God's word as conveyed by Moses. Although we know that the journey was filled with incidents of the people's rebelliousness, nevertheless, at this moment, the relationship of Israel and God was how it always should be — one of trust and harmony, like a bride and groom.

D'rash: Personal Reflection

THE FESTIVAL OF DENIED FREEDOM

The Torah reading for Pesach, especially as interpreted by the Sages, is one of total triumph. It celebrates the release from bondage and envisions a future in which this celebration will be repeated year after year by a free people.

The midrashic compilations created by the Sages came into being after Israel had experienced the Babylonian exile, after the Second Temple was destroyed, and after the Roman exile had begun. Celebrating Pesach under those conditions would have had a very different feeling. Instead of being a free people enjoying the redemption that had come to them, the Israelites were downtrodden. At such a time the Sages thus emphasized the hope of future redemption, going so far as to contend that God too participates in the exile of Israel and will realize this future redemption both for the Israelites and for God.

As a Jew brought up in America, where Jews by and large did not feel oppressed or enslaved, and who then moved to Israel, where Jews live "as a free people in our own land," as the national anthem, "Hatikvah" (The hope), puts it, I have never experienced a Pesach seder under any such difficult conditions. The closest I ever came to that was in Spain in 1959.

I was serving as a chaplain in the United States Air Force, stationed at a Strategic Air Command (SAC) base in South Dakota. At that time American troops were stationed in Spain and North Africa, and it was decided to hold a seder for all these American Jewish service personnel in Madrid near a SAC base. Oddly enough, I was the closest SAC Jewish chaplain to that base, and so I was assigned to go to Spain and hold the seder in Madrid. First I flew to the East Coast, and from there I flew to the base in Spain. American Jewish service personnel from North Africa were also flown in to join those already in Spain.

For logistical reasons, the seder was to be held in a school building in Madrid rather than at the base. The base, however, provided all the new dishes and utensils we needed, while the Jewish Welfare Board shipped us *Haggadot* and kosher supplies.

Knowing there was a Jewish community in Madrid, I sought out and met with the local leaders. None of them were Spanish natives. All had come to Spain during the Second World War, escaping from the Nazis in France, Holland, and other countries. As they told me their stories, I learned that although Franco was a Fascist and had risen to power with the help of Nazi Germany, he had wisely remained neutral during the war and had not closed his borders to refugees. Jews who managed to get there—usually coming over the mountains from France—were permitted to remain.

Many of them had prospered in Spain and were content. They had a synagogue in Madrid. Under Spanish law at that time only Catholic churches were permitted to be seen by the public as houses of worship. Synagogues, like Protestant churches, could exist but were not allowed to display any symbols or signage to indicate what they were.

At the meeting I invited members of the community to join us for the seder. They were enthusiastic about the idea, but the government's permission was required for their attendance, and unfortunately, that permission was denied. No reason was given for this arbitrary decision, but then a dictatorship is never required to explain itself. Were officials somehow afraid that the Jewish locals' exposure to people who lived in a free country would create or add to their dissatisfaction? Whatever the reason, the air force was given strict orders that only Americans were to be permitted to enter the building where our seder was being held. To enforce that ruling, armed members of the Spanish Civil Guard were stationed at the entrance and examined the credentials of everyone who wished to enter, making certain that no Spanish citizens joined us inside.

And so it was: several hundred American servicemen and service-women attended the seder I conducted in the cafeteria room of a school in Madrid, while outside, members of the Spanish Civil Guard carefully checked that no Spanish Jew would be part of our festivities. In the meantime, the local Jewish community held its own seder in the Goya Room of a local hotel.

Our seder was a wonderful event for all those Jewish service personnel far away from home, but a shadow had been cast on it by the government-imposed limit on the Madrid Jewish community's freedom. Pesach is Ḥag ha-Herut—the Festival of Freedom. A seder conducted while armed guards stood outside to prevent Jews from America and from Spain from celebrating together was an unpleasant contradiction in terms.

Yom ha-Shoah

The Cry of the Lowly

PSALM 10

*Why, O Lord, do You stand aloof, heedless in times of
trouble? The wicked in his arrogance hounds the lowly—
may they be caught in the schemes they devise! . . . Rise,
O Lord! Strike at him, O God! Do not forget the lowly.*
—Psalm 10:1–2,12

P'shat: Explanation

There is no official liturgy or Torah reading for Yom ha-Shoah, which
has the official title the Memorial Day for the Shoah Martyrs and
Heroes. In 1959 the Knesset of Israel created this holiday to commemorate the Holocaust. Officials selected the date of the 27th of Nisan
because of its connection with the Warsaw Ghetto uprising, which
began on the 14th of Nisan, the day before Passover. Such a memorial
would have been inappropriate on Passover, so a date shortly after
the holiday was chosen.

The vast majority of Jewish communities in the world accept and
observe this day of commemoration, even though there is no one liturgy that all follow. Psalm 10 is frequently recited because it seems
so appropriate; it could have been written by a victim of the Shoah.
It calls upon God to rescue the innocent and punish the wicked who
are perpetrating this terrible crime and causing so much suffering.
The psalm concludes with the assurance that God hears the cry of
the lowly and downtrodden so that "men who are of the earth [will]
tyrannize no more" (Psalm 10:18).

It may be that in the long run evil is defeated, but sometimes it is too late. To our great sorrow, this was the case with the six million Jews who were murdered by the most efficient killing machine ever devised by the wicked of the earth.

D'rash: Exposition of the Sages

"The voice of your brother's blood cries out to Me from the ground" (Genesis 4:10). Said Rabbi Shimon bar Yochai: A parable. It may be likened to two gladiators striving with one another before the emperor. If the emperor wished, he could have separated them. But he did not wish to do so, so one overpowered the other. As he was being slain, the gladiator cried out, "I demand justice from the Emperor!" Thus—"The sound of your brother's blood cries out to Me."
—Genesis Rabbah 22

In the Cain and Abel story, after Cain murders his brother, God curses Cain for what he has done. There is no indication that God could have prevented this.

Shimon bar Yochai gives the words "The sound of your brother's blood cries out to Me" a daring interpretation. He sees this as a protest on the part of the slain brother's blood, a protest against God, as it were, who, like the emperor, did not prevent the killing. Bar Yochai is raising the question that so many ask: Why did God not prevent this? Or, as the Psalmist put it, "Why, O Lord, do You stand aloof?"

Indeed, the voices of the six million call out for justice. Why didn't God intervene? We have no answer, only the sound of silence. Yet to say that God could have saved the Jews but did not or, even worse, that God did not *want* to save them is surely blasphemy. Perhaps the most we can say is that by giving human beings free will, God created a situation in which, in the short run at least, the wicked can indeed succeed.

What kind of a world would it be if God prevented every such act? A very different one from the one we know. What is to be remembered here is God's warning to Cain, before Cain commits the world's first murder, that "sin crouches at the door" but that "you can be its master" (Genesis 4:7). This implies freedom of choice—but also includes the advice, indeed the imperative, to make the right choice and not give in to sin.

The Shoah is the prime example of human beings ignoring that divine command and bringing catastrophe because of it.

D'rash: Personal Reflection

LESSONS OF THE SHOAH

My bar mitzvah took place in June 1946, a year and a half after the liberation of Auschwitz. I recently came across the brief talk I gave at that ceremony. A central point in it was that because of the murder of six million Jews, it was more important than ever for me to devote myself to the well-being of the Jewish people and the preservation of Judaism and its way of life.

What impelled me to say that? My own family had no immediate connection to the Shoah. If we had relatives in Europe who had perished or survived, we did not know of them. The closest personal contact I had with survivors was visiting a camp for Jewish displaced persons whom the United States had permitted to come to America on a temporary basis. They were taken to a facility not far from Syracuse, where I lived, and not permitted to leave it. The Syracuse Jewish community organized itself to help them, visiting and bringing the people whatever they needed. My family would do that on Sundays.

Seeing my bar mitzvah speech made me realize that my concern with commemorating the Shoah has been with me since that early point in my life. In the early 1960s I published articles in various Jewish journals suggesting new ways to observe Yom ha-Shoah and urging my fellow rabbis to hold Yom ha-Shoah services in synagogues and not only in the general community, as was the typical practice of the time. Annually, in my own synagogue in suburban Chicago I created an elaborate service that included readings from Holocaust literature and the use of slides, documentary films, music, and other media. Many congregants participated in the readings, which involved long rehearsals and preparations. These well-attended services became a high point of the year.

Later, after making *aliyah*, I was part of a group of Israeli Conservative rabbis in the early 1980s who created and published a special service for Yom ha-Shoah held in all the Masorti (Conservative) synagogues in Israel on that date each year. Later, in 2003, when I was president of the International Rabbinical Assembly, together with the Schechter Institute we created *Megillat HaShoah*, "The Holocaust Scroll," a special text to be read each year on Yom ha-Shoah in Masorti synagogues worldwide. Each of its six chapters addresses a different aspect of the Shoah. It serves the same purpose for Yom ha-Shoah as the book of Lamentations does for Tisha b'Av: it is a special text that is read year after year to commemorate the event.

The service begins with my prayer:

> The ark of Torah, of faith, of learning, stands empty and bereft.
> We have come here to remember those who cannot be forgotten.
> We have come to speak of that which cannot be spoken but must not be left unsaid.
> We have come to remind not others but ourselves of what was done and what was not done.
> We have come to ask questions that cannot be answered but cannot be left unasked.

As someone who was born the year Hitler came to power, I suppose I have always felt that I was spared only because of my grandparents' decision to emigrate from Eastern Europe to America at the end of the nineteenth century. Otherwise, that fate would have awaited me in Europe. I had a life of ease and comfort, while those born in Europe at the same time suffered through the Shoah and lived or died in ways I could not imagine. The least I could do would be to memorialize them and to teach the lessons of the Shoah. We are to "never forget" and ensure that this "never [happens] again."

But there is more. Remarkably, the lesson of Egyptian slavery as imparted in the Torah is that because we suffered as strangers in Egypt, we must never treat strangers in our midst that way. Similarly, the lesson of the Shoah is that because we suffered from the Nazi calumny that some humans are actually less than human and therefore can be eliminated, we must never believe—and always protest—any such teaching. The blood of six million martyrs cries out against silence in the face of such evil. All human life is sacred.

Yom ha-Atzmaut

Land of Milk and Honey

DEUTERONOMY 26:1–12

*I acknowledge this day before the Lord your God that I
have entered the land that the Lord swore to our fathers
to assign us. . . . He brought us to this place and gave
us this land, a land flowing with milk and honey. . . .
And you shall enjoy, together with the Levite and the
stranger in your midst, all the bounty that the Lord your
God has bestowed upon you and your household.*
—Deuteronomy 26:3,9,11

P'shat: Explanation

Yom ha-Atzmaut—Israel Independence Day—is a new holiday on the
Jewish calendar established only in 1948. It is held on the Hebrew date
of the declaration of Israel's independence, the 5th of Iyar.

Since it was established by the Knesset, Israel's parliament, it really
began as a civil rather than a religious holiday. It has, however, been
incorporated into the religious festival cycle by all the various Jewish
religious streams (with the exception of most ultra-Orthodox groups,
which do not acknowledge it as such).

Each community, however, makes its own decisions as to how Yom
ha-Atzmaut is to be commemorated. Some recite the *Hallel* prayer;
others recite it but without a blessing. Some include a special section
in the *Amidah*, the central prayer, describing the miracle of the creation of the State of Israel. Some have a Torah reading (and those that
do tend to choose different sections to read); others do not.

The reading I have cited above is common in Israel where I live. The beginning of the section Ki Tavo' in Deuteronomy, it describes the ceremony of bringing the First Fruits to the Temple, accompanied by a declaration made to the priest, to whom the basket of fruit is given. The fruit is a physical symbol of our having come to the land and our now enjoying its fruits. The declaration itself is a brief recapitulation of Jewish history: our earliest ancestors were wanderers who went down to Egypt and were enslaved there; they cried out to God, who freed them and then brought them to a land "flowing with milk and honey."

D'rash: Exposition of the Sages

Rami ben Ezekiel once visited Bene-Brak. He saw goats grazing under fig trees. Honey was flowing from figs and milk ran from [the goats] and they mingled with one another. "Indeed," he said, "this is 'a land flowing with milk and honey'!" Rabbi Jacob ben Dostai said: It is three miles from Lod to Ono. I once went there early in the morning and was wading up to my ankles in fig-honey. Resh Lakish said: I once saw milk and honey flowing in Sepphoris and it extended over an area sixteen by sixteen miles. Our Rabbis taught: In the blessed years of the Land of Israel, an area of fifty cubits by fifty cubits would yield fifty thousand kor [of grain] while Zoan [in Egypt] even at its best yielded no more than seventy. . . . Even Hebron, the rockiest ground in the Land of Israel, was seven times more fertile than Zoan, the most fertile place in Egypt! Rabbi Zera went up to the Land of Israel and could not find a boat to ferry him across the river [Jordan], so he crossed grasping a rope. When someone sneered at him . . . he replied, "Should I not rush to enter the place where even Moses and Aaron were not allowed to enter?"

—Tractate *Ketubbot* 112a

These are but a few of the many sayings found in the Talmud praising the fertility of the Land of Israel and demonstrating the Sages' love for the land. The Sages often used extravagant language to emphasize that the Torah's words concerning the land were accurate; it was more fertile and more to be praised than any other land. Similar passages both in the Talmud and in ancient midrashim make the same point, going so far as to state that even the stoniest and least fertile part of Israel, namely, Hebron, which was good only for a burial ground, was better than Zoan, the best part of Egypt. Unfortunately, these accounts are not exactly accurate, but on the other hand, the land is a good land that can sustain excellent crops when properly handled. And it does have both milk and date-honey in abundance.

The Sages also tell us the story of Rabbi Zeira, a third-century Sage from Babylonia who, feeling discontented with his life in the Diaspora, left to study and teach in the Land of Israel. He was so impatient to reach the land that he could not even wait for the ferry to take him across the river. He contrasted himself to Moses and Aaron, who, for all their greatness, were never able to enter the land. Now that he was so privileged, how could he possibly wait even an instant?

This charming story emphasizes the importance of dwelling in the land and the idea that living there is a great privilege.

D'rash: Personal Reflection

WELCOME TO THE LAND

Although we made *aliyah* to Israel as a family in 1973, my wife and I first visited Israel in the fall of 1955. As part of my Jewish Theological Seminary rabbinical training, I was permitted to spend a year in Jerusalem studying at the Hebrew University and participating in a special program the seminary ran there.

As was common at that time, we did not come by plane but by ship. Together with another rabbinical student and his wife, we crossed the

Atlantic and landed in France, traveled through Europe, and then in Italy boarded another ship that would take us to Haifa.

After a rather stormy voyage, we were due to arrive there early that morning. A bit like Rabbi Zeira, the four of us arose at dawn and stood on the deck to catch our first view of Israel. We were very excited when Haifa came into view and could hardly wait for the ship to dock.

Passport control was then a much simpler and more personal affair than it is now. We went into a shed of some sort. One man was there, sitting behind a desk. He took my passport, looked at me, and, before he stamped it, said, "Ma Shlom Yehudi?" — literally, "Is all well with a Jew?" (the Hebrew version of the well-known Yiddish phrase "Vos macht a yid?"). This simple greeting startled me for a moment. In the Diaspora the term "Jew" has pejorative connotations. I was not used to being called "Jew" in such a positive and friendly way. I realized then what it meant to be in a land of our own, to be home. Many years later, when deciding to come on *aliyah,* I still recalled the deep impression that simple Hebrew greeting "Ma Shlom Yehudi?" had made upon me. I never forgot it.

A highlight of our year was Yom ha-Atzmaut. We watched as Israel's eighth Independence Day began with a ceremony dedicating a huge elaborate menorah, the symbol of the state, that had been erected in a small park near the building on King George Street housing the Knesset. (Now it stands near the monumental Knesset building in the government compound.) After that, a brief ceremony commemorating Israel's fallen soldiers was held.

Then we joined the hordes of people streaming into the center of Jerusalem, where everyone sang and danced throughout the night. This was not part of a planned celebration but the extemporaneous outpouring of feeling on the part of Israelis who had struggled for so many years to achieve independence. They did not take it for granted.

Since the state was then so young, the exuberance of the celebration was less elaborate but much more spontaneous than it has since become. Those celebrating the creation of a Jewish state for the first time in two thousand years were those who were responsible for making it happen—and those who had paid the price for it.

The next day we traveled by bus to Haifa to view the official military parade. It was impressive to see the ranks of soldiers, both men and women, striding down the avenue. The idea of a Jewish army defending a Jewish state was still a novelty and a source of pride for someone like myself who had never seen such a thing before. (Looking back, the military equipment so proudly displayed was nothing like what Israel has now, but it was enough to permit Israel's massive sweep into Sinai the following August in response to the Palestinian terrorist incursions into Israel that had occurred over that entire year.) We returned to Jerusalem that night, tired but exhilarated by our participation in Yom ha-Atzmaut in the place where it all happened.

Even though Yom ha-Atzmaut in Israel is now much more elaborate, organized, and populated with events than it was in 1956, the newness and freeness of the celebration that year would be difficult to reproduce. Nevertheless, I still feel that of all the holidays in the Jewish year, Yom ha-Atzmaut is the only one that must be celebrated in Israel in order to be truly realized. We have been able to do that since making *aliyah* in 1973, and the few times that, for one reason or another, I have been elsewhere on that date, I have truly missed being in Israel—I have felt a void. Going on a picnic in England or joining a synagogue-based celebration in New York is no substitute for a simple barbecue with friends in Jerusalem. No matter what is done, nothing can compare with simply being there and sharing the day with others who also feel, and live, the importance of having achieved independence and renewal after two thousand years.

Shavuot

The New Covenant

EXODUS 19:1–20:23

*"'You have seen what I did to the Egyptians, how I bore you
on eagle's wings and brought you to Me. Now, then, if you will
obey Me faithfully and keep My covenant, you shall be to Me
a kingdom of priests and a holy nation.' These are the words
that you shall speak to the children of Israel." Moses came and
summoned the elders of the people and put before them all
that the Lord had commanded him. All the people answered
as one, saying, "All that the Lord has spoken we will do!"*
—Exodus 19:4–8

P'shat: Explanation

Although in the Torah the holiday of Shavuot is not connected to
any historical event, the Torah reading for that day recounts the ceremony held at Mount Sinai when the Decalogue was proclaimed by
God and accepted by the people of Israel. The reason is that at some
point during Second Temple days, the Pharisaic Sages determined
that the events at Sinai took place on Shavuot. The Torah says it was
in "the third new moon after the Israelites had gone forth from the
land of Egypt" (Exodus 19:1). That was, after all, the month in which
Shavuot is celebrated, and so the Sages designated Shavuot as "the
time of the giving of our Torah."

The significance of this event, called in Hebrew *ma-amad har Sinai*—
"the ceremony at Mount Sinai"—is summed up in the words spoken
before the Decalogue is revealed. The people have come to Sinai, as
God told Moses at the burning bush that they would (Exodus 3:12), in

order to enter into a covenant with God. If they accept that covenant, they will become "a kingdom of priests and a holy nation." By declaring "All that the Lord has spoken we will do!" the Israelites indicate their acceptance. At that moment the die is cast, and the very nature of the people of Israel is transformed.

Previously, God had entered into a covenant with Abraham upholding that his progeny would become a great nation and be granted a homeland. Now, a new covenant, the covenant of Sinai, goes much further: binding this nation to the service of God and the observance of God's commandments. The nation therefore became a holy nation and all the people became priests, that is, dedicated to the service of the Lord.

D'rash: Exposition of the Sages

Rabbi Yose said, "Judah would expound the verse, 'The Lord came from Sinai' (Deuteronomy 33:2) thus: Do not read it that way but rather 'The Lord came to Sinai' to give the Torah to Israel. But I do not interpret it that way but rather thus: 'The Lord came from Sinai' like a bridegroom who goes forth to meet the bride."
". . . and they took their places below the mountain" (Exodus 19:17). This teaches that the mountain was pulled up from its place and they came and stood under it, as it is said, "You came forward and stood under the mountain" (Deuteronomy 4:11). Of them it says in the writings, "O my dove, in the cranny of the rocks, hidden by the cliff" (Song of Songs 2:14).
— Mekhilta Ba-Hodesh 3

". . . and they took their places below the mountain" (Exodus 19:17). Rav Avdima bar Hama said, "This teaches that the Holy One held the mountain over their heads like a vat and said to them, 'If you accept My Torah all will be well, but if not — this will be your grave!'"
— Shabbat 88a

There are two accounts of the events at Sinai that we celebrate on Shavuot: one from Exodus and the other from Deuteronomy. In both the people are described as standing *b'tahtit ha-har*—usually translated as either "below" or "at the foot of" the mountain. However, the word *b'tahtit* can literally be taken to mean "underneath" the mountain. The *Mekhilta*, edited ca. 300 CE, presumes that literal meaning; therefore, the text is seen as describing the people as actually standing under Mount Sinai when the Decalogue is proclaimed. The mountain thus becomes a great wedding canopy. Another saying in the *Mekhilta*, by Rabbi Yosi, makes this clear: God is depicted as a groom who leaves his place under the mountain in order to escort his bride back under the *huppah*, as is customary in Jewish weddings.

Rabbi Yosi's saying is an interpretation of the verse in Moses's blessing to the people in Deuteronomy containing the phrase "The Lord came from Sinai." Some Sages found this phrase problematic. Why would the Lord be coming *from* Sinai? Should it not have said that God came *to* Sinai in order to give the people the Torah? Rabbi Yose, however, sees this as describing how God, who was already at Sinai, left it in order to escort Israel back to Sinai for the ceremony, just as a groom stands under the *huppah* and then goes from it to lead his bride under it.

A later source, the Babylonian Talmud, contains a different interpretation of the phrase *b'tahtit ha-har*. The fourth-century Amora Rav Avdimi also takes it literally: the people stood under the mountain. But in his eyes Sinai is not a *huppah*, a symbol of love. Rather, he perceives it as a threat: if the people had refused to accept the Torah, the mountain would have been dropped on them, and it would have become their grave!

There could hardly be two more different interpretations of the Sinai event, and neither approach is precisely depicted in the Torah's account. On the one hand, in the Torah the agreement is entered into willingly; there is a choice and not coercion. On the other hand, it is still an awesome and fearful moment. When the people experience the lightning and thunder they say to Moses, "You speak to us, and we will obey; but let not God speak to us, lest we die" (Exodus 20:16).

The Sages went beyond that simple meaning, making it either a terrifying threat or a blissful wedding.

Which was it to be? A *huppah* or a death threat?

At stake here was more than the proper interpretation of a word. Rather, it was the Jewish understanding of how Israel attained a special relationship with God, becoming a kingdom of priests and a holy people. Were we coerced into it, threatened with extinction if we did not agree? Or were we led into it as a result of a loving relationship, wooed, as it were, by God, who loved Israel?

Fortunately, the wedding imagery triumphed. The people's love was returned, and the "marriage" took place at—or even under—the *huppah* of Sinai.

The Rabbinic understanding of the Sinai covenant as a marriage ceremony between God and Israel became so widely accepted in Jewish tradition that the custom emerged of erecting a *huppah* in synagogues on Shavuot and reading a marriage document (*ketubah*) between God and Israel during the festival service. We are what we are not because of force and coercion but because of free choice and love. That is what our Judaism is all about.

D'rash: Personal Reflection

THE DIVINE MARRIAGE

The Israel Museum in Jerusalem once held a beautiful exhibition of medieval illuminated *ketubot* from many different Jewish communities. As I viewed them I tried to read the names of each bride and groom and the location of the wedding. It was like taking a stroll through Jewish history in Europe, Asia, and North Africa.

Eventually, I came to one *ketubah* that puzzled me because its wording seemed to be different from the usual text. When I saw the names of the happy couple, I understood why: the groom was the Holy One Blessed Be He and the bride was Israel. The date was Shavuot and the place was Mount Sinai. I realized that this *ketubah* was based on that

Rabbinic midrash in which the Torah's simple account of the Sinai encounter is transformed into a divine marriage ceremony.

History has given us enough examples of attempts to force religious observance on people: threats of hellfire and damnation and, worse, executions by religious authorities. In modern times, fanatic religious groups have also used force in the attempt to coerce religious obedience. I like to believe that the Sages of Israel rejected that path and chose instead to emphasize love as the greatest motivation for observing religious commandments. What could be more symbolic of that than a *ketubah* between Israel and God?

When we celebrate Shavuot in our synagogue, decorated with flowers and greens in accord with the tradition that Mount Sinai bloomed when the Torah was given, the congregation stands when the Decalogue is read. For me, this is more than simply listening to a reading from the Torah. It is, rather, a moment to experience what happened then, to stand with my people under the *huppah*, entering into our relationship to God, and to hear the reading of the *ketubah* that outlines our responsibilities and our loving relationship. I was not there, although the Sages said that the souls of all Jews who would ever be born were present at Sinai, but at least I can feel as if I am renewing those wedding vows.

If one takes being a Jew seriously, I think it is not sufficient to learn about the creation of a new covenant at Sinai. One needs to experience it as a personal event in one's own life and to renew that commitment every year on the anniversary of the day when it first took place. Certainly for me, standing under the *huppah* of Sinai is the ultimate experience of being a part of the Jewish people and continuing its tradition of seeking to transform the world into a true realm of God.

Selected Bibliography

This brief selected bibliography contains the names of books that will help the reader understand the history of the Sages and their methods of interpretation of the Torah. It also contains the names of some English translations of Rabbinic works of biblical commentaries and legends.

Bialik, H. N., and Y. H. Ravnitzky. *The Book of Legends*. New York: Schocken Books, 1992.

Cohen, Gershon. "The Talmudic Age." In *Great Ages and Ideas of the Jewish People*, edited by Leo Schwarz. New York: Modern Library, 1956.

Cohen, Shaye J. D. *From the Maccabees to the Mishnah*. Philadelphia: Westminster Press, 1987.

Finkelstein, Louis. *The Pharisees*. 2nd ed. Philadelphia: Jewish Publication Society of America, 1962.

Flusser, David. *Judaism of the Second Temple Period: Volume 2: The Jewish Sages and Their Literature*. Jerusalem: Magnus Press, 2009.

Ginzberg, Louis. *The Legends of the Jews*. Philadelphia: Jewish Publication Society of America, 1954.

———. *On Jewish Laws and Lore*. Philadelphia: Jewish Publication Society of America, 1955.

Glatzer, Nahum. *The Rest Is Commentary*. Boston: Beacon Press, 1962.

Goldin, Judah. *The Fathers According to Rabbi Nathan*. New Haven CT: Yale University Press, 1955.

———. *Studies in Midrash and Related Literature*. Philadelphia: Jewish Publication Society, 1988.

Halivni, David Weiss. *Midrash, Mishnah, and Gemara*. Cambridge MA: Harvard University Press, 1986.

Hammer, Reuven. *Akiva: Life, Legend, Legacy*. Philadelphia: Jewish Publication Society, 2015.

———. *The Classic Midrash*. Mahwah NJ: Paulist Press, 1995.

———. *Sifre Deuteronomy*. New Haven CT: Yale University Press, 1986.

Heschel, Abraham Joshua. *Heavenly Torah as Refracted through the Generations.* New York: Bloomsbury, 2007.

Kadushin, Max. *The Rabbinic Mind.* New York: Jewish Theological Seminary, 1952.

Lieberman, Saul. "Rabbinic Interpretation of Scripture," In *Hellenism in Jewish Palestine.* New York: Jewish Theological Seminary, 1994.

Montefiore, C. G., and H. Loewe. *A Rabbinic Anthology.* Philadelphia: Jewish Publication Society, 1960.

Moore, George Foot. *Judaism.* Cambridge MA: Harvard University Press, 1946.

Schechter, Solomon. *Some Aspects of Rabbinic Theology.* New York: Behrman House, 1962.

Urbach, Ephraim. *The Sages: Their Concepts and Beliefs.* Jerusalem: Magnus Press, 1975.

In the JPS Daily Inspiration Series

A Year with the Sages: Wisdom on the Weekly Torah Portion
Rabbi Reuven Hammer

A Year with Mordecai Kaplan: Wisdom on the Weekly Torah Portion
Rabbi Steven Carr Reuben
Foreword by David Teutsch

To order or obtain more information on these or other Jewish Publication Society titles, visit jps.org.